Veil

Dress, Body, Culture

Series Editor **Joanne B. Eicher,** *Regents' Professor, University of Minnesota*

Advisory Board:

Ruth Barnes, *Ashmolean Museum, University of Oxford*
Helen Callaway, *CCCRW, University of Oxford*
James Hall, *University of Illinois at Chicago*
Beatrice Medicine, *California State University, Northridge*
Ted Polhemus, *Curator, "Street Style" Exhibition, Victoria & Albert Museum*
Griselda Pollock, *University of Leeds*
Valerie Steele, *The Museum at the Fashion Institute of Technology*
Lou Taylor, *University of Brighton*
John Wright, *University of Minnesota*

Books in this provocative series seek to articulate the connections between culture and dress which is defined here in its broadest possible sense as any modification or supplement to the body. Interdisciplinary in approach, the series highlights the dialogue between identity and dress, cosmetics, coiffure, and body alternations as manifested in practices as varied as plastic surgery, tattooing, and ritual scarification. The series aims, in particular, to analyze the meaning of dress in relation to popular culture and gender issues and will include works grounded in anthropology, sociology, history, art history, literature, and folklore.

ISSN: 1360-466X

Previously published titles in the Series

Helen Bradley Foster, *"New Raiments of Self": African American Clothing in the Antebellum South*
Claudine Griggs, *S/he: Changing Sex and Changing Clothes*
Michaele Thurgood Haynes, *Dressing Up Debutantes: Pageantry and Glitz in Texas*
Dani Cavallaro and Alexandra Warwick, *Fashioning the Frame: Boundaries, Dress and the Body*
Thomas S. Abler, *Hinterland Warriors and Military Dress: European Empires and Exotic Uniforms*

DRESS, BODY, CULTURE

Veil
Modesty, Privacy and Resistance

Fadwa El Guindi

Oxford • New York

First published in 1999 by
Berg
Editorial offices:
150 Cowley Road, Oxford, OX4 1JJ, UK
70 Washington Square South, New York, NY 10012, USA

Paperback edition reprinted in 2000

Berg is an imprint of Oxford International Publishers Ltd.

Library of Congress Cataloging-in-Publication Data
A catalogue record for this book is available from the Library of Congress.

British Library Cataloguing-in-Publication Data
A catalogue record for this book is available from the British Library.

ISBN   1 85973 924 5 (Cloth)
        1 85973 929 6 (Paper)

Typeset by JS Typesetting, Wellingborough, Northants.
Printed in the United Kingdom by Biddles Ltd, King's Lynn.

It is hoped that this book equally reaches those who decided to veil, those who refused to unveil, those who refused to veil, those who traditionally always veiled, and those who never ever veiled.

Contents

Transliteration and Translation   ix

Preface   xi

Part 1: Veiling in Perspective

1   Introduction   3

2   The Veil in Comparative Tradition   13

3   Ideological Roots to Ethnocentrism   23

Part 2: Dress, "Libas" and "Hijab"

4   The Anthropology of Dress   49

5   Sacred Privacy   77

6   The Veil in Social Space   97

7   The Veil Of Masculinity   117

8   The Veil Becomes a Movement   129

9   The Sacred In The Veil: *Hijab*   147

Part 3: The Resistance of the Veil

10   Reactions To The New Trend   161

11   Contexts Of Resistance   169

12   Veiling And Feminism   177

Notes   187

Bibliography   215

Index   235

Transliteration and Translation

No system of transliteration is followed, except for the HAMZA and 'AYN, which are marked here by the apostrophe as a convenience to nonspecialists. Although some Arabic words or names, such as Mecca, Muhammed or Koran, have become common English words, in this book I use the spelling adopted by the *American Journal of Islamic Social Sciences* to approximate better the Arabic pronunciation of these words, so that they are spelled Makka, Muhammad, and *Qur'an*.

Most Arabic words are printed in Italics. In some instances, when it is relevant to the meaning, I specify the syllable stress in parentheses following an Arabic word. Also, for each new Arabic word, its triliteral root follows it in parentheses.

I carefully scrutinized existing English translations of the Qur'anic text relevant to my analysis, and examined it against the context of the other sources utilized – the original Arabic *Hadith* narratives and the Arabic *Tafsir*, ethnography and historical accounts. I discovered that often shades of meanings and nuances embedded in the original text are lost in the translations or slightly modified – enough to alter the meanings significantly for this anthropological analysis. Possibly it is some English-translated segments that are responsible for recurring clichés in scholarship, particularly on charged topics such as women and dress. Most translation of the original Arabic Qur'anic and *Hadith* text and of other non-Islamic Arabic sources is my own.

Preface

This study[1] was born out of fieldwork on the contemporary Islamic move-ment. It is an analysis, and re-analysis, of data embedded in an original synthesis of ethnography, history, Qur'anic text, *Hadith*, and *Tafsir*. It is not simply a descriptive ethnography of veiling, or a "community study" of a community in which veiling is practiced, with a focus on women. I have been engaged in fieldwork and research on this subject since I began a field project on the Islamic Movement in Egypt in the 1970s. This was before the formation of Women's Studies, when little background research was con-veniently available to researchers on issues related to gender. I worked progressively and published on the subject, placing gender and veiling in a larger cultural context.

Veil was not my original choice for this book's title. For a number of reasons my original intent was to write a book about *Hijab*, the word in the Arabic calligraphic art on the cover. "Veil" has no single Arabic linguistic referent, whereas *Hijab* has cultural and linguistic roots that are integral to Islamic (and Arab) culture as a whole. But the publisher preferred *Veil* to *Hijab* for reader accessibility and familiarity. From a marketing angle, the publisher rightly finds *Veil* more marketable, even sexy. I was not persuaded by the marketing argument.

As I reflected further on the matter I realized that my own resistance to using the word "veil" stems from the same bias that entraps many scholars. The veil is avoided as a subject of study because of what it stands for ideologically or for its association with Orientalist imagery. And while the word "veil" is found in many – too many – titles, scholarly discussion of it occupies a few pages, even paragraphs, in most works. In most, the veil is attacked, ignored, dismissed, transcended, trivialized or defended. This reaches hysterical proportions in the media, where a hostility has developed against the veil (often under the guise of humanism, feminism or human rights) from Saudi Arabia (after the Gulf War contact) to Iran (after the Islamic Revolution), and is now concentrated on the Taliban as they consol-idate their power over Afghanistan. Much of what is said is ethnocentric (often a personalistic vision reflecting the fears of the authors) and shows no understanding of how such movements are contextualized in global politics – the rise of the Taliban, for instance, being a product of the CIA's activities during its struggle against the Soviet Union in the Cold War period. This bias, and misinformation, also prevented a full anthropological analysis, thus further hindering an adequate understanding of the veil, its roots, and its meaning in its sociocultural context.

I came to realize during the course of my research on the subject that veiling is a rich and nuanced phenomenon, a language that communicates social and cultural messages, a practice that has been present in tangible form since ancient times, a symbol ideologically fundamental to the Christian, and particularly the Catholic, vision of womanhood and piety, and a vehicle for resistance in Islamic societies, and is currently the center of scholarly debate on gender and women in the Islamic East. In movements of Islamic activism, the veil occupies center stage as symbol of both identity and resistance.

The title of the book is *Veil*, then. This work will privilege the veil with a full analysis and understanding. It is not a defense of or an attack on the veil – rather it is a scholarly effort to bring about a fuller understanding. Instead of replacing *Hijab* as the subject of this book, *Veil* integrates it as an aspect of the study of the veil and embeds it in the larger framework of the anthropology of dress. *Hijab* is more culturally specific, and embodies cultural levels of meaning as well as social aspects of relations, and is better understood when embedded in the more holistic context. Extracting the study of the veil from Area, Women's, and Religious Studies, and embedding it instead in the anthropological study of dress, deprovincializes and de-exoticizes it. In accomplishing this I am particularly indebted to Joanne Eicher and her various collaborations with others for their research and their publications, which pioneered the contemporary, systematic study of the domain of dress. Building on the framework they developed from comparative cross-cultural research, namely a socio-cultural communication model, I incorporated insights from an analysis of the Arab notions of *libas* and *hijab*. The resulting framework deals with material, sociocultural, and symbolic aspects of the veil.

By the time this book was being written, much background research on gender in the Middle East had been explored and compiled, in the works of Leila Ahmed, Margot Badran, Fatima Mernissi, Lila Abu-Lughod and others, as Women's Studies gained momentum. I found some of these works useful, particularly for locating Arabic references, and for relevant background historical material focusing on gender. I also consulted primary sources. However, since this is not primarily a historical study, I also relied on secondary sources that included material relevant for my analysis. Ahmed's historical research exploration on gender provided an invaluable resource.

My work differs from existing works, however, in its goal (to understand veiling, not gender), in the overall interpretation of historical and religious materials, and in the analysis.

A holistic understanding of humankind calls for comparative data from all available sources deemed relevant for understanding the meaning people themselves attach to their cultural constructions (see Schweizer 1998). I examine the veil in many contexts and synthesize many sources of data. In addition to ethnography and historical materials, this study consults three Arabic textual sources in their original form and language – the *Qur'an*, the *Hadith*, and the *Tafsir* – and integrates them through ethnographic analysis of contemporary and historical material to produce an understanding of the varied body of the relevant materials.

A word about text. "Text" has been used in this book to refer to written Islamic scripturalist material, namely (and minimally) the *Qur'an*, the *Hadith*, and the *Tafsir*. Islam has many other bodies of text. I do not use "text" to refer to written documents produced by the anthropologist or in the metaphorical sense of "culture as text" that was in vogue recently. *Tafsir* is the body of *Exegesis* or Interpretation generated by Islamic scholars and experts.

Ordinarily in Middle Eastern Anthropology, Islamic text is left out, both as data and in the analysis. A few Qur'anic *Suras*, particularly the ones pertaining to the subject of women, are routinely and uncritically referenced from secondary sources, their English translation unchallenged, and their meaning presumed. Critical inquiry into the content of Islamic textual sources has been left to scholars of religion, students of Islamic Studies, and researchers in Middle East Studies.

The procedure I used in exploring text was contextual and relational. Segments of text relevant to my subject were examined against other segments in the same source. That is, a relevant concept that is located in a particular *ayah* in a *sura* was examined against its presence in other *ayahs* in the same *sura* and also in other *suras*. Information in the *Qur'an* was examined against *Tafsir* and in *Hadith*. This procedure had to be systematic to yield the observations and meanings I was able to derive. These are then examined against ethnography.

The approach in this book bridges the two orientations to Middle Eastern phenomena – that of scholars of Religious and Islamic Studies, who rely heavily on textual sources, and that of anthropologists of the Middle East, who rely heavily on contemporary ethnography, making marginal use of texts from secondary or English-translated sources.

It is a widely held perception that Islamic text is far removed from the lives of the people, and therefore irrelevant to anthropological studies of Muslims. Geertz, in his classic book *Islam Observed* (1968), wrote that Islam is scholastic, legalistic, and doctrinal. He distinguished "religiousness" from "religious-mindedness," which he described as being held by religious convictions and holding them. Religious-mindedness is the celebration of belief rather than assertions of belief. Scriptural Islam was classified as the Great Tradition, and lived Islam in combination with folk practices, the Little Tradition. Antoun (1968: 171) defined the former as Islamic law and Qur'anic ethics; and lived Islam, the Little Tradition, according to Antoun comprised village customs and beliefs (1968: 671). Lived Islam meant particularistic beliefs and rituals that some might call folk beliefs or superstition, and they include "saints" festivals, fate, baraka, "the hand of Fatima," or "nebulous things," as Geertz called them, wondering whether there are "any pigeons in . . . these pigeonholes" (Geertz 1968: 23). Antoun considered them analytically separate levels of thought and action. Anthropologists tended to focus on particularistic elements when studying religion in Muslim communities. Others imagined it possible to study the Middle East without including religion. In either orientation, Islam was held apart.

The anomaly, then, is the fact that Muslim people in most communities studied by anthropologists prayed (five time a day), fasted (every day of the month of Ramadan every year), and mobilized their social and material resources at great cost to enable elders in the family to go on the lifetime pilgrimage to Makka. Even remote groups (such as the Rashayda bedouins) annually celebrated the *'Eid* as an important occasion. Yet there is resistance against acknowledging the existence of such an Islamic dimension in daily life. These practices were dismissed as "nominal" Islam.

Leaving scriptural Islam out of ethnography was in part due to a "localizing" orientation that makes the anthropologist focus exclusively on the "local" culture. These reified divisions of local understandings into religiousness and religious-mindedness, or the Great versus the Little Tradition, misdirected studies. But there is also the factor of the non-observability of certain phenomena, which is a function of theory and methodology. Observability, as different from visibility, is a function of tools of discovery and procedures of analysis.

Many such spurious divides were conceptually imposed on Islamic society: in addition to the Great and Little Traditions, folk and formal culture, public and private, honor and shame, culture and nature, and scriptural text and ethnography. But the anthropology of our ancestors, going back to Ibn Khaldun, was not so bounded, so fixed, so polarized. It developed out of a dynamic process of knowledge, building from many sources – any sources. Its mode of analysis is unique in its synthesis and its science.

In ordinary life people integrate a multiplicity of dimensions. Muslims live according to rhythmic patterns alternating between sacred and secular space and time in daily life and throughout the life cycle. Islamic text, far from remaining frozen in Islamic scholars' specialized teachings and writings, spreads to ordinary folk through forums of collective worship and public media, and is transmitted through socialization and by oral tradition. It enters the cultural constructions that shape thinking and influence ordinary lives.[2] Separating formal text from ethnography in the study of Muslims, no matter how traditional their lifestyle, misrepresents and distorts the reality.

These are problems that face studies of non-Islamic societies as well. I carried out long-term intensive fieldwork, thirty-two months of field research and twelve years of observation, among the valley Zapotec of Oaxaca. They too are considered only "nominally," (in this case) Catholic. I too, at first, engaged in "localizing" my study by separating out formal elements of Christianity from daily practices. But ultimately the conceptual approach I formulated to describe their system of rituals was integrative, and shows how the Zapotec draw upon various corpora of belief, including formal elements of Catholic beliefs. Analysis was not built on polarities, but on complementary oppositions mediated dynamically in a way that integrated the various corpora. It is a "living" process in which some occasionally see contradictions, contest them, and seek means to resolve them. The believing process is live, though perhaps not observable in anthropological analysis if the tools are not sharp enough.

This awareness guided my subsequent long-term fieldwork project on the Islamic Movement. Fieldwork among activist youth *Islamiyyin* in Egypt since the 1970s led me to approach Islam as a living phenomenon and the *Qur'an* as a living document. Recurrently throughout human history, purist movements led by individuals or groups have risen against "syncretized" versions that people themselves weave or are forced to adopt by a dominant group imposing a "controlling process" (Nader 1997). The United States may not be fully cognizant of the impact it has in provoking extremist reactions when it employs heavy-handed methods against Muslims, nor is there a willingness to acknowledge the corrosive effect that Israel has on the region and Islamic politics. As earlier in South Africa and Algeria, eventually people rise from submission, recapture governance, and liberate their lands from occupation. Islamic movements, like many movements occurring cross-culturally, undergo processual phases from extreme disruption to routinized stabilization. We have witnessed Iran move out of the former into the latter (as the United States is now seeking to forge relations with Iran) and the Taliban move into the former after victory over the Soviet Union. Many African-Americans brought to the West in slavery were originally Muslims in their homelands; many Christians in southern Spain were Muslims in Andalusia before the Inquisition. They were Christianized as part of an effort to pacify the area.

Many such areas are currently undergoing Islamic revival movements. The revitalization of religious traditions is active today almost everywhere. Sometimes this results in violence. Some seek to recapture their sacred identity. Revitalization is a visible feature of Islam today, as it has been since its first moments of formation in Arabia. Populist movements are revitalizing processes, often carried on at high cost.

Since dress code (and veiling) is a salient part of the movement, I examined the veil more closely. To go beyond appearance and visibility, I developed procedures for observability. The veil, it turns out, is a complex phenomenon. So I embarked on a journey from history, to scriptures, to ethnography, to poetry, to photography – a journey that left me breathless. I searched through different bodies of data and across national borders. How far back does the evidence for this practice go? Who practiced it? Is it the same phenomenon? Does it have the same meaning across eras, empires, and religions? The quest for answers became a voyage of discovery.

The exploration of the vast cultural-regional area (Greek, Byzantine, Mesopotamian, Egyptian, and Arabian) for comparative contexts of veiling and gender ideology was in search of patterns, regularities, and contrasts in practice and meaning. I had in previous publications examined historical (archeological) materials to identify ideological roots to contemporary cultural traditions in the Arab Gulf region and in Egypt. I incorporated my observations from these studies into the present work. For several decades now, scholars in Middle Eastern Studies, such as Afaf Marsot among others, have suggested Mesopotamian/Persian roots for veiling and Hellenic/Byzantine roots for seclusion. More recently, Leila Ahmed has used a gender perspective to examine these two regional complexes, which she organized using geographic divisions such as Mesopotamian and Mediterranean Studies. Instead of geography, I structured Chapter 2 in this book ("The Veil in Comparative Tradition") thematically. Five themes are discerned from among the materials on ancient traditions in the region that characterize contrastive contexts: complementary, exclusionary, hierarchical, egalitarian and seclusionary. This differentiation underlies the understanding of veiling as presented in this work. One discovery during my overall exploration was that the veil, reified into a material form of a single origin, had become appropriated by studies of gender, which overlooked veiling by men and its larger cultural context. This study is not to be a book on gender or Islam, but is an exploration of the veil as it is embedded in Islam, culture and society.

The veil is situated at the intersection of dress, body, and culture. I drew upon the holistic paradigm of communication developed for the cross-cultural study of dress. This expanded the possible range of ways of looking at the veil. The nonmaterial, intangible component was subjected to symbolic analysis, not by indulging in, as Bateson put it "an orgy of interpreting symbols" (1958 [1936]), but by examining in detail the various bodies of data for the various contexts, historical, ethnographic, visual, and textual, that yield meaning about the sacred and not just the material.

Observations deriving from the texts were examined against data from ethnography. Concepts and premises emerging in the analysis of ethnographic data and established as central to understanding the subject are grouped according to common qualities or on the basis of Arabic etymological affinities. For example, *hurma-haram-harim* (sanctity and privacy) is such a grouping. This is then connected to concepts of *hishma-tahashshud* (restraint, respect and dignity) to develop understanding of core notions of sanctity, sanctuary, respect and privacy in a way that is characteristically Arabo-Islamic.

My argument, developed in Part II of this book, is that veiling in contemporary Arab culture is largely about identity, largely about privacy – of space and body. I contend that the two qualities, modesty and seclusion, are not adequate characterizations of the phenomenon as it is expressed in the Middle East. In their social setting, veiling proxemics communicate exclusivity of rank and nuances in kinship status and behavior. Veiling also symbolizes an element of power and autonomy and functions as a vehicle for resistance. It was no accident that colonizing powers and the local state both consistently used the veiling of women as their "field of operation" or as an element in a "controlling process." Ironically, as the textual research in this study shows, "purifying" campaigns of emergent Islamic movements, such as the Taliban, are now at the stage of establishing themselves politically, at first regionally and then internationally, through membership in the United Nations. They are consolidating control over their society and what counts in it – and that means women. They are not examining the *Qur'an* for fundamentals about Muslim life. When they do, they will find a kinder model. Extremist forces, along with the whole world, are watching the United States' upheaval over the sexual adventures in the White House. People worldwide are also watching, and reading on the internet, how American culture has ultimately produced the kind of disturbed young woman who engages in what many consider sexual perversions in seeking men in power. What kind of values, family, womanhood lead to that? The effect of such a real-life drama produced by a superpower in a worldwide theater is not to be underestimated. After all, less realistic dramas, such as "Dallas," had had their effects in the 1970s on the nonwestern viewing world.

In sum, many cultural domains and methodological tools inform this study: original fieldwork-based ethnography (my own and that of others); Islamic textual sources; visual analysis; linguistic analysis; cultural analysis; and the ethnographic analysis of historical materials. The study of contemporary veiling (since the 1970s) draws on my own fieldwork in Egypt and observations from research trips I took to many parts of the Arab East, South Asia, and Andalusian Spain. The scope of this research provides insights as to the manner in which all the bodies of data used here are analyzed. Veiling is set in historical, cultural, and Islamic textual contexts. Social science, like science in general, builds on existing knowledge furthered by new data and original re-analysis. The notions of "primary data" and "original analysis" carry methodological significance. In social anthropology, the primary source is traditionally field-discovered ethnographic data; for a historian it is archival materials; and for an archeologist, the products of excavations. But all bodies of data, primary, secondary, ethnographic or textual, are amenable to anthropological analysis. Anthropology provides both primary data and methodological tools for the analysis of any data. Its orientation is characterized by a specific perspective based on mastery of cultural knowledge. I contend that anthropology, in particular, has the rigor and the framework and disciplinary tools most suited for this kind of synthesis – to combine a wide range of approaches and bodies of data in analysis.

My analysis of the veil was gradually enriched through the many national and international lectures I was invited to deliver since the publication in 1981 of my fieldwork-based research on the Islamic Movement in Egypt. But I owe the immediate crystallization of the idea that led to this book to the presentation I was invited to make by Dr Thomas Blakely in the Visual Research Conference, a conference he envisioned and annually organized and chaired. It is a two-day (pre-American Anthropological Association annual meetings) forum sponsored by the Society for Visual Anthropology of free intellectual exchange unhampered by time limits. The title of my visual presentation was "Transparency of Veil." The discussion that followed provided the impetus for this book.

I am grateful to a number of people. Former student, and now colleague, William C. Young generously, freely and meticulously provided photos and additional commentary on his published works on the Rashayda. I also discovered a meeting of minds with another former graduate student at UCLA, now a colleague, Nicole Sault. Building on her ethnographic experience with the Zapotec, my other cultural area of research, Dr Sault published a work that cross-culturally examines the notions of body and self. I also thank Drs Tarek and Hisham Fathi for providing original Arabic calligraphic artwork made by local Egyptian artists who work in their architectural offices in Cairo, and Ali Konyali and Levon Mardikyan for assisting in providing slides and postcards of miniatures from the Topkapi Palace in Istanbul, Turkey.

I acknowledge the research assistance on contemporary ethnographic and historical material on Mesopotamia provided by a student in my Middle East class at the University of Southern California, Meggan L. Torrey. My research assistant, Courtney Mykytyn, a graduate student of Anthropology at the University of Southern California, provided invaluable assistance in the phase of identifying visual elements for the book and in seeking and obtaining permissions.

I thank Richard Kurin, Director of the Center for Folklife and Cultural Studies at the Smithsonian Institution, for supplying photos taken by Daphne Shuttleworth of the Sebou' ceremony in Egypt from the archives of the Center, and Daphne Shuttleworth for her drawings of the two gendered Sebou' pots. I appreciate, too, permission for the use of photos and text by Jay Ruby, former editor of *Studies in Visual Communication*. In casual conversation with my colleague Yvonne Haddad as to which of two projects in progress I shall finish first, Veil or Islamic Feminism, she instantly and crisply said, "Veil. People do not understand it. After Veil they will understand Islamic Feminism." She is right, and that is the order I assumed. Finally, I am privileged with warm unconditional support by my husband and colleague Professor Dwight W. Read.

I also owe much to Berg Publishers: to the peer reviewers to whom the press sent my manuscript and whose comments helped clarify my observations and sharpen my analysis; to Joanne Eicher, who, since hearing my presentation of initial findings, took an interest in the work and encouraged its development into a book; and to Kathryn Earle, whose excitement about the publication lent support and encouragement and whose painstaking editing improved the manuscript in many ways, making the task of production infinitely more pleasant.

A final comment about imposed conceptualizations. This work dissociates itself from two notions widely imposed on the Islamic movement. The first is "fundamentalism," an imposed notion deriving mainly from Western Christianity that is conceptually inappropriate, ethnographically inaccurate, and ethnocentric. The second is "Islamism" (first used by Marçais in 1928), a construct – also by Western scholars – that appropriates and monopolizes debate on the Islamic movement, framing it outside the context of Islam. When fundamentalism was revealed to be ethnocentric, Islamism was adopted as the substitute. Yet there is no equivalent to "Islamism" and "Islamist" in discussions of Christianity – there is no "Christianist" movement, and no "Christianism." But in studying Islam, "Islamic" has become "Islamist" and "Islam" "Islamism." In the local vernacular *Islamiyya* and *Islamiyyin* are the terms used. The revival movements in the Islamic world do not constitute a phenomenon external to Islam – they are legitimately Islamic. In my analysis they are approached as a process consisting of several phases developing over decades in response to internal and external sociopolitical events, as a dynamic aspect of Islam, and in contexts of liberation and resistance.

Part 1

Veiling in Perspective

Introduction

Despite the inclusion of the word "veil" in the titles of many publications, the veil as a phenomenon has been treated in a perfunctory manner, as a homogeneous object, a material element of clothing almost exclusively embedded in gender, and distorted by ethnocentric accounts, or studied from the perspective of Women's Studies alone. In the two approaches – ethnocentric and Women's Studies – veiling in the Middle East is considered an element in a material/ideological set of presumably connected practices and institutions making up the complex *veil-harem-eunuchs-seclusion-polygamy*. This set is presented (L. Ahmed 1992: 17, 18) as having originated millennia ago and spread across the Persian, Mesopotamian, Hellenic, and Byzantine civilizations, from Achaemenid[3] rule, to Greek, Parthian,[4] and Sassanian[5] in successive invasions, presumably having been borrowed between ruling dynasties throughout the region, eventually to become ordinary social practices. From a feminist perspective, this complex set of institutions is considered either a direct cause or expression of women's oppression through the ages. Western-ideology feminists (in the East and the West) have dominated the discourse on the veil, viewing it as an aspect of patriarchies and a sign of women's backwardness, subordination, and oppression.[6] This uni-dimensional approach narrows the study of the veil to single-context analysis and leads to a distorted view of a complex cultural phenomenon.[7]

First, the assumption that veiling practices passed from one area to another in a "relay" style[8] is over-simplistic. The notion of innovation solely by diffusion and contact has long been discarded by anthropologists, who have discovered that many if not most significant cultural developments in human history occurred by processes of independent invention. There are also processes of assimilation and syncretism that come into play in situations of encounter.[9] At any rate, unless the search is scientific (archeological) or recognizably ideological/mythical and the evidence is established by scientific methodology, there are limits on the value of considering origins, particularly of a single material object.

Secondly, it is analytically unproductive to connect the several institutions *veil-harem-eunuchs-seclusion-polygamy*, because each element may have had its own history, role in society, and cultural meaning. There is sufficient evidence to indicate that we are dealing with multiple phenomena, layers of meaning, and diverse contexts. Each cultural region in the different eras used the same or similar elements in a different way and gave veiling a different meaning.[10] Looking at these institutions separately allows for a more focused and comprehensive exploration of the veil in a cross-cultural (ethnographic) context, based on available evidence, and permits an analysis within a conceptual framework grounded in premises established in anthropology.[11]

Thirdly, grouping the veil with other institutions confines study to veiling by women. Ethnographic evidence supports the presence of veiling practices among men in the pre-Islamic and post-Islamic Arab East. In order to understand the phenomenon of veiling one must include veiling behavior by both sexes. Moreover, most existing descriptive accounts of the veil are in works focusing on women, not on the veil. That is, even veiling by women is neither adequately covered nor well understood. Existing works rarely go into any detail, the kind of detail that is necessary for understanding the veil's nuanced communicative dimension. There are three ethnographic exceptions: veiling by Tuareg men, by rural Muslim Indian women, and by the Rashayda bedouins. These, along with the ethnographic material on Yemen by Carla Makhlouf (1979) and the social historical account of Mamluk Egypt, will provide the case studies data for the analysis presented in Chapter 5. Unni Wikan's (1982) ethnography on Omani gender discussed below is also a study in detail.

Given the shortage of detailed and adequate ethnography on veiling behavior I find myself compelled to use whatever is available to supplement my own ethnographic observations and analysis. I use the Muslim Indian ethnography on veiling in my analysis because of the detail it supplies of veiling behavior's communicating kinship status, thus extending the ethnographic cases from Muslim societies beyond the Arabic-speaking cultural region. Finally, there is not a single ethnography, in print or visual, devoted to the systematic study of the veil or veiling practices.[12] Many major works on Middle Eastern women make no mention at all of the veil or veiling behavior. Dress in general was not the subject of study, and was often not even mentioned in studies using the approach of analyzing symbols or political economy. Looking at sustained works by a single anthropologist shows that studies (such as for example those by Aswad 1967; 1974; 1978) that deal with many dimensions of society, including economic and political power, and that focus mostly on women's lives, can yet be completely devoid of any mention of women's dress. Incomplete descriptive accounts of the veil are to be found scattered through numerous more general works on women.[13] Many traditional ethnographic works, most of them not focused on women, yielded interesting observations and a few valuable insights on gender and veiling-related practices.[14] In all, however, veiling was peripheral to the focus of study. A few documentary films[15] by non-anthropologists (Fernea 1982; Kamal-Eldin 1995) have focused on the veil because of its recent revitalization in Egypt and the Islamic world.

There are four notable exceptions to this neglect of studying dress in the Middle East: Kanafani's (1983) analysis of the aesthetics of food and clothing in the United Arab Emirates; Rugh's (1986) survey of dress in Egypt; Weir's (1989) study of Palestinian dress; and Young's (1996) ethnography of dress (including ornament and body decoration) among the Rashayda. Most recently, a welcome edited collection came out using dress in the Middle East as its theme (Lindisfarne-Tapper and Ingham 1997a). Kanafani's study presents a description of the ritualized serving of meals, with its "range of complementary and contrasting tastes, textures, and colors" constituting a nonverbal communication system (1983: 106–7). Rugh documents the diverse manifestations of Egyptian *baladi* (an Arabic word meaning "folk," but which stands for "traditional local") dress in an attempt to show how Egyptians "read" clothing to identify regional, socioeconomic and religious identities. Her goal was to discover how dress "provides a code which can decipher the complexities of social structures and the values on which they are based" (1986: vii–ix, 4–5). Weir's coffee-table book is a visual feast – a photographic essay with detailed information about the social significance of dress for both sexes, it consistently uses native names of clothing articles and descriptions while contextualizing the various cultural uses of dress, such as in Palestinian weddings and boys' circumcisions (1989: 20). The work was part of a major museum exhibition held in London. It is a photographic record through its dress of Palestine as an ancient, continuing and richly diverse culture. Young's study, an ethnography on the Rashayda[16] rather than on dress *per se*, comprises the most systematic set of original contemporary data collected in the field and analyzed within the conceptual paradigm of anthropology. It places dress in society and culture as a whole.

The present work is devoted to the phenomenon of the veil, which is examined within the anthropological framework developed for a cross-cultural analysis of dress. Rather than an isolated material object or practice, the veil will be analyzed comprehensively within a holistic analytic approach that situates it in the multidimensional contexts of dress – the material, the spatial, the religious – as a mode of communication that builds on cross-cultural, cross-religious and cross-gender knowledge.

Etymology of Veiling

The English term "veil" (like its European variants, such as *voile* in French) is commonly used to refer to Middle Eastern and South Asian[17] women's traditional head, face (eyes, nose, or mouth), or body cover. As a noun *veil* derives, through Middle English and Old North French, from the Latin *vēla*, pl. of *vēlum*. The dictionary meaning assigned to it is "a covering," in the sense of "to cover with" or "to conceal or disguise." As a noun, it has four usages: (1) a length of cloth worn by women over the head, shoulders, and often the face; (2) a length of netting attached to a woman's hat or headdress, worn for decoration or to protect the head and face; (3) a. The part of a nun's headdress that frames the face and falls over the shoulders, b. The life or vows of a nun; and (4) a piece of light fabric hung to separate or conceal or screen what is behind it; a curtain.

In another reference source[18] the range of meanings under "veil and veiling" is organized under several broad headings: A. *Interpersonal Emotion*: (1) celibacy; (2) covering in the sense of cover; (3) covering in the sense of shade; B. *Modes of Communication*: (1) hiding in the sense of disguise; (2) concealment, conceal, or concealed; (3) deception, sham; C. *Organic Matter*: (1) screen; (2) invisibility; (3) dimness;(4) darkness; (5) dim sight. The final category is D. *Dressing* in "Space and Dimensions." It is interesting that "veil as dress" is last on the list of significations. There is a separate grouping called *Religion: Canonicals* that includes vestures; covering; seclusion; monastic; occult. (On "Veil of Veronica" see Apostolos-Cappadona 1996).

In sum, the meanings assigned in general reference works to the Western term *veil* comprise four dimensions: the material, the spatial, the communicative, and the religious. The material dimension consists of clothing and ornament, i.e. veil in the sense of clothing article covering head, shoulders, and face or in the sense of ornamentation over a hat drawn over the eyes. In this usage "veil" is not confined to face covering, but extends to the head and shoulders. The spatial sense specifies veil as a screen dividing physical space, while the communication sense emphasizes the notion of concealing and invisibility.

"Veil" in the religious sense means seclusion from worldly life and sex (celibacy), as in the case of the life and vows of nuns. This Christian definition of the Western term "veil" is not commonly recognized. Although evidence shows that the veil has existed for a longer period outside Arab culture, in popular perception the veil is associated more with Arab women and Islam.

In Arabic (the spoken and written language of two hundred and fifty million people and the religious language of one and a half billion people today) "veil" has no single equivalent. Numerous Arabic terms are used to refer to diverse articles of women's clothing that vary by body part, region, local dialect, and historical era (Fernea and Fernea 1979: 68–77). *The Encyclopedia of Islam* identifies over a hundred terms for dress parts, many of which are used for "veiling" (*Encyclopedia of Islam* 1986: 745–6).

Some of these and related Arabic terms are *burqu', 'abayah, tarhah, burnus, jilbab, jellabah, hayik, milayah, gallabiyyah, dishdasha, gargush, gina', mungub, lithma, yashmik, habarah, izar.* A few terms refer to items used as face covers only. These are *qina', burqu', niqab, lithma.* Others refer to headcovers that are situationally held by the individual to cover part of the face. These are *khimar, sitara, 'abayah* or *'immah.* To add to this complexity, some garments are worn identically or similarly in form by men and women, and the same term is used in both cases. Some are dual-gendered while others are neutral-gendered. For example, both women and men wear outer garments such as cloaks and face covers (L. Ahmed 1992: 118; El Guindi 1995b). As an example, *lithma* is the term for a dual-gendered face cover used in Yemen by women and associated with femaleness, yet it is also worn by some Bedouin and Berber men and associated with virility and maleness. Other examples include the neutral-gendered terms *'abayah* or *'aba* of Arabia and *burnus* of the Maghrib – overgarments for both sexes.

All this complexity reflected and expressed in the language is referred to by the single convenient Western term "veil," which is indiscriminate, monolithic, and ambiguous. The absence of a single, monolithic term in the language(s) of the people who at present most visibly practice "veiling" suggests a significance to this diversity that cannot be captured in one term. By subsuming and transcending such multivocality and complexity we lose the nuanced differences in meaning and associated cultural behaviors.

It is worth noting that neutral-gendered or dual-gendered dress among Arabs is not associated with unisex identity, behavior or attitude. Even when similar or identical in form, dress items are "worn" differently by women and men, who "carry themselves" differently in ways that are understood culturally. The line between cultural femininity and cultural masculinity is maintained through gait and body language. Gender markers are not hidden when wearing neutral-gendered or dual-gendered dress items.

An interesting case that highlights these points on Arab gender marking is that of the *xanith* (henceforth spelled *khanith*) studied by Unni Wikan (1977, 1978, 1982) in Sohar, Oman. The term *khanith*, which the Omani use to refer to men who are effeminate or display effeminacy, derives from the Arabic root *kh-n-th.* Other variants used elsewhere among Arabic-speaking groups, as in Egypt for example, include *mukhannath.* In her ethnographic study of Sohar, a northern coastal town of Oman, Wikan describes how *khanith*, though anatomically male, does not stand exactly for a man. The term stands for males who are not "men enough" for Omani woman to veil to. And while they perform sexual services for men, they are not considered women and their services are homosexual in nature.[19]

Dress is a marker that determines the position of *khanith* on the cultural scale of manhood and womanhood. The Omani man wears a *dishdasha* (a long-sleeved, ankle-length white shirt). "A Xanith wears a dishdasha . . . but it is sewn differently and is made out of different color fabric" (Wikan 1982: 173). The *dishdasha* worn by men is always in plain white fabric. Women wear patterned cloth in bright colors. "Like women's dress the dishdasha worn by a Xanith has a swung waist," but, unlike the clothing of either men or women, "that of the Xanith is made out of unpatterned cloth in pastel colors . . . Men and women wear head covers. A Xanith does not" (1982: 173). The differences appear in other aspects of dress. "Whereas men cut their hair short and women wear theirs long, Xaniths keep theirs medium long. And whereas men comb their hair backward away from the face and women comb theirs diagonally forward from a central part, Xaniths comb theirs forward from a side part, and they oil it heavily in the style of women. Men always have their arms covered, women may privately reveal from elbow to wrist, but Xaniths characteristically expose their lower arms in public" (1982: 173). Perfume is another area of dress that reveals interesting commonalties and differences. "Both sexes wear perfume, especially at celebratory occasions. They also wear perfume during intercourse. The Xanith is generally heavily perfumed and uses heavy make-up that draws attention to himself" (1982: 173). This would fall within the notion known in Islam as *tabarruj* (exhibitionist behavior and dress), which describes pre-Islamic society and is frowned upon. Exhibitionism is reinforced by the "affected swaying gait" made easy by the close-fitting garments (1982: 173).

I contend that the institution and phenomenon of *khanith* (which in some ways resembles the institution of the *hijra* in India (see Nanda 1990), with which Oman had been historically in contact through trade and intermarriage) is an element in the structure of Omani culture that plays a mediating function between the two culturally unambiguous genders of man and woman. It is a construction that combines elements from both genders, yet is distinct from each. It shares properties from each gender, yet is separate from both. This contrasts with India's *hijra*, who dress and appear like women, and constitute a construction that plays a different role in the culture than that played by *khanith* in Arab culture. The latter is a construction that shares features with both in order to bring out the differences between them, as it were. *Khanith* reinforces the bounded gender duality characterizing Arab culture.

Noteworthy is the observation that in Oman *khanith* may be transitional in the life cycle of men. A *khanith* may switch back to being "a man" and engage in heterosexual marital unions. Womanhood, however, is permanently unambiguous – one is born a woman and moves from phases of virginity to maturity in marriage. Significantly, a *khanith* is forbidden by law to dress like a woman, and is particularly forbidden from wearing a *burqu'* (woman's face mask), which is a material and symbolic element representing womanhood.

In the context of women wearing men's clothing items, as in Egypt, neutral-gendered headgear or overgarments in Arab society should not be seen as connoting the unisex style (in apparel and behavior) adopted in Western culture. Unlike Western unisex practices, wearing men's headgear or overgarments is not perceived as making women less feminine. Rather it shifts the marker from the material to the behavioral in body and movement. Femininity tends to overtake male garments worn by women, and its maleness is redefined, not only becoming female, but also erotically charged.

Perhaps that is the reason why in conservative religious circles crossing sartorial gender lines is disapproved of. Some cases are documented in which women are criticized for publicly wearing male overgarments and headgear. For example, Ahmed mentions an edict "issued in Cairo in 1263 forbidding women to wear *'imamahs* (male headgear) and other masculine clothing" (L. Ahmed 1992:118). Conservative religious authorities disapproved of sartorial gender-crossing. Authorities called on families and husbands to put an end to the practice. Interestingly, sanctions were not consistently or strictly enforced in the case of Egypt. A hundred years after the 1263 edict, conservative jurists were still disapproving of women in Cairo wearing male headgear. Ahmed notes that the medieval jurist/scholar Hajj (1929),[20] was criticizing the Cairo women of his time for wearing *'imamah*s in his writing about a century after the 1263 edict (L. Ahmed 1992: 118).

One way to organize the many elements of clothing subsumed under the category "veil" is to classify them according to the body parts they conceal. Using this classification we would have a three-part typology of head cover, face cover, and body cover. However, some items serve in a number of ways and conceal several parts. Careful ethnography shows how headcovers are manipulated subtly to cover face and communicate specific messages and relations. Perhaps, to avoid such overlap, a better approach would be to identify veiling behaviors and meaning. In this case, I propose classification by what the veil reveals, what it conceals, and what it communicates. This approach seeks meaning beyond the material quality of the item.

The Veil in Women's Studies

The Western word *veil* is "sexy" and marketable in the West. It thus tends to be overused, invariably out of or without context, in titles of books, articles, conferences, press, films[21] and popular literature[22] in a way disproportionate to the relative significance of the veil in Middle Eastern affairs, and irrespective of the quality of knowledge about the veil. Some scholars of Islam have expressed concern that "veil" has come to replace "crescent" as a symbol of Islam in the West, which is outrageous.[23] Rather, the veil has come to replace the earlier obsession with "harems" and *hammam*s. "Harems" and *hammams* then and the "veil" now evoke a public sexual energy that early Christianity, puritanist Western culture, and contemporary elements of fundamentalist Christianity have not been able to come to terms with, comprehend, or tolerate. In the West *harem, veil, polygamy* envoke Islam and are synonymous with female weakness and oppression.

Those concerned see a disproportionate emphasis given to the veil in contemporary publications on the Middle East, at the expense of other major issues of significance in the overall discourse on Islam and women. Ironically, while a plethora of publications on women in the Middle East has appeared since the 1970s, they have contained only occasional passages on the veil. Examining the literature, however, shows that while "veil" is used in many titles, most publications on Middle Eastern women focused on gender or women's roles, not the veil. Makhlouf's *Changing Veils* (1979), which is among the more sensitive early ethnographies, is a good example. The discussion on veiling in Yemen was covered in under ten pages (pp. 30–8) out of 103 pages of the book. The ethnography is primarily on Yemeni women. And similarly, while the veil was discussed by Leila Ahmed (1992), the focus of her work, as its title (*Women And Gender In Islam*) accurately indicates, is on gender. Other studies on the veil situate it in the context of gender and focus exclusively on women.

Confining the study of the veil, just like the study of women, to the domain of gender in lieu of society and culture narrows the scope in a way that limits cultural understanding and theoretical conceptualization. A trend developed out of area studies and women's studies in the seventies that led to a flood of works on women in the Middle East (see the bibliographic work on the subject by Kimball and von Schlegell 1997) that described and recorded exclusively women's lives, women's experiences, women's poetry, and women's attitudes.[24] Such a singular focus assumed that the lives and contributions of women had been ignored and neglected and a gap needed to be filled. Henrietta Moore (1988) corrected that misperception with regard to anthropology: "women have always been present in ethnographic accounts, primarily because of the traditional anthropological concerns" (Moore 1988: 1). Earlier Edwin Ardener (1975a: 1) noted that "at the level of 'observation' in fieldwork, the behavior of women has, of course, like that of men, been exhaustively plotted: their marriages, their economic activity, their rites and the rest." The problem, they argued, was not a lack of record or description of women's roles and contributions but how their lives and experiences had been represented. Using the "add-women-and-stir method" (Boxer 1982: 256; Moore 1988: 3) has not yielded conceptually refined studies on women in general, nor, I add, on Middle Eastern women[25] in particular.

Studying the veil within gender suffers similar limitations. There is too much focus perhaps on the "who started it" orientation. Did Islam introduce the practice? Did Jews veil or not? Was not veiling documented during the Persian/Mesopotamian period? Generally it has become accepted in scholarly circles that the practice of women's veiling already existed in the Mesopotamian/ Mediterranean region. Stern (1939a: 108) emphatically observed that "Muhammad did not introduce the custom of veiling." According to Hansen (1967: 71) "seclusion and veiling are phenomena . . . foreign to the Arabs and unknown at the time of Muhammad." The issue of origin was addressed by many in the 1970s and 1980s (see for example Marsot 1978: 261–76; Dengler 1978: 229–44; El Guindi 1983: 79–89). Ahmed carried out a survey (begun in 1982 and completed by 1992) of ancient and modern historical materials and came to the same conclusion – that Islam did not introduce veiling. But then Ahmed shifted from origin to institutionalization, stating that, despite its presence for millennia in the Mesopotamian/ Mediterranean region (not Arabia), veiling "seems *not* to have been *institutionalized until Islam* adopted it," that veiling is *"evidently very congenial to Islam,"* that "as an institution, *it is Islamic,"* and that prior to Islam it was *"an occasional custom"* (1982:523, emphasis added). Yet these remarks are contradicted in Ahmed's own works. Ahmed conducted an extended survey of its wide and continued use from people to people for millennia prior to Islam. Her research shows how veiling and seclusion were part of an institutional structure and ethos in Greek and Byzantine societies. In what way, then, can it be considered an *occasional custom* and *not an institution?* If it is not an institution, how did this custom manage to remain "outside" the societies that generated rules and laws about it? As Ahmed herself stated, the rules on veiling in Mesopotamia were spelled out millennia ago in such detail that they specified which women must, and which could not, veil – all carefully detailed in *Assyrian law* (L. Ahmed 1992: 11–30). What do we make of the fact that special laws about the practice of veiling were literally inscribed in stone? It could not have been only a *passing* custom, nor does evidence support the claim that the *"veil is congenial to Islam."* What is particular and unique to Islam, as distinguished from other cultural and moral systems, that would assign to it a predisposition to veiling? Can ethnography uphold such a claim?

Clearly a practice that can be called veiling, and that is apparently similar in form and function, existed in all these cultures. But it is also evident in my ethnographic analysis of the historical record that veiling was and is a practice that is differentiated and variable, with each variant deeply embedded in the cultural systems. Perhaps the whole issue should be reframed. Is it the same veil that is being documented throughout the millennia? Does the practice have the same meaning when situated in contexts of different cultural ideologies, different societies, different times? The issue becomes, then, not whether it was a passing custom or whether we can consider veiling an institution or not, but rather what is the meaning of the veil in the various historical and cultural contexts and what does the phenomenon reveal about the culture within which it is embedded at any time in history. By shifting the focus it becomes meaningless to claim that the veil was institutionalized only after Islam adopted it from Mediterranean, Balkan and Mesopotamian influences.

Another casualty from exclusively focusing on women is dropping men out of the picture. Stern (1939a), consulting Lichtenstadter,[26] mentions evidence in pre-Islamic Arabia of veiling by men, which is interpreted as being for protection from the harm resulting from envy. For example, the poets (probably from fifth-century Arabia) Abdul Rahman (called Waddah) and al-Kindi, among others, are described as having their faces veiled in festivals[27] (Stern 1939a: 108). But veiling by men in Arab culture is excluded in discussions framed within the paradigm of Women's Studies. The commonly produced linkage of *harim* with seclusion and sex derives from a perspective that embeds the phenomenon of the veil (and its assumed environment, the harem) in the sphere of gender, rather than in the holistic contexts of society and culture. First, the ethnographic evidence explored in this study shows that veiling occurs without seclusion and seclusion occurs without veiling. Second, my analysis of the historical record reveals that seclusion of women more accurately describes Christian (Mediterranean/Balkan) culture than Muslim society. And in the Christian culture seclusion is more associated with religion and religious concepts of purity – both absent in Islam. Finally, there is a need to fill the historical gap in the scholarly coverage of women's roles. This, however, is best accomplished by developing adequate tools for holistic analysis that embed the study of the veil in culture and society at large, rather than in the narrow sphere of gender, turning it exclusively into a study of the veil as an isolated article or one on women's veiling alone.

2

The Veil in Comparative Tradition

What begins as a quest for an object that at first seems intangible usually turns out to have a more prosaic origin. Perhaps it is true of all knowledge.

Fra Mauro, sixteenth-century monk and cartographer to the court of Venice (Cowan 1996: 106)[28]

I discern five distinctive patterns that characterize different cultural traditions in which the veil and veiling behavior had different functions and meaning. The case of ancient Egypt is discussed for perspective and because it seems, as noted by many scholars, to be the only Mediterranean/ Middle Eastern society on record in which women show no evidence of head or face covering.[29] This exception does not extend to Jews, though, as Leila Ahmed (1992: 523) claims: ". . . [the veil] . . . appears to have been occasionally in use among all the peoples of the area, from the Greeks to the Persians, with the only clear exceptions being the Jews and the Egyptians." Existing evidence (both Biblical and scholarly, as in Goitein's multi-volume study, 1967, 1978, 1983 on Medieval Jewish Egyptians in the eleventh century) seems to support the presence of veiling among Judaic women from a period prior to Christianity through to the modern period. Jews are not singled out though, as the different patterns I distinguish are based on cultural traditions (such as Persian, Egyptian, etc.) rather than religious faiths (such as Jewish, Christian, or Muslim).

The patterns are (1) complementary, as in Sumeria; (2) exclusionary and privileging as in the Persian–Mesopotamian case; (3) egalitarian, as in Egypt; (4) hierarchical, as in Hellenic culture; and (5) seclusionary, as in Byzantine culture. These themes are revealed through the analysis of data from sources in philosophy, theology, law, mythology, ethnography, and history. They are explored here in historical-cultural contexts and against ideological premises that together produce distinctive meanings of womanhood. Images of self and body are considered pertinent to the role of the veil and the meaning of veiling.

13

Sumerian Gender Complementarity

In an earlier publication I analyzed a poetic myth that tells of the creation of Dilmun, the ancient region that is today's Bahrain[30] (El Guindi 1985b: 75; for text selections in English; Kramer 1961). Its use of symbolism suggests roots for patterns that seem to have continued over the centuries. Dilmun's creation results from the union of a male and a female deity. *Enki* is the water god who gives water to *Nimsikil*, his wife and the goddess of the land. Her fields and farms become abundant with crops and grain, and her city becomes a vibrant harbor full of boats and trading activity. Water is "alone" without land and land is "infertile" without water. Dilmun is created when the land is impregnated by water in marital union, giving birth to abundant life. This duality and complementarity of gender roles has persisted since ancient times and is replicated in modern times in the sexual division of labor: men at sea, performing sea activities,[31] women on land, performing land activities. Diving and trading took men away from home for long periods during pearling seasons. Women were *de facto* heads of household with responsibilities in internal and external affairs. They represented the household in the community, and engaged in income-producing activities, both domestic and extra-domestic, such as fishing or diving (Naggar 1981: 6, 14; Rumaihi 1976: 25). This autonomy, independence and authority can be seen in contemporary rural Shi'a villages in Bahrain where "each home is locked with a padlock ... [and] each woman carried the key to her house tied to her *headcloth* or to *one of her braids*" (Hansen 1967: 40, emphasis mine). It is particularly interesting that the symbol of control and autonomy, the key to the house, is attached to woman's "dress" – i.e. headcover and hair braids. This theme connecting "veil" with power emerges elsewhere as well and will be discussed later.

Assyrian/Persian Class Exclusivity

Using the primary source for Assyrian law (the Code in English translation) [32] it becomes evident how Assyrian law reveals a connection between veiling and social stratification. It states which women *must* and which *could not* veil. Exploring a number of relevant laws one can discern the following differentiations: "ladies-by-birth" (noble women) versus "concubines and servants"; respectable, married women versus "harlots"; free women versus slaves. Law 40, according to Driver and Miles (1935: 407) states that: "Women, whether married or [widows] or [Assyrians] who go out into the (public) street [must not have] their heads [uncovered]. Ladies by birth ...

whether (it is) a veil (?) or robe or [mantle?], must be veiled; [they must not have] their heads [uncovered]. Whether . . . or . . . or . . .[33] shall [not] be veiled [but], when they go in the (public) street [alone], they shall [surely] be veiled."

In other words, women of nobility *had to* veil. Servants, according to the Laws, had to veil too, but *only* when accompanying noble women. The law is clear on the prohibition of veiling for slave-girls. Law 40 in the Middle Assyrian Laws states that "slave-girls shall not be veiled" (Driver and Miles 1935: 409). In contrast, "a hierodule, whom a husband has married, must be veiled in the (public) streets but one, whom a husband has not married, must have her head uncovered in a (public) street; she shall not be veiled" (Driver and Miles 1935: 407). That is, former "sacred prostitutes" have to veil after marriage. *Common prostitutes and ordinary slave-girls are never permitted to veil publicly* (Driver and Miles 1935: 128, my emphasis).

Ahmed, citing Meek (1950: 183), describes the penalty when veiling rules are violated. "Those caught illegally veiling were liable to the penalties of flogging, have pitch poured over their heads, and have their ears cut off" (Ahmed 1992: 14). Penalties for violation of veiling laws were so severe that one might look at them as a high-cost investment in support of the social system. In the case of slave-girls, Law 40 states that "he who sees a veiled slave-girl . . . and has let her go (and) has not arrested her (and) brought her to the entrance of the residency, (and) charge (and) proof have been brought against him, he shall be beaten 50 stripes with rods; his ears shall be pierced (and) a cord shall be passed through (them) and be tied behind him; the informer (?) against him shall take his clothes; he shall do labour for the king for 1 full month"(1935: 409). For harlots, "He who sees a veiled harlot shall arrest(?) her; he shall produce (free) men (as) witnesses (and) bring her to the entrance of the residency. Her jewelry shall not be taken (from her, but) the man who has arrested her shall take her clothing; she shall be beaten 50 stripes with rods, (and) pitch shall be poured on her head. Or, if a man has seen a veiled harlot and has let her go (and) has not brought her to the entrance of the residency, that man shall be beaten 50 stripes with rods; the informer (?) against him shall take his clothing; his ears shall be pierced (and) a cord shall be passed through (them) and be tied behind him; he shall do labour for the king for 1 full month" (1935: 409).

Out of veiling laws a pattern emerges revealing a highly stratified social system based on class, moral and marital status, and respectability. Clothing is used in both prohibition and in punishment. And, as the next Law shows, ceremonial veiling is a vehicle for mobility. Law 41 states that: "If a man will veil his concubine (?), he shall summon 5 (or) 6 of his neighbours to be present (and) veil her before them (and) shall speak, saying: 'She (is) my wife'; she (thus becomes) his wife. A concubine (?) who has not been veiled before the men (and) whose husband has not spoken, saying: 'She (is) my wife', (is) not a wife but (still) a concubine (?). If a man has died (and) his veiled wife has no sons, the sons of concubines (?) (become his) sons; they shall take a share (of his property)" (Driver and Miles 1935: 411). The man's act of veiling (or not veiling) a woman is a means by which a woman's status shifts. Analogous to this is the rite of conferring new status upon college graduates through the ceremonial donning of the cape over the gown by a college official as each student walks up to the stage, shakes hand with the official and receives the "blank" certificate substitute. By publicly veiling the woman, the Mesopotamian man declares her as wife, and thus confers upon her a status of respectability and exclusivity.

Clearly, wives and daughters of high-ranking men of the nobility had to veil in Mesopotamia. As Ahmed puts it "upper-class women enjoyed high status and legal rights and privileges . . . influenced events and had real power over men and women of lower ranks . . . and could indeed even emerge as rulers" (1992: 15).[34] Importantly, Ahmed describes how ordinary women were trained as scribes and "worked as potters, weavers, spinners, hair-dressers, agricultural workers, bakers, singers, musicians, and brewers . . . [and] owned and managed property in their own name" (1992: 16). They had power as priestesses who lived together in conventlike institutions. The analogy with Catholic Christianity is limited, since marriage was not forbidden to these priestesses.

Ahmed adds, citing Gerda Lerner (1986), that emphasis must be put on the differentiation between "'respectable' women and those who were publicly available" (L. Ahmed 1992: 14). But I see the primary feature reflected in Assyrian society to be the class divide. Special dress marked the aristocracy, and hence lower-class women and disreputable ones were prevented by legal sanction from using the dress markers of the reputable and aristocratic women. Within this context the veil was a mark of exclusivity, status, privilege, and privacy. While there is resemblance in form, the case was different in classical Greek society, which is briefly discussed next, in terms of ideological foundations, women's status and attitudes toward womanhood.

Hellenic Gender Hierarchy

In terms of ideological foundations for Greek society I build on Ahmed's research (Ahmed 1992) and present my analysis of Aristotle (384–322 BCE) as a key ideologue whose influence was widespread beyond Greek society and endured through the ages into the Western world. First, his stature as philosopher lent credence to his ideas, which codified social values and practices of Greek society. Secondly, these ideas were woven into a cultural construct of gender. Finally, his influence extended beyond Greek society in three directions:

- Aristotelian premises took root in Christianity as it developed into the Byzantine empire.
- They penetrated medieval Arabic, Muslim and Jewish thought, when Greek philosophy was being translated, critiqued, and integrated by Arab scholars during the peak of Islamic Andalusian civilization in Spain.
- Greek principles of society and government, including gender ideology, laid many of the foundations of Western thought and society.

These Ideological foundations to classical Greek society provide the roots for the subsequent Byzantine construct of gender. Ahmed writes that "Aristotle's theories conceptualized women not merely as subordinate by social necessity but also as innately and biologically inferior in both mental and physical capacities – and thus as intended for their subservient position by 'nature'" with defective bodies which render them "impotent males" whose contribution to conception is that of matter not soul, and hence inferior (1992: 29). This view of "woman as nature," presumed universally applicable, pervades contemporary Western thinking, even in anthropology. By extension the male "is by nature superior, and the female inferior; and the one rules and the other is ruled" (Aristotle, quoted in Ahmed 1992: 29).

Consistently with the Aristotelian view that the primary purpose of marriage is reproduction, Ahmed describes Athenian law as requiring a female heir "to marry the next of kin on her father's side – even if she was already married – to produce a male heir for her father's *oikos* (family, house)" (1992: 28). Women were not allowed to buy or sell land, or make purchases in the market. Properties passed to women as gifts of inheritance, but were administered by male guardians (1992: 29).

Ahmed, using Pomeroy (1975) as her source on the free women in classical Greek society (550–323 BCE) in Athens prior to Christianity, describes them as having been "secluded so that they could not be seen by men who were not close relatives. Some women were even too modest to be seen by . . . relatives" (Ahmed 1992: 28). Similar to contemporary rural Greece as described in ethnographies, Ahmed writes, "Men and women led separate lives, men . . . in public areas, such as the marketplace and the gymnasium, while 'respectable' women stayed at home. Women were expected to confine themselves to their quarters and to manage their household . . . *Their clothing concealed them from the eyes of strange men*" (1992: 28, italics added).

Women are described as segregated in rooms situated inwards, away from the street and separated from the public area of the house. They covered their heads with a shawl and were admired for their silence and submissiveness (Ahmed 1992: 28). Hellenic society is presented here as characterized by gender hierarchy and asymmetry in ideological and social space.

Egyptian Gender Equality

Most feminists accept the premise of gender equality as a quality of ancient Egyptian society. The rights and egalitarian conditions enjoyed by Egyptian women, says Vercoutter, shocked the conquering Greeks. He observes that as Greek and Roman mores and laws spread, Egyptian women lost most of their rights (Vercoutter (1965–7). In Ahmed's survey of gender in ancient societies, she uses Pomeroy to describe Egyptian attitudes and laws regarding women at the time of the Greek conquest. According to Jean Vercoutter, arguing from a New Kingdom (1570–950 BCE) document], ". . . the absolute equality before the law of the man and the woman appear clearly. Doubtless this equality is at the source of the general belief in the privileged position of the woman in Egypt, in comparison with the feminine condition in other civilizations of Antiquity, and this deserves to be examined more closely" (Vercoutter 1992: 119(1), quoted in Ahmed 1992: 31).

Pomeroy (1984: xv) compares gender in Egypt, classical Greece (Athens 500–323 BC), Hellenistic[35] societies, and the later Roman Republic. Ahmed argues that after the Greek contact with Egypt Hellenistic women's position improved. Citing Pomeroy (1984: 119–20), Ahmed sees them as "freer . . . treated more equally in law . . . not secluded . . . nor did traditions inhibit them from associating with men" (1992: 29). Comparing women in Ptolemaic Egypt with Greek and Roman women, Pomeroy describes them as full participants in the economy, who owned property and transacted property and financial dealings on their own behalf. They were not secluded, nor was their role in society described as primarily reproductive (1984: 171, 173). Pomeroy justifies her choice of Athens "since women were more restricted and theories about their inferiority and difference from males more eloquently framed . . . such was the case in Classical Athens, where respectable women were relegated to domesticity (1984: xvii).

Eventually, the status of Ptolemaic Greek women improved, according to Pomeroy, perhaps through their choosing to transact contracts following Egyptian law; or possibly Greek law may have changed to correspond to Egyptian law (1984: 119–20, cited in Ahmed 1992: 29). In addition to rights in legal transactions by which women owned, bought, inherited, administered, and disposed of property, favorable changes were made in marriage contracts. Women could terminate marriages, as did men and husbands were forbidden to be polygamous. They were also prohibited from entertaining mistresses or concubines, and were required to return dowries and pay fines in case of divorce without just cause (1984: 97, 94, cited in Ahmed 1992: 30).

As noted by Ahmed, Marsot and others the decline of the position and rights of women in Egypt occurred long before Islam and even Arab conquest, mostly with the encroachment of European influence occurring in the Christian era.

Byzantine Seclusion

While recognizing that seeking origins for particular practices entails tracing a linear or simple path, I am describing particular ideological climates and specific historical conditions that serve as fertile ground for developments of ideas and institutions that appear similar in form but yield distinct meanings in new contexts. Byzantine society is important in this study because of historical encounter and contact between the Byzantines and the Persians in the region that is now the Middle East, establishing traditions that flowed into what became Islamic civilization, creating continuities and discontinuities. It also represents a significant development in Christian thought and practices. A brief summary of broad developments in Christianity reveals elements that assist in understanding the difference in meaning between practices in Christian culture and similar ones in Muslim culture. But this also serves as a backdrop to contextualize the Euro-Christian gaze that developed in later contexts of empire.

Using primary and secondary sources, Brown (1988) devoted an entire study to the practice of permanent sexual renunciation – continence, celibacy, life-long virginity – that developed among men and women in Christian circles in the period from a little before the missionary journeys of Saint Paul, in the 40s and 50s AD, to a little after the death of Saint Augustine. He mentions that Clement of Alexandria, a Christian writer at the end of the second century, summed up pre-Christian and Christian notions of the body this way: the human ideal of continence, set forth by the Greek philosophers, teaches one to resist passion, not to be made subservient to it, but Christians "went further – the ideal is not to experience desire at all" (1988: 31).[36]

Consistently with ancient Greek notions about womanhood,[37] Brown discusses Jewish folk wisdom, which stresses "the seductive wiles of women and the disruptive effect of the claims that women made upon the men as the bearers of their children and the sharers of their bed . . . (stirring up) the lust and jealousy that pitted males against each other. Accordingly, the Jewish group of Essenes, a sect settled at Engeddi near the Dead Sea, abandoned women and adopted lives of permanent continence" (1988: 38, 39).

Ahmed (1992) briefly discusses the cultural climate reflected in the writings of early Christian ideologues, particularly Michael Psellos (the eleventh-century Byzantine author and political figure) as cited in Grosdidier de Matons (1967). Veiling and body covering is mentioned in three contexts in Psellos mentioned in Ahmed (1992). One observation is about his mother at her daughter's funeral, when she raised her veil in the presence of men for the first time in her life (Grosdidier 1967: 28–30, cited in Ahmed 1992: 27). A second concerns "the Cesarissa Irene ... [so] scrupulously observing the imperative of concealing the flesh that she covered even her hands" (1967: 25). And the third refers to a tenth-century Byzantine patrician defending his daughter's custom of going to the baths, explaining that she went out "veiled and suitably chaperoned" (Ahmed 1992: 27; citing Grosdidier de Matons1967: 28–30).[38]

The nature of men and women as constructed in early Christianity is summarized in the conceptualizations of three primary interpretations discussed in Pagels (1988: 2–4): those of Gnostic Christians, Orthodox Christians, and St Augustine. Gnostic Christians take Adam and Eve to represent two distinct elements in human nature – the psyche, or soul (as the center of emotional and mental life) and the higher self or spirit. Some authors take Adam as the higher spiritual self and Eve as the soul, but in other texts Eve is the higher spiritual self. "[I]n order to recognize the true Eve (one's spiritual self) one must repudiate any relationship with the 'other woman' who embodies the passions; and that Eve must repudiate involvement with 'the other men', 'the adulterers' in order to receive her 'true bridegroom'" (Pagels 1988: 4).

Orthodox Christians look at Genesis as history with a moral and Adam and Eve as actual historical persons, the ancestors of our species. "From the story of their disobedience, shame and punishment, each of the orthodox teachers ... [Irenaeus, Tertullian[39] and Clement] ... derives specific moral consequences. They use the story to warn against disobedience, to encourage chastity and to interpret the hardships of human life, from death to male domination, as the just consequences of our first parents' sin. The words of Tertullian addressed to his 'sisters in Christ' [were] ... 'You are the devil's gateway ... Do you not know that you are each an Eve? The sentence of God on your sex lives on in this age; the guilt, necessarily, lives on too' " (1988: 5).

"The Orthodox insist central to the story is the issue of human freedom. Tertullian agrees – the whole point of the story of Adam and Eve is that God gave us free will. As Justin put it: We who once delighted in immorality, now embrace chastity alone ... Justin celebrates the Christians' freedom from internal domination by passion ... Methodius depicts the whole of human history, ever since Eden, as a progressive evolution of human freedom – the life of voluntary virginity" (1988: 5).

Considered the most influential of all interpreters, Augustine (354–490) changed the message. "His teaching radically breaks with his predecessors" (1988: 6). He reads in Genesis a story of human bondage. "Adam's desire for autonomy became the very root of sin ... the forbidden fruit itself ... Since the Fall it is lost entirely" (1988: 6). Augustine, according to Pagels, envisions that Adam and Eve "received the body as a servant [and that] ... After Adam and Eve disobeyed ... they felt, for the first time, a movement of disobedience in their flesh, as punishment in kind for their own disobedience to God" (1988: 7). In addition, when God created Adam and Eve "they enjoyed mental mastery over the procreative process – procreation 'like a handshake' " (1988: 7). Pagels states that according to Augustine, "spontaneous sexual desire is proof and penalty of original sin [implicating] ... the whole human race, except Christ, who alone was born without libido, without the intervention of semen (which he believed transmits libido)"(1988: 7). Ever since experiencing sexual desire, "Adam has sprung wildly out of control, marring the whole of human nature" (1988: 7).

Pagels connects this construct with controversy over sexuality. There is no lack of controversial issues, she writes: "Consider, how those New Testament sayings on creation that are attributed to Jesus and Paul have touched off controversies concerning sexual practice, ranging from marriage, divorce and celibacy to gender and homosexuality – controversies that have lasted for millennia" (1988: 11).

As an illustration of how current this controversy[40] is, there is a recent story in the United States: the artist Robert Gober has had an unnamed exhibition at the Museum of Contemporary Art's Geffen Contemporary in Los Angeles, known as MOCA, which features a sculpture of the Virgin Mary that is described by art critic Christopher Knight in the *Los Angeles Times* on 9 September1997 as follows: "the Virgin's midsection has been pierced by a spiraling tube of bronze culvert pipe ... Hollow, the conduit makes the sculpture into another cruciform shape. An inescapable image of phallic penetration merges with the mysterious void of her womb."

On 22 September 1997, a rebuttal in the *Los Angeles Times* was written by the Capuchin Franciscan Father Gregory Coiro, director of media relations for the Roman Catholic Archdiocese of Los Angeles: "the Blessed Virgin Mary is pierced by what looks like a huge hollow screw ... by exploiting the image of the Mother of God, Gober has thus gained entry into the pantheon of vulgar artists who traffic in abusing sacred symbols and offending religious believers." Critiquing the critic, Father Coiro writes: "let's bypass the lofty art critic verbiage and call a spade a spade . . . my ignorance of high art prevents me from being able to appreciate how profaning the holy and visually raping the virginal can lead to some cathartic resolution" for the artist. Most telling is the sentiment expressed by Father Coiro in which he states that the artist could have expressed his disdain against the Catholic Church and its teachings, but "why take it out on the Madonna?" Clearly it is *profaning by sexualizing* that challenges the sensibilities of fundamental Catholic premises.[41]

In this chapter I have explored gender ideology, class ideology and veiling in the ancient traditions of the Mediterranean and Persian/ Mesopotamian regions. This led to my identification of five distinguishing patterns setting the background for understanding the prevailing ethnocentrism that has distorted understandings of Arab culture.

The revealed differentiation in patterns also deconstructs the previously linked complex of practices and institutions, namely harem, seclusion, veiling and sexuality. In Chapter 3 I discuss the institution of the harem in its social, cultural and historical setting against the context of the ideological roots underlying the ethnocentrism that colored the lens of the gaze at Arab culture and Islam.

3

Ideological Roots to Ethnocentrism

Orientalism, both pictorial and literary . . . has set the stage for the deployment of phantasms – a central figure emerges, the very embodiment of the obsession: the harem.

Malek Alloula, *The Colonial Harem* (1986)

Harem: Fact and Fantasy

The Euro-Christian gaze at Muslim culture, whether expressed by word or picture, has been a gaze of violence, dominance, distortion and belittlement, whether by travelers, missionaries, scholars or occupying soldiers (see Mabro 1996 [1991]). Some critics have seen through the colonial gaze, exposed it and deconstructed it. In the perceptions of many, veil, harem, seclusion and unbridled sexual access constitute a linked whole. This is particularly so in the colonial construction of the colonized East. Some feminists, in their defense of women, end up reproducing this same construction when they reaffirm the imagery of the sexual character of harems. The feminist construction of the harem as a sexual institution is not dissimilar from the colonial and Orientalist position which Alloula, in his book *The Colonial Harem*, characterizes as the "phantasmic absence of limitation to sexual pleasure" (1986: 49) or "carnivalesque orgy" (1986: 62).

The Colonial Harem is a study of colonial postcards carried out by the Algerian writer Malek Alloula. He collected picture postcards, arranged them by topic, and annotated them for study. The postcards were made in Algeria by the French during the first part of this century and were sent by French tourists and occupying settlers to Paris with personal messages. The postcards depicted Algerian women staging the colonial fantasy of the French. The study, observed Barbara Harlow in her introduction to the book, "reveals an intense preoccupation with the *veiled* female body" as part of a "phantasm" that cannot be dissociated from the political agenda of the French colonial project (Harlow 1986: xv–xvi, emphasis added). Alloula, she notes, tried to force the postcard "to reveal what it holds back (the ideology of colonialism) and to expose what is repressed in it (the sexual phantasm) . . . [and uncover] the colonial perception of the native" (1986: 4–5). It becomes evident how the postcard "fully partakes in colonial violence" (see Figure 1).

162. - SCÈNES et TYPES. — Femme Arabe avec le Yachmak.
SCENES and TYPES. — Arabian woman with the Yachmak.

Figure 1 Studio-made postcard image representing a colonial assault by the French Occupation on Islam and Muslims. The colonials, during their occupation of Algeria, are subverting dress and privacy to undermine the colonized culture. From the series of colonial postcards by the French from1900-1930 in Algeria. By permission, from *The Colonial Harem* by Malek Alloula, University of Minnesota Press, 1986.

Unlike Alloula, who exposes the colonial gaze through his analysis of postcards, Fatima Mernissi, a Muslim feminist sociologist, reaffirms this Euro-Christiano-centric perspective when she describes the Muslim harem. In her attempt (1993) to explain "the revolt" of the *jawari* (slaves) in the Abbasid[42] harem she does so in sexual terms: "[It] was deep and enduring, because it *operated on the level of emotions and sex, of eroticism and sensuality* " (1993: 39, emphasis mine). Mernissi admirably uses Arabic scholarly sources for locating historical facts, but she then leans on Christiano-European feminist ideology to interpret them.[43] It is an ideology that considers "harem" to be the ultimate locus of female oppression and subordination, thus reducing a complex sociopolitical structure purely to gender and sexuality. Mernissi explains "why the harems were full of *jawari* [slave women] at the time of the great Muslim conquests" (1993: 54) by resorting to polygyny and the ruling that puts a limit only on the number of free women taken as wives and not on slave women. From this rule she looks at the reality of the harem primarily as a sexual institution and a locus for polygynous alliances (marital or sexual).

The notion of seclusion dominates writings on Middle Eastern women. Doumato also links the harem to female seclusion. She writes: "The ultimate expression of female seclusion is the harim (harem) system" (1995: 19). And, like many observers on Middle Eastern women, she sees both as part of an aristocratic way of life in which allowing one's wife to remain at home is a mark of luxury and status. However, Doumato does point out that seclusion characterized poor Saudi women as well, not just the nobility.[44]

Leila Ahmed (1982), in an attempt to balance extreme positions, mentions two aspects of the harem: a women's bonding aspect and the aspect that "permits males sexual access to more than one female" (1982: 524). There is irony in the use of the word "harem" itself. The English term *harem* (stress on first syllable) is a distortion of the Arabic word *harim* (stress on the second syllable) – a derivative of the same root (*h-r-m*) that yields the Arabic/Islamic notion of *haram* (stress on second syllable), which means "sacred." Both *harim* and (the Turkish term) *haramlik* refer to the women of a household and to women's quarters, as opposed to guest (and men's) quarters, which are called *salamlik*. This sacred quality embedded in the meaning of the term used to refer to women and women's quarters (see El Guindi 1981a, 1983, 1985, 1986b, 1987), which was not previously widely recognized by Western authors, has in the 1990s begun to be incorporated in writings. Doumato (1995: 19) does mention the cultural meaning of the original term *harim* being "both the area of the home in which women dwell and the women of the family, the word connoting sacredness and inviolability."

The multidimensional nature of harems emerges in the Memoirs of the feminist Huda Sha'rawi, in which her description of her life in the *harim* reveals an atmosphere of large household management, marital alliances, life and death events, and involvement in national politics, rather than a locus of sexual orgies. Both father and husband were legally polygynous. There was no sexual access to slaves and servants. The remark by Badran (1995a: 5) that "[t]he eunuch was answerable to the master alone, whose women and children he protected and whose orders he obeyed ... [and] exercised considerable power over women, even to the extent of controlling their access to their own money" is not supported in Huda Sha'rawi's own memoirs (Sha'rawi 1981 (Arabic); Shaarawi 1987). Badran's own primary subject – Huda Sha'rawi – provides a different nuance to the picture.[45]

Much useful information can be discerned from Sha'rawi's description of the *harim* that was her home before and after marriage. *Harim* is the Arabic word referring to the women's quarter in the household of her natal family (Sha'rawi 1981(Arabic); Shaarawi 1987). In a specific but very revealing incident she related how she wished to go on vacation to Alexandria. Her husband tried to prevent her by blocking access to funds, at which point her mother, who lived in the same household in her own private quarters, inter-vened. She released funds for her daughter's trip and made arrangements for her stay in Alexandria against the wishes of her husband, who did not accompany her. The eunuch, along with the maids, accompanied her. Clearly the "matriarch" of the household prevailed, and the eunuch could not exercise any serious power over Huda's movements or finances. Nor in this case could her husband (Sha'rawi 1981: 88–9, my free translation).

As does Ahmed, Badran recognized the quality of gender awareness that emerged out of the harems. In her examination of Egyptian feminism in the nineteenth and into the twentieth century she located "the roots of ... Egyptian feminism ... [and the] site of the first emergence of women's 'feminist awareness' ... [in the] urban harem" in which upper and middle-class women lived (1995b: 4).

Looking at the phenomenon of the harem from the perspective of gender alone and through the ideological lens of feminism strips it from its cultural context and from society at large. Badran's comments are a good example. She wrote: "[a]mong the wealthy upper classes, elaborate architecture as well as large household establishments catered to the maintenance of strict divisions between the sexes. Eunuchs[46] (castrated male slaves) guarded women and children, accompanied them if and when they went outside, and controlled all entries into the household" (1995b: 5). This uni-dimensional ideological view about *harims* and the role of eunuchs is challenged by insights from anthropology that place the phenomenon in the larger sociocultural context.

In his anthropological analysis of the Ottoman court and harem, Alexander Moore (1992) situates the harem in the context of a successful dynastic rule of over 600 years that was supported by a complex but sophisticated governing bureaucracy. In AD 1250 a band of nomadic Turks from central Asia arrived in northwestern Anatolia (today's Turkey). They fought against both Christian Byzantines (the Eastern Roman Empire) and Muslim Seljuk Turks. Later, the sultan Mehmet the Conqueror took the city of Constantinople in 1453 (1992: 382–4).

Numerous scholars have noted that a system that separated the sexes and secluded women, who were guarded by eunuchs, is neither indigenous to Arab society nor to Islam. It was fully in place from the Byzantine period when the Ottomans took over. Goodwin observes that prior to the Ottomans women in Greece "were confined to a *gynaecium* " (1997: 84). He adds that when the Ottoman sultans conquered Byzantium they accepted certain elements, including the exact design of the Byzantine royal guard uniform, from the Byzantine system, to become "the emperors of New Rome, in all but name." "The gallery of Hagia Sophia," Goodwin states, "remained the place for women" (1997: 152).

Goodwin accordingly considers the Ottoman harem to be "a reflection of the Byzantine *gynaecium*" (1997: 121). My analysis suggests that this is not quite the case. While aspects of form continued or were borrowed, the meaning and content of relations shifted dramatically during the Ottoman period. Melman (1992 [1995]) challenges the common view of the *haramlik* (women's quarters in household or palace) which had occupied a special place in the "sexual geography of travelers" as central to a sensual Orient. She describes the sexual geography this way: "[T]he harem as the *locus* of an exotic and abnormal sexuality . . . a microcosmic Middle East, apotheosizing the two characteristics perceived as essentially Oriental: sensuality and violence" (1992: 60, emphasis in original). She attributes this distortion to the fact that the Middle East is seen as a political threat and Islam as a possible alternative to Christianity. "[T]he early Ottoman sultans," she explained, "modeled the *harem-I humayun* (or Imperial Harem) [including the use of eunuchs] . . . on the Byzantine *gynecea*" (1992: 60; also see Stowasser 1984; Penzer 1936). For perspective, Melman makes the points that "the Greeks had sequestered females in separate *gynecea*" and "the Hebrews had been polygamists" and that "the evangelical missionaries who preached the abolition of the harem well knew that the Scriptures abounded with examples of plural marriages" (1992: 60). Yet the attack on Islam and European charges about polygamy persisted. As Harlow puts it: "a major thrust of the medieval European attack on Islam was an *argumentum ad hominem* directed at . . . Prophet Muhammad . . . for indulging in polygyamy"

(1986: xv). It has been stressed in modernist Islamic writings that the *Qur'an* limited polygyny and recommended monogamy because of the significance of the constraining condition in the same passage of exact quantitative and qualitative equality among wives. Ironically, Melman adds: "Indeed nowhere in the Old or New Testament is polygamy explicitly prohibited – except once, in St. Paul's admonition to bishops and deacons not to espouse more than one wife at a time" (1986: 60).

Melman's observations are supported by many scholars who claim that the institutions of the harem, with eunuchs and enforced seclusion of women, were strongly in place during the Byzantine rule, and were adopted and adapted by the Ottomans after their conquest of Constantinople. I would caution, as I have earlier regarding the practice of veiling, that the harem institution is not monolithic, and cannot be reduced to a cultural artifact that passed in a linear succession from dynasty to dynasty or civilization to civilization. The specific reference above is to the direct adoption of a Byzantine governing structure that the Ottomans became heirs to after conquest. And even despite this direct inheritance the Ottoman ruling harem had a different character. The marked quality becomes not seclusion but complementary structures of governance and management, one by men and one by women.

Moore (A. Moore1992: 382–401) describes the sultan's imperial household as the center that supplied all the civil, military, and service corps. It contained two parallel structures: the gate and the harem. Building on Byzantine institutions already in place, the Turks developed a patrimonial principle: instead of breeding thousands of royal kinsmen – a model Saudi Arabia experimented with but eventually needed to supplement with imported labor – they recruited and trained slaves. Christian boys went to the Gate and European girls went into the harem. All were slaves, many from the Byzantine era, others newly recruited or acquired. "In the nineteenth century they were mostly Circassian girls from Georgia on the Black Sea" (1992: 392) aspiring to a better life, who were acquired or sold.[47] Goodwin (1997) reports that by the end of the sixteenth century, "Tatars were the chief suppliers and slavery was the main support of the Crimean economy. In 1578, 17,000 slaves were imported . . . [and trade existed] between Antalya and Alexandria . . . [during which the] boys were deprived of their manhood in Coptic monasteries (such mutilation was abhorrent to a Moslem)" (1997: 106).

Moore (1992) sees the harem as the mirror image of the gate. They were both schools for training. They had paths of advancement and were graded by rank and achievement. The grand vizier himself was a gate slave. Women in the harem spent much time "learning the arts of courtly gentlewomen" (1992: 392). He defines the harem as "more of a school for officials' wives than a residence for the sultan's consorts" (1992: 392–3). Goodwin supports this view and conceptualizes the harem as "a pyramid at the apex of which the Valide sat in far from lonely state, since all important business passed through her hands" (1997: 129). Sayyid-Marsot writes that the harem was certainly a "place where order reigned, where everyone was assigned a task, and where administrative skills were necessary to direct and guide the numerous servants, slaves, and retainers" (1995: 40).

Eunuchs were castrated men who served both in the harem (under the authority of the head woman sultan) and the sultan in the inner court; they served women and men in a system in which a particular structure was to be maintained (A. Moore 1992). That female slaves were under the immediate authority of the women they served, rather than male masters, is supported in chronicles of other periods in Islamic history. Administratively, according to Goodwin, the Ottoman harem and the Palace School ("where the elite boys were trained for the chief offices of the empire") were until 1582 under the same administration of the white eunuchs. The structure of training was also identical, particularly in form. "Both had affinities with the guild system ... [T]he young girls were admitted to the Harem as *acemi*, which was the same term as that used for the boys and meant cadet rather than recruit. Like the pages, they were *kul*, or members of the larger family of the sultan, rather than slaves who could be bought or sold. The white eunuchs could propose which graduates from either school might be married to each other" (Goodwin 1997: 129, 131).

The eunuchs of the harem, who along with the princes, were the only men to live there, had their entire genitals removed. In the inner court eunuchs who were less drastically altered waited on the sultan. From these ranks graduated the highest officials of the empire (A. Moore 1992).

The master–slave relation was special. "Since many Ottoman slaves were manumitted, a freed man had a special relationship with his former master and could be adopted into the family. The Abbasid dynasty [of Baghdad] was so voracious that the family had 33,000 kin. Patronage was merged with procreation. Manumission was contractual" (Goodwin 1997: 105). The powerful women of the Abbasid period are well known – Harun al-Rashid's mother, his cousin and wife Zubaida, and his sisters. Chronicles of this period attest to the extent to which the mother exercised authority in affairs of state. Men of high positions had access to the Caliph's mother. In various Islamic eras evidence shows that men frequently sought favors by going through wealthy or powerful women. These women "could get powerful men removed from office, engaged in wheeling and dealing in the marketplace, and were fabulously wealthy" (Abbott 1946: 137 ff., cited in Sayyid-Marsot 1995: 12).

In the Ottoman harem the highest-ranking officials are the *valide* sultan,[48] or the sultan's mother, and the head black eunuch, or *Kisler agha*. Goodwin puts *valide sultan* (equivalent to queen mother) at the very top of the pyramid structure. As mother of the sultan, she ruled the harem. Next came *hasseki sultan* (chief royal lady), a princess who is a mother of sons, followed by *hasseki kadin* (mother of daughters). The top two women become secluded upon the death of their sons. The *kadin* could remarry on the death of the sultan (for more on the power of women in the harem and the role of the *valide sultan* see Goodwin 1997: 121–50; see Fanny Davis 1986 on the Ottoman lady).

Mernissi points out how Islam introduced the innovation of declaring the son of a slave woman and a free father to be free. "[H]er husband could no longer sell her after the birth of a child and she became free after his death . . . [Her] children had the same rights and privileges as those born of a free mother. They could inherit a share of the father's possessions equal to that of the other children according to the prescriptions of the *shari'a* [Islamic law]. The *jawari* . . . [made] certain that their sons could inherit everything, even the throne" (Mernissi 1993: 57). Sayyid-Marsot mentions that historiographers of the Ottoman period refer to it "as the age of women or Sultanate of Women, in which mothers of sultans . . . were the real rulers. When the man on the throne had been incarcerated in a 'golden cage', a palace, from puberty until he came to the throne, with only women and eunuchs for companions, women and eunuchs played a powerful role in affairs of state" (1995: 12).

The princesses, or the daughters and sisters of sultans, also bore the title of sultan, and they practiced monogamy. Their husbands could not have another wife. The sultan's mother, who was in origin a slave, could in her new status "hold audiences with state officials, travel publicly around the city (properly veiled . . .), endow mosques and support charities, [engage] in politics, and . . . statecraft" (A. Moore 1992: 393).

Mernissi (1993) describes harems in Fatimid Egypt in which "[the princess and head of the empire] was adorned by hundreds of *jawari* [female slaves] who had the task of making her even more beautiful. They draped her in tunics of the finest silk, linen and royal brocade, specially designed by an industry that served only the dynasty" (Mernissi 1993: 159–60; see also Stillman 1986: 742–7)

Many travelers to Turkey and other parts of the Muslim East, whose views on Islamic culture have been influenced by a puritanist Christian environment, have totally missed the dynamic complexity of the system of parallel hierarchies characterizing the harem and its women's special privileges. "It was the harem on which they focused with fascination and loathing . . . eliciting pious condemnation for its encouragement of sexual laxity and immorality" (L. Ahmed 1982: 524).

As Sayyid-Marsot puts it: "Nineteenth-century Western authors who discovered 'exoticism' of the 'Orient' pictured Egyptian women either as sex objects as did Gérard de Nerval or as '*odalisques*' à la Ingres, reclining in harems and passing the time in intrigue and eating *rahat lukum* (Turkish delight)" (1995: 39, italics added). She rejects the harem–monastery analogy: "in no way did a harem resemble a monastic order" (1995: 40). In 1931 Crawley wrote: "a Muslim woman takes the veil, just as does a nun" (1931: 76). This is an example of a very commonly presumed analogy that results from examining the veil as object with universal (Christian) meaning. So the veil of the nun and the veil of the Muslim woman are presumed identical. Nothing can be more different than these two veils. The difference is in the meaning, the symbolism, the ideology, the constructed womanhood, and the notion of sexuality.

But there is another aspect to such a comment – the tendency ethno-centrically to impose Christian constructions on Islamic understandings. Underlying much of this prevalent imagery is a set of attitudes influenced by the Christian construct of moral goals. Both Islam and Christianity provide moral systems to restrain improper and disorderly behavior that threatens the sociomoral order: Christianity chose the path of desexualizing the worldly environment; Islam of regulating the social order while accepting its sexualized environment.

The moral standards of Islam are designed to accommodate enjoyment of worldly life, including a sexual environment. It posed no tension between religion and sexuality. Different challenges present themselves to Islam and to Christianity. In their accounts of travels, scholars and writers with a Euro-Christian background had difficulty comprehending the challenge that Islam has taken upon itself in opting for the latter path. The fertile imagination that embellishes accounts of "baths and harems and veils" is woven out of an internalized culture of a desexualized society. It is interesting that many have seen a resemblance between the extravaganza around President Clinton over the Monica Lewinsky case and the witchcraft hysteria in Salem three hundred years ago. There is a parallel in the sexual element underlying both. Arthur Miller (1998) writes in the Opinions section of *The Daily News* in the United States: "witch hunts are always spooked by women's horrifying sexuality awakened by the superstud devil. In Europe where tens of thousands perished in the hunts, broadsides showed the devil with two phalluses, one above the other. And of course, mankind's original downfall came about when the filthy one corrupted the mother of mankind" (Miller, "Opinions," *The Daily News*, 16 Oct. 1998). The Christian vision was formed to attain a state of purity and moral perfection – a concept linking sex, religion, and moral order in a way that is Christian, not Islamic – particularly not in the sense of the Islam of the revelational original source, the *Qur'an*.

In accordance with the Christian ideals discussed earlier, the idea that members of the same sex can be socialized to have close, intimate, confiding, and private relations without necessarily sexualizing them is incomprehensible. Ahmed noted this component of bonding in the harem of later times in the Arab world. She describes the harem as "a system whereby the female relatives of a man – wives, sisters, mother, aunts, daughters – share much of their time and their living space [so that] women have frequent and easy access to other women in their community" (L. Ahmed 1982: 524).

In her ethnography on women in North Yemen, Makhlouf describes how women's separate sphere constitutes a "source of support and even of power" (1979: 25). These women are actively exchanging information in their daily visiting and do have a role in informal political decision-making. Between the *'asr* (afternoon) prayer and the *'isha* (evening) prayer women are out of their homes going to the *tafrita* (women's visit) where women gather in friends' homes dressed up for the occasion; they enjoy each others' company, listen to music, tell stories, smoke the hookah, chew *qat* (*Catha edulis*)[49] and exchange valuable information (see Makhlouf 1979: 21–30). "The all-female groupings . . . constitute the universe within which girls and women of all ages spend the greatest part of their lives. From . . . childhood, girls . . . participate in an inter-generational world with their mothers, aunts and grandmothers" (1979: 24).

In a novel based on the true experiences of an American woman married to a Saudi upper-class man, the author makes sensitive observations about this quality of life in a woman's world. Alireza describes the atmosphere of privacy (Chapter 10), intense story-telling (1971: 133–6), the sharing and getting along, house help, slaves, and social life (1971: 140, 161–3). The intensity in the women's world at times seemed to suffocate her, as she had been socialized in a culture of individualized space and isolation from large family life. She called it "suffocating groupness" (1971: 141, 151) and being "married to the family rather than to Ali" (1971: 207). With all the detail in her description, there was no mention of lesbian relations, or sexual lewdness.[50]

American culture particularly before the 1970s socialized men and women in a climate that idealized heterosexuality and encouraged competitive tension among members of the same sex while it also discouraged public display of emotion. It also cultivated sex as the only expression of intimacy against a long ideological tradition that envisioned sex as defiling or impure. It is no wonder that the feminist movement was not only a movement to liberate Western women from entrenched domesticity, but in large part to liberate their sexuality as well from ideological and religious "chastity belts." But American women confronted a barrier against their full liberation in the absence of an established cultural foundation that encouraged the development of nonsexual female friendships. Realizing this, women consciously began to establish networks and to form consciousness-raising groups. In the process, they discovered that without cultural support there was much to be learned and unlearned before building trust and developing personal, non-organizational, bonds. I contend that developments leading to a phase of cross-sex antagonism and open same-gender sex is not unrelated to the absence of cultural foundations for same-gender friendships.

In contrast, the culture into which Arab women are socialized provides a deep-rooted, culture-based foundation for asexual "solidarities" outside a feminist environment – asexual[51] but warm and supportive and accompanied by much physical touching. Such bonds provide the conditions needed for other kinds of solidarities.

It is within a Euro-Christian climate of thought and ideology that sense is made of the antipathy expressed toward the culture into which travelers "entered" in fantasy from behind the closed doors. Alloula views the colonial postcards, the "comic strip of colonial morality" (1986: 4) whose golden age lies between 1900 and 1930, after which their mission was taken over by colonial cinema and tourism, as "nothing more than an *innocuous* space in which the sexually repressed characteristic of colonialism can surface or pour itself out at any moment" (1986: 130, n. 15. emphasis in original).

The colonial postcards staged Algerian women to evoke images about women's quarters as "prisons" (1986: 17–26), naked bodies and "sub-eroticism" (1986: 105–24) and "oriental sapphism" (1986: 95–104) (see Figure 2). Out of such fantasies, Robert Withers (1905 [1619]) describes urban women's baths this way: "much unnatural and filthy lust is said to be committed daily in the remote closets of the darksome baths: yea women with women; a thing incredible" (1905: 247(1) as quoted in L. Ahmed 1982: 525).[52] Goodwin (1996) raises doubt about Withers as a source for a number of reasons. Withers is purportedly the translator for the primary documents by Ottaviono Bon, who was sent to Istanbul as Bailo, or Venetian representative both of the Senate and of Venetian subjects (Bon 1996: 12). Withers seems to have translated Bon's original accounts, but "added over 50 lines to [the] text in the edition of 1625 and yet another 250 lines appear in the 1650 version. These add 10 per cent to the length of the book . . . additions [which] have nothing to do with Bon but a great deal to do with the young translator's somewhat abrasive humour" (1996: 17–18).

Lady Montagu is the woman traveler who is repeatedly cited by scholars as having a more perceptive image of Turkish life. She challenged common

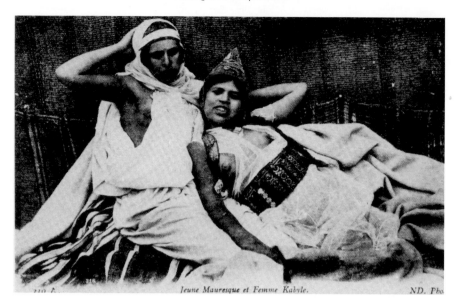

Jeune Mauresque et Femme Kabyle.

Figure 2 Studio-made postcard image of "Moorish and Kabyle" women invoking lesbianism in the harem, as an example of the colonial and Euro-Christian gaze at Muslim women. From the series of colonial postcards by the French from 1900–1930 in Algeria. By permission, from *The Colonial Harem* by Malek Alloula, University of Minnesota Press, 1986.

perceptions of the harem as a locus of women's oppression and licentiousness. In 1717 she was in Turkey with her husband Edward Wortley Montagu, British Ambassador Extraordinary to the Court of Turkey and representative of the Levant Company. In an article on Lady Montagu, Elizabeth Fernea wrote: "Robert Halsband, her most recent biographer, has pointed out that [in 1717 Lady Mary] was among the first to suggest that Muslim women were not benighted 'others' bound by a cruel code of restriction and oppression, but might have values and customs that were worthy of, if not emulation, at least of study and respect" (Fernea 1981: 330, citing Halsband 1965b: vii).

Lady Montagu recounted a visit to a Turkish bath, clearly refuting popularly peddled statements about the baths, particularly in men's travel accounts. In a letter Lady Mary wrote: "I went to the [Turkish] bagnio about ten o'clock. It was already full of women . . . without any distinction of rank by their dress, all being in the state of nature, that is, in plain English, stark naked, without any beauty or defect concealed. Yet there was not the least wanton smile or immodest gesture amongst them. They walked and moved with . . . majestic grace" (Halsband 1965a: 313 as quoted in Fernea 1981: 330). Lady Mary described the bath as "the women's coffee-house" (1965a: 313), relating by analogy the women's world and the men's world.

Jean August Dominique Ingrès, the French painter, was purportedly inspired by Montagu's account when he made his famous painting *Le Bain Turc* (1862), now in the Louvre. Ahmed (1982: 526) sees it as reviving "the lesbian theme" recurrently imagined by other male travelers and artists in connection with the women's world, as "two women fondle each other in a frankly sexual caress." Women as *odalisques* was a common style of painting Muslim women, communicating the imagery of leisure, luxury, voluptuousness and non-Christian womanhood. The term *odalisque*, according to Alloula, began to appear in French at the beginning of the seventeenth century, but ironically it derives from the Turkish, *odaliq (oda* meaning chamber*)*, which means "chambermaid." The term is "metamorphosed by Orientalist painting . . . into the sublimated image of the one enclosed by the harem . . . the prohibited space is endowed by Western imagination with a strong erotic connotation" (Alloula 1986: 130, n. 24; see also d'Huart and Tazi 1980; Maurel1980; Verier 1979).

Ironically, the original description by Montagu that purportedly provided the inspiration for *Le Bain Turc* was about the impression created in the Turkish women in the bath by her restricted manner and dress. "I saw," Lady Montagu wrote, "they believed I was so locked up in that machine [referring to the confining undergarments of corsets and girdles], that it was not in my own power to open it, which contrivance they attributed to my husband" (Halsband 1965a: 314). Her observations suggest both her and their awareness that dress and fashions (particularly the Western ones at that time) can oppress women and abuse their bodies. It is fascinating that the views of the women in the bath about Lady Montagu's "tight-lacing" and "corseting" were identical to Western feminist objections to them.

To the ethnocentric Western traveler, particularly in earlier centuries, the women's world of baths must have presented a shock to European sensibilities stretching fantasies to the limit. Western male travelers (except perhaps a few male physicians mentioned occasionally) had no access to such private activities as women's baths and harems, yet took the liberty of writing reports and letters as if they had. Alloula observes that the colonial postcard is created with "elaborate" staging that presupposes and gives the illusion that the photographer is inside the place of confinement. In the absence of mass media, the postcard fills the gap and adds "chatter to colonialist discourse" (1986: 44). He adds, "what the postcard proposes as the truth is but a substitute *for something that does not exist*" (1986: 129, n. 10, emphasis in original), neither photographically nor in real life. Like travelers' writings, these tell more about them (their fears and repressions) than about Middle Eastern life. The impact of the fabricated image, as in the case of the colonial postcards, is the illusions sent from the colony to the mother country, that is, "to a public incapable of questioning its truthfulness" (Alloula 1986: 129). In this case, the postcard becomes the source of information, the expert voice, the authority on the subject. The impact is expressed in the comment by Clot Bey,[53] when he writes: "In Europe it is generally imagined that the harem is a kind of place of prostitution, the exclusive theatre of the most numerous sexual pleasures and stultifying debauchery of a people sapped by libertinage" (1840 (2): 395, translated in Sayyid-Marsot 1995: 173, n.12). Alloula's quote from Jean Thevenot, *Voyage du Levant (1665)* confirms this image: "This great idleness causes the women to be depraved, and they apply all of their mind to the search for means of distraction" (Alloula 1986: 95).

The bath and harem then, the veil now,[54] generate strong reactions and fabulous fantasies[55] and a recurrent frenzy in the media.

There is a European discomfort with institutions and practices that are presented in Christian ideology as immoral, and that challenge puritanist asexualized models of gender life and relations. In Christian gender ideology, the notion of purity, translated into practiced asexuality, is reflected in the Christian institutions of female seclusion, celibacy,[56] and the virgin birth, all of which develop into restrictive womanhood and dress (see Armstrong 1995). From this perspective, close gender relations are automatically interpreted as sexual. But these are assumptions based on certain facets of Christian thinking and teaching, not on the reality of Muslim life.

In sum, it is argued in this chapter that the notion of "seclusion" is not appropriate for describing Arab and Muslim women's lives, and that it more appropriately represents Christian and Mediterranean religious life. The picture indiscriminately painted in colonial constructions of "sexual orgies" is deconstructed, revealing the ethnocentrism (and Euro-Christian ideological basis) behind these assumptions. Examining the meaning of the word *harim* as it plays out in Arab culture brings out the crucial component of sacredness, which radically shifts the emphasis from presumed sex. An ethnographic exploration of the *harim* further casts doubt on the common perception of it as a woman's indulgent world. It reveals a structure of governance, management, and negotiation in a relational setting of gender complementarity. The harem is about women and men, society, and politics in a particular culture, not women, sexualized life, and seclusion.

The next section continues discussion of the ideological basis to existing understandings of veiling among Muslim women by presenting the Western Evangelical missionary project in the Middle East – its goals and methods for "reforming" Oriental womanhood.

Orientalism and Christianism

The Orientalist imagery permeated writings, paintings, postcards and photographs, allowing observers to penetrate women's privacy in Arab societies, and showing them behind the walls and barred windows, as Alloula so compellingly demonstrates in the colonial postcards he presents. Photography was one instrument that, by what Graham-Brown (1988: 70) calls a "leap of imagination" gives the illusion of revealing the hidden and forbidden, while creating "the mythology" which Edward Said (1978) calls an "orientalized Orient."

Said observes that the Orient was invented by Europe and became part of its self-definition since it (the Orient) is "the source of its [Europe's] civilizations and languages, its cultural contestant" (1978: 1). In turn, the Orient provides Europe with a contrasting basis against which Europe's identity can be constructed. Orientalism, he writes, is about "dominating, restructuring, and having authority over the Orient – because of Orientalism the Orient was not (and is not) a free subject of thought or action" (1978: 3; see also the synthesis on Orientalism by Philippe Jullian 1977).

On the one hand, Muslim women are presented as caged, inaccessible and imprisoned behind walls and bars, hidden from men; yet travelers, explorers, artists and scholars had produced an enormous volume of paintings, photos, postcards, and writings depicting these women in detail. George Sandys (1905 [1619]) is quoted in Ahmed (1982) describing Muslim women in the sultan's harem. "[I]t is not lawful for anyone to bring ought in unto them with which they may commit the deeds of beastly uncleanness; so that if they have a will to eat cucumbers, gourds, or such like, they are sent in unto them sliced, to deprive them of the means of playing the wantons" (Sandys 1905 (1619): 347 as quoted in Ahmed 1982: 534). Hasib (1996), expressing a Muslim woman's view, explains such distortions about Islam and Muslims as an attitude of hostility prevalent in the West towards Muslims, and claims that "Muslim women are ironically held as exotic sexual objects by the west, more so than other women in the world." She explains that this attitude is due to "Islam's great political and military challenge to Christian Europe during the Middle Ages and the Renaissance" (see also Gaudio and Pelletier 1980).

Ahmed and Sayyid-Marsot, among others, question the reliability of writings on Muslim women by Western male observers who were almost certainly denied access to women's quarters and private life (harems and baths). Graham-Brown explains this: "'[H]arem scenes' were studio reconstructions composed by the photographer. In this respect, the photograph, like the painting or engraving, was a figment of imagination, which assumed the privileged position of the voyeur entering this closed and private space, and allowing the viewer to do likewise" (1988: 74). Alloula also discusses the studio staging of "models" as the material for the colonial postcards.

An interesting observation regarding the question of access to women's private quarters in Muslim society is found in Huda Sha'rawi's Arabic memoirs, (*Muthakirat Huda Sha'rawi*, 1981) in which she recounts how her French mentor/friend Mme Rushdi was discussing negative tales circulating among the "foreigners" in Egypt about Egyptian character and morals. She commented that the *hijab* engendered hostile remarks and was being misinterpreted. Therefore, many travelers carried wrong impressions when they left Egypt and subsequently wrote falsehoods. Their views were informed by the mistaken assumption that they had visited the harems of respectable families when in fact they were deceptively taken to brothels (1981: 80, my free translation).

Examples such as this of a constructed imagery, whether based on real or imaginary landscapes, have shaped outsiders' understandings of Middle Eastern women and their private lives. The *hammam* or public bath, as Melman puts it, for example, "came to *apotheosise* the sensual, effeminate Orient . . . the *loci sensuales* in the erotically charged landscape" (1992, 1995: 89). Hasib's comment about women being the target of distortion is quite pertinent, since the Middle East has public baths for men and not just women, yet the male Western descriptions were mostly silent on men's baths, which they would have had access to, focusing in an obsessive way on women's harems and baths, which they could not have had access to, although a persistent current of thought in Europe linked men's Turkish baths with male homosexuality (D. Phelps, personal communication). Yet Arab men's memory of visits to the bath is described as luxurious, nourishing, satisfying and asexual.

The reality of women's baths is sensitively described in a novel based on real-life experiences by al-Idlibi (1988). She writes of her grandmother's experiences in the women's bath in Syria. The story is about a household in which a struggle for authority exists between the aging husband's mother and the maturing wife. The grandmother was in her seventies, yet had never once skipped her monthly trip to the public bath, known locally as the "market bath." She considered the baths to have a "delicious ambience about them which [those] who had never experienced it could not appreciate" (1988: 19). Then one day the granddaughter decided to join her grandmother in her monthly visit to the bath, curious to discover its "secret." The episode is described in this way:

Grandmother led me by the hand to the room where her massive trunk was kept. She produced the key from her pocket and opened the trunk in my presence – this was a great honor for me, for the venerable trunk had never before been opened in the presence of another person – and immediately there wafted out of it a strange yet familiar scent, a scent of age, a smell of the distant past, of years which have been folded up and stored away. Grandmother drew out of the depths of the trunk a bundle of red velvet, the corners of which were embroidered with pearls and sequins. . . . She handed me a wine-colored bath-wrap decorated with golden stars [and] white towels decorated . . . with silver thread. . . . She called the servant to carry the bundle containing our clothes and towels, and the large bag which held the bowl, the soap, the comb, the sponge-bag, the loofah, the soil of Aleppo, and the henna which would transform my grandmother's white hair to jet black. (al-Idlibi 1988: 21)

This series of events set the backdrop for the bath event. First, there is the female generational struggle for authority in the household; second, there is the generational difference in attitude, in which the grandmother maintains the time-honored tradition of going to the public bath (even if he she had to go alone) while the wife finds it backward and a sanitation hazard; third, the ritual passage of the daughter into the tradition by being privileged in becoming the first to attend the opening of her grandmother's trunk and being given a "gift" (originally part of the grandmother's lavish trousseau) of dress items for her first entry into the public bath.

Off they walked together, granddaughter and grandmother, servant following. The market bath was nearby the house. A little plaque above the door of the bathhouse read in poetic rhyming Arabic "whoever the Divine Blessing of health would achieve, should turn to the Lord and then to the baths of Afif" (1988: 21). The imagery of the bath, second only to the divine and associated with health, is one factor. The social and ritual aspects are the more dominant considerations in the memory and imagination of the people who experience it closely in their culture. Many a young woman nostalgically and fondly remembers the special day of the bath accompanying her mother, often described as a "day like the feast." They entered the bathhouse.

Social status, cultural knowledge, ritual initiation and passage, and dress emblems are aspects of the complexity embedded in the experience of warmth, scents of ginger, roses, jasmine and oils, motion of naked bodies, soothing sounds of fountain water, reflections from large wall mirrors, colored rugs, splendid Arabo-Islamic design tiles, colors, fogging steam, and cross-currents of women's voices telling stories, building alliances, forging relations, or eating with their children in a corner, unable to drown the children's laughter, crying, and screaming; here body, self, and culture become one. Arabic calligraphy reads "cleanliness is part of faith" (1988: 22). Al-Idlibi writes:

> Our maid hastened to undo one of our bundles, drawing out a small prayer rug, which she spread out, on the bench. My grandmother sat down on it to get undressed. . . . My grandmother urged me to undress. I took off my clothes and wrapped myself in the wine-colored bath-wrap. . . . Women sat around . . . busily engrossed in washing, scrubbing, and rubbing. . . . As she [grandmother] left the baths there was a certain air of haughtiness in her step, and she held herself proudly upright. . . . She was enjoying the esteem which was hers only when she visited the market baths. At last I understand their secret . . . (1988: 22, 27)

Not all writings on Muslim women by Western males were negative. In his *Aperçu général sur l'Egypte* (1840: 395), Clot Bey is quoted in Sayyid-Marsot (1995) as attempting to correct distortions in commonly held views about Egyptian women and the harem. "One errs; a severe order, a rigorous decency, reign in the harem, and make it, in many ways, *similar to our monastic establishments*" (1988: 173, n. 12, italics added). In correcting the image of Middle Eastern women, Clot Bey evoked the analogy with a Christian institution, namely Christian monasteries, to communicate the qualities of order, rigor and decency.

It is interesting, however, that the analogy is with an institution that is not only not Islamic, but is contrary to fundamental orthodox notions of Islam, which do not prescribe a separation of religious life from worldly life. This is a gentler and indirect "gaze," one that is softened by being Christianized in imagery. The Orientalist cultural enterprise that Said writes about takes in "the whole of India and the Levant, the Biblical texts and the Biblical lands" (1978: 3). It is the basis of a particular gaze that finds expression through different Western insitutions.[57] One such institution is the Western Christian proselytization project. Here the gaze is Euro-Christiano-centric,[58] dress is central to it (see Baizerman, Eicher and Cerny 1993 for more on Eurocentrism in dress), and women are its focus. Its target, like that of the Orientalist project, is the Orient – Japan, China, India, and North Africa, and extends deeper to Central Africa.[59]

An article by a photographer (Kaplan 1984) describes the "lantern slide presentations" that were made (citing the Stereopticon Department) to convey "information, humor and inspiration" (1984: 61) and to recruit converts and seek funds for missionary activity. These slides are selected from the scientific library of the United Methodist Church.[60] The sixty-minute program called *Enlightened Women in Darkened Lands* was one of many scripts presented as lantern slide shows during the 1920s and 1930s[61] in local churches to raise revenues and further missionary recruitment. Illustrated lectures provided information about how people abroad *dressed*, worked, and played (1984: 61).

Kaplan evaluates *Enlightened Women in Darkened Lands* as one of the more sophisticated lectures in the collection, made about 1921, which is not only multicultural but cross-cultural as well. "It is organized around five regions or countries: North Africa, India, China, Japan, and Central Africa. The slides contain, along with images, text that introduces the customs and religion of a country. Charts and maps ... illustrate the rise of Muslim conversions throughout Africa. Word slides declare the gender inequalities existing in non-Christian cultures" (1984: 63) and construct a story of the variety of women's oppression around the world. The presentation includes an Arab man selling beautiful women in an open market in Makka, the holiest city in Muslim religion. The use of this Arab man undoubtedly sends a message about Islam and Arab men and women. But Kaplan makes the additional point that this Arab man stands for all non-Christian, Oriental men, and that he could be a "priest in India, a father in China, or a husband in Japan" (1984: 63).

The implication is that wherever men have subjugated women, the state religion, not men, should be held responsible, and that a woman's role, in the home and in society, is dictated by religion (1984: 63). It is interesting to note the striking resemblance between the Christian missionaries' argument that female subjugation is caused by official religion and some Western feminist positions.[62] As presented, slavery, child marriage, and prostitution have one thing in common – all are non-Christian practices. The point made here is that "if men and women would convert to Christianity, their culture would have an opportunity to liberate itself and prosper" (1984: 63). The contrast between *enlightened* and *darkened* in the project's titles is revealing.

A photo called *Beautiful Women, North Africa*, with penciled notations and revisions made for a presentation held in 1981, shows two Arab women who, as Kaplan emphatically points out, "are unveiled"[63] (1984: 63). However, the photos show the two women wearing headdresses, substantial jewelry, and clothing that is loose, unfitted, long-sleeved, and ankle length – qualifying as "modest" by traditional standards. One woman is in profile and looks beyond the camera, and an older woman has her hands clasped in front of her cautiously and looks at the camera (see Figure 3). It is pointed out that in the missionary lecture the fact that both are wearing "elegant costume and jewelry" is presented as betraying their vulnerability to the "wealthiest and craftiest and lewdest man" (Kaplan 1984: 63). The complete original caption formulated as part of the lecture presentations follows:[64]

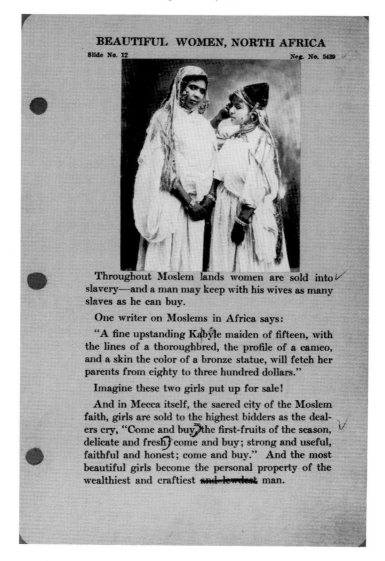

Figure 3 From missionary lanternslides with original commentary and marked edits, representing Arab women from Algeria. From *Journal of Visual Communication* (discontinued), by permission from editor Jay Ruby.

Throughout Moslem lands women are sold into slavery – and a man may keep with his wives as many slaves as he can buy. One writer on Moslems in Africa says: "A fine upstanding Kabyle maiden of fifteen, with the lines of a thoroughbred, the profile of a cameo, and a skin the color of a bronze statue, will fetch her parents from eighty to three hundred dollars."

Imagine these two girls put up for sale!
And in Mecca itself, the sacred city of the Moslem faith, girls are sold to the highest bidders as the dealers cry,
"Come and buy, the first fruits of the season,
Delicate and fresh; strong and useful;
Faithful and honest; come and buy."
And the most beautiful girls become the personal property of the wealthiest and craftiest [and lewdest] man.

[Brackets mark edits on original photo text.]

Photo and text suggest that marriage is equated with slavery – a fate awaiting even the most "refined." In this context, dress is used to communicate status, as well as the opposite point that even the "unveiled," here signifying "refined," cannot escape such oppression and slavery. Since both women wear headcovers, the "veil" must specifically mean "face cover" to the author.

In contrast, the series of photos labeled *Bible Woman*, such as *Bible Woman, Africa*, shows emancipated converted women who travel to tell the story of Christ. As women they are seen to have access and can penetrate the innermost recesses of the non-Christian oppressed women, according to the slide, to reach "the *secluded* women, the *slave* women and the *outcaste* women" (Figure 15, Kaplan 1984: 75, emphasis added). The chosen terms are evocative. The combination of select missionary vocabulary and Orientalist photography constructs illusions and contrasts between Christian[65] and non-Christian cultures. *Secluded* is suggestive of Muslim Arab woman, *slave* of African and *outcaste* (with an "*e*" instead of the common spelling "outcast"), obviously, specifically, and deliberately targets India. "Slavery" is used interchangeably with "oppression," to describe the conditions of non-Christian women. Through the visual medium of word and picture slides, clothing is used as a vehicle to construct an image world and communicate a message about people from the non-Christian world.

The slide text describes the Bible woman (that is, the converted) as noble and unselfish, a "new woman emerging from the old darkness into the light of Christian civilization" (Figure 15, Kaplan 1984: 75). The photo *Bible Woman, Africa* shows a barefoot African woman dressed in foot-length draped cloth worn over a long-sleeved knitted sweater with a simple headwrap – solid, white, simple, and neat: the converted Christian African. The caption says:

The Bible woman travels among her sisters telling the old, old story of Christ and his wonderful love. She can reach the secluded women, the slave women and the outcaste women, as the men, either missionary or native, can never hope to do. And into the most hopeless soul and the darkest home, she brings the joy and the brightness of the Gospel ... What womankind owes to these noble, unselfish women, no one can ever estimate; but theirs is the reward of a new woman emerging from the old darkness into the light of Christian civilization. (Kaplan 1984: 75)

It is relevant in this context to mention another woman traveler to the Middle East who, in this case, challenges the presumed superiority of Christians. Lady Duff Gordon, who lived in Egypt in 1862, wrote in her letters from Egypt that Christians are not more permissive than Muslims in matters pertaining to women and family. She described the situation: "the Copts have but one wife, but they shut her up much closer than the [Muslims]. They are strict monogamists; males are circumcised before baptism and it was long the practice to circumcise females also" (L. D. Gordon 1969: 55).

The final photo in the missionary lectures is called *Elizabeth Ryder, Missionary Baby*. The photo shows a cute white toddler "costumed" in Japanese native dress standing in the midst of a garden, holding a Japanese umbrella and looking at the camera charmingly while laughing and throwing back her head. She looks neat, clean, and pure. The accompanying text states:

The world will never know what womanhood and girlhood owe to this bright little mission tot in far away Japan, dressed in native costume. Her smile spreads wherever she goes – it is truly contagious. The world will never know the whole story of the sacrifice of thousands of other children like her in mission lands – away from schools and association with children of their own race and age.

But some day the world will take off its hat and bow in reverence to the missionary wife and missionary baby, apostles to suffering womanhood.

Then there is a long list of noble Christian women who have spent their lives working for their sisters in other lands. Their names are many and glorious – only a few typical women in a few fields can be mentioned in the brief compass of this lecture.

In the field of medical missions women stand preeminent. (Kaplan 1984, on back cover)

Notions of Western Christian sexuality and Muslim sexuality are relevant to the attitudes described above. Foucault, in *The History of Sexuality*, dehomogenized Western sexuality by putting it in historical context. He describes how at the beginning of the seventeenth century there was more openness and frankness about sex. "[S]exual practices had little need of secrecy; words were said without undue reticence, and things were done without too much concealment; one had a tolerant familiarity with the illicit. Codes regulating the coarse, the obscene, and the indecent were quite lax compared to those of the nineteenth century. It was a time of direct gestures, shameless discourse, and open transgressions, when anatomies were shown and intermingled at will, and knowing children hung about amid the laughter of adults: it was a period when bodies "made a display of themselves'" (1980: 3). But this changes to "monotonous nights of the Victorian bourgeoisie . . . [and] [s]exuality was carefully confined; it moved into the home" (1980: 3).

The sexuality and dress of the Victorian woman was the subject of much controversy. The subject of tight-lacing and corsetry in the West received much attention in costume history and was the center of controversy among feminists, puritanists, and antifeminists. The argument by feminists focused on the confining, restraining function of clothing in turning women into "slaves."

Kunzle considers reformist moves against corseting and tight-lacing anti-feminist, thus turning the argument on its head (1977: 570). He thus associates feminism with corseting and tight-lacing, whereas most feminist women were arguing for the liberation of women's body from such constrictions. A dominant component of the new wave of feminism in the 1970s as it was manifested in the United States and Europe was to "liberate women's body and sexuality." The public exposure of more of the body and the liberating of breasts from bras created quite a stir. Looking at feminism and dress differently, Kunzle calls Rousseau and Napoleon and Renoir the enemies of the corset, and gives as the reason that they are "generally autocratic males with a low opinion of the female sex and an attachment to the concept of the 'natural woman', that is, one dedicated to home and children" (1970: 570). Jean-Jacques Rousseau considered "stays" as a means to sexualize the body and the corset as abusive of maternal nature. Orson Fowler accused tight-lacing not only of ruining the health, inducing consumption, and causing sterility but also of "exciting the 'organs of Amativeness' and developing a wholly unchristian erotic sensibility" (1898: 35 ff.). It is worth noting how the "natural," the "maternal," and the "asexual" seem to be linked in these observations. The expressed concern about the "unchristian erotic sensibility" is an example of the prevalent ideology elucidated earlier in Chapter 2, that combines a fundamentally Christian puritanist belief and a dominant West constructed as a standard lens through which to project the world of the East. As demonstrated in the pictures of the harem in colonial postcards, the quest for the harem is the Euro-Christian quest for the exotic inferior other – an obsession forcefully and vigorously expressed in the series grouped by Alloula as "the exhibition of breasts" of Arab women, or "an anthology of breasts" (1986: 105–26).

My overall intent is to analyze the veil, the subject of this book, as an aspect of dress contextualized in society and culture. Part I established patterns that underlie misperceptions and misconceptualizations about Middle Eastern women. Questions are reframed to bring out qualities and orientations that more adequately characterize the culture. Part II explores dress as it is cross-culturally described in the ethnography, and as it has been approached as an anthropological subject. Dress is then examined in Arab conceptualization and usage showing its place both in social and in sacred culture and drawing upon notions of privacy. After establishing the study of dress as the anthro-pological framework for the study of the veil, I discuss veil and veiling behavior in various contexts and across genders, drawing upon multiple bodies of knowledge. This is followed by the analysis of the role of the veil in the contemporary Islamic movement and the sacred meanings of *hijab* that connect it with cultural notions of sanctity and privacy. Part II ends after an ethnographic analysis is presented of the veil as dress, as a symbol of identity, as a code for communication, and as a vehicle for Islamic resist-ance, leading to a full discussion, in Part III, of the role of the veil in resistance movements and in feminism.

Part 2

Dress, "Libas" and "Hijab"

It is only shallow people who do not judge by appearances.
The true mystery of the world is the visible, not the invisible.

Oscar Wilde, *The Picture of Dorian Gray* (1891)

4

The Anthropology of Dress

Dress in Theory and Ethnography

I consider in this chapter how dress has been dealt with ethnographically and theoretically. In the course of this exploration it became evident that relatively little attention has been given to the study of dress as a topic in and of itself in anthropology, and ethnographic descriptions of dress are rare. Whatever ethnographic materials existed remained scattered in records and studies, perhaps because of the relatively secondary significance attached to dress in comparison with other aspects of society and culture, such as kinship, law, marriage, religion, etc. Ethnographic and anecdotal accounts on dress remained fragmented, awaiting adequate conceptual tools to provide them with some coherence. A framework for the study of dress was needed.

The few attempts to develop approaches to study dress varied in their impact on anthropological studies. In a unique approach to dress, Kroeber (1919) studied clothing, particularly women's fashion, in a pioneering (and classic) study that used a systematic quantitative approach. This study has subsequently been expanded (1957; Kroeber and Richardson 1940). However, this kind of study has never been replicated by others. As is noted by Eicher and Roach-Higgins, Kroeber developed "methods for measuring properties of dress and searching for ways to link historical fluctuations in properties of dress to fluctuations in other cultural phenomena" (1992: 21). On a much narrower scale, there is a study by Robinson on men's beards approached in terms of fashion fluctuations (see Robinson 1976), as a one-time effort that was not sustained or extended.

Another kind of work is a rather neglected publication by Crawley, which was compiled and published in 1931 (1931; also see Crawley 1912). It devoted a substantial section to dress, providing detailed documentation of cross-cultural customs and explanations given for customs when available. In this work, Crawley formulated his own ideas, borrowing from existing paradigms and critiquing others. These ideas, although sometimes inconsistent, can be considered a rudimentary framework foreshadowing the contemporary study of dress. His approach was influenced by the social evolutionary tradition that emerged during the 1860s, eventually turning into a dominant paradigm. Studies within this tradition traced customs in different societies and interpreted them using doctrines or premises that make up a universal framework of development for human culture. These are: the doctrine of survivals, seeking origins, the comparative method, the psychic unity of humankind, and the uniform stages of development from savagery to barbarism to civilization.

Crawley accepted the general evolutionary framework, but expressed reservation about seeking origins in the case of his study of dress. He considered "the genesis of dress" (1931: 2) to be too speculative. He nevertheless adopted a scheme of social evolution and development, adding a psychological dimension to it. "[W]hen once instituted, for whatever reasons or by whatever process, dress became a source of psychical reactions, often complex, to a greater extent than any other material product of intelligence" (1931: 1). He seems, however, inconsistently to accept the notion that clothing "originated" in a decorative impulse that characterized "the natural [primitive] man." Without dwelling on origins he explores existing formulations about dress in primitive society. Borrowing from Stanley Hall (G. S. Hall 1898: 366) he discusses multiple functions of clothing – "protection, ornament, and Lotz's self-feeling" (1931: 77), adding that "the subject's material personality is increased by clothing, and his psychical reaction is proportional to [it]. The result is a rich complex of self-consciousness, modesty, and self-feeling" (1931: 12).

His exploration of cross-cultural ethnography led him to identify certain functions of dress, which he called "hypotheses." They comprise decoration, protection and concealment. He observed that "in the most primitive clothing [there is] a curious interchange of concealment, protection, decoration, and advertisement [presumably meaning attraction]" (1931: 12). Crawley seems implicitly to accept the ornamentation (or decoration) hypothesis, which states that "the natural man will undergo any trouble, any discomfort, in order to beautify himself to the best of his power [and that] . . . "the less body-covering . . . the greater the tendency to painting, scarification, and tattooing . . . [as if (here Crawley refers to Gautier)] . . . having no cloth to embroider, they embroider themselves" (1931: 6, 22).

I find the ethnography of the contemporary Hageners of New Guinea to be relevant to this idea. They indeed "embroider themselves," but not because of the absence of cloth or clothing, as the hypothesis presented by Crawley states; rather, according to the study by Strathern and Strathern (1971), they select their bodies, rather than cloth or any other material crafts, as the canvases through which "statements about social and religious values are made" (1971: 1). Here body painting is connected to the individual and to society. Hagener men and women decorate themselves as "referents to the two sets of significant values in Hagen society – clan solidarity and prestige and individual wealth and well being" (1971: 1).

The case of the Rashayda bedouins is also relevant. Systematic data[66] collected by William Young during his fieldwork among the Rashayda[67] show how this Bedouin society uses dress, the body, and the tent as canvas upon which group identity and differentiation are "painted." Weaving, decorating and embroidery are done by the women. They use their bodies, those of their camels and livestock, and their shelter (the tent) to mark the symbols of group identity. Branded, embroidered, or tattooed, the Rashayda communicate their membership in a tribal branch by a particular shape brand[68] or a particular design or pattern on dress or tent (Young 1994, 1996).

The protection hypothesis discussed by Crawley proposes the invention of clothing as a protection for the body against harsh weather and the environment. It connects clothing and the notion of harmony with the environment, using the idea of fitness and balance. The final hypothesis in Crawley's formulation is the concealment hypothesis, which presumes a stage of barbarism in which wives became the property of men. He quotes Ellis (1897), who wrote: "the garment appears . . . a moral and physical protection against any attack on his [the husband's] property" (i.41 quoted in Crawley 1931). The hypothesis states that male jealousy instituted clothing for married women. He also quotes Ratzel, who wrote: "the first to wear complete clothes is not the man, who has to dash through the forest, but the married women" (Ratzel 1896–8: i. 93–4, quoted in Crawley 1931: 8). Crawley comments that for Ratzel "The primary function of her [a woman's] dress is to render her unattractive to others, to conceal her body from other men's eyes" (1931: 8).

Crawley criticizes the concealment hypothesis. According to him, it leaves out the elements of mystery and attraction that he proposes accompany concealment (1931: 11). By that he means that concealment of the body by clothing brings out an aura of mystery and enhances attraction, rather than what is purported in the hypothesis, namely that it makes bodies unattractive.

The point made by Crawley about mystery from concealment finds support in contemporary ethnography on veiling by Muslim women. For example, Papanek observes that "the social distance imposed by the covering enhances what is already seen as feminine in the culture: sexuality, a special sense of vulnerability . . ." (1973: 296). Carla Makhlouf makes a similar point when she cites a daily newspaper in her ethnography on Yemen as an example of the seductiveness of concealment. The daily newspaper *Al Thawra* published the view that "the *sharshaf* had ceased to be a modest garment and that it 'showed' the charms of the women by so strongly evoking them" (1979:

33). Other observations by Makhlouf confirm this quite common cultural view of the concealment of the woman's body as enhancing feelings of sexuality (see also Mernissi 1975). One male informant related how "what had first attracted him to her [his wife] was a short glimpse he had of her face when she once happened to lift her veil" (1979: 33).

Dress was not consistently treated by anthropology's British and American founders, who advocated the social evolutionary framework. In their survey of treatment of dress in anthropology, Eicher and Roach-Higgins observed that Morgan, in *Ancient Society* (1877), "devoted a chapter to the 'organization of society on the basis of sex' but offered no comment on how dress may be related to such social organization, or the interpersonal conduct it implies. Instead, he followed his special interest in kinship designations almost exclusively in the discussion . . ." (1992: 25, n.9). So they engaged in an interesting exercise of mentally mapping dress onto Morgan's evolutionary scheme: material and non-material progress "made in each of the six stages of social evolution that culminated in the attainment of the seventh stage: civilization. These six preliminary stages included three levels of savagery and three levels of barbarism" (1992: 25, n. 9). From this evolutionary scheme Eicher and Roach-Higgins imagined how Morgan would have fitted in dress and meticulously formulated stages that would have included a conception of the evolution of dress: "Briefly, he saw humans entering the first social level of savagery naked, the first level of barbarism in skin garments, and arriving at civilization in woven garments" (Eicher and Roach-Higgins 1992: 25, n.9).

Others would see human beginnings in a different way. In the edited work by Barnes and Eicher (1992b), Dransart has an article in which she describes the beliefs about the mythical origin of the Andean peoples (1992b : 145–63), whose ancestors entered this world "fully clothed, wearing the dress which identified the sex and ethnic origin of the wearer" (1992b : 145). Thus the Andeans, like other groups, construct their beginnings using dress, and make a connection between dress, gender, and ethnic origin. As ethnography shows, this association is quite common. Not all human groups, however, "enter this world," like the Andeans, fully clothed, nor do all groups conceive of beginnings as heterogeneous.

Eicher and Roach-Higgins also examined Charles Darwin's contribution to the subject. They observe that "In *The Descent of Man*, and *Selection in Relation to Sex*, Darwin attributed developments in dress by both sexes to a general inborn similarity in the mind of 'man'. At the same time, he perceived innate differences in attention paid to dress by men and women, attributing to females a 'greater delight' in activities of dress than men (Darwin, C., n.d.: 884, 901)" (1992: 24, n. 7). These ideas are further elaborated in *The*

Expression of Emotions in Man and Animals, where, they observe, Darwin proposed that males are less sensitive about how dress is viewed than are females. "This explanation, although based on a belief in innate differences, led him a step away from a strictly evolutionary stance regarding sex differences in dress" (1992: 24, n.7). Eicher and Roach-Higgins found in this concept an expression of "a rudimentary social-psychological viewpoint, greatly resembling that of contemporary symbolic interactionists, who posit that people's self-evaluations of their presentations of the outwardly observable self are learned through their social interactions with other people" (1992: 24, n. 7).

Edward B. Tylor (*Primitive Culture*, 1871) was not much concerned about dress except for mentioning a few historical changes in its form, but only as examples of his premise of "cultural survival" as an aspect of the stages of social evolution. He downplayed the social significance of dress and its observable survivals. But, according to Eicher and Roach-Higgins, subsequent generations of researchers on dress from different disciplines "regularly included virtually obligatory sections on such survivals in their work" (1992: 24, n. 8).

Over 500 years earlier, Ibn Khaldun, an Arab scholar who in 1377 developed "the science of culture," included dress in his formulation. On the basis of the social history of Maghribi Islamic culture he developed a theory of culture change in which dress is one of the distinguishing and transformative elements in the transition between *'umran badawi*[69] (elemental culture) and *'umran hadari* (civilizational culture). He proposed dress as an item of basic need that becomes more elaborate and rich as societies become more sedentary, urbanized, and leisurely. He wrote that "the inhabitants of the desert restrict themselves to the necessary in food, clothing, and mode of dwelling" (1958: 249). Simple societies develop and their conditions change, leading to acquisition of wealth and comfort in excess of their needs. "They use more food and clothes . . . they build large houses, and lay out towns and cities for protection . . . use varied splendid clothes of silk and brocade and other [fine materials]" (1958: 250).

In *The Principles of Sociology* (1879), another evolutionary scholar writing in the second half of the nineteenth century – Herbert Baldwin Spencer – devoted three chapters to the topic of dress, one of the more lengthy treatments of dress, which, according to Eicher and Roach-Higgins (1992: 25, n. 6), anticipated an ethnography of dress. As an evolutionist, he explored dress, classified it by type, and then fitted types to points on the evolutionary scale. He distinguished primitive people from nineteenth-century Western Europeans, whom he considered to be "representatives of higher levels of social evolution" (1992: 25, n.6).[70]

It is interesting to consider nineteenth-century evolutionary thinking against the context of Ibn Khaldun's fourteenth-century theory of culture change. In his theory the civilized state was represented by the "high" civilizations of the Middle East – Egypt and Mesopotamia, reaching a regional civilizational peak during the caliphal period of Islamic civilization. However, his theory, while developmental, is not lineal nor formulated on the basis of a presumed progression from lower to higher, from inferior to superior. Ibn Khaldun's theory does not conceptualize culture as a lineal progression from primitive to civilized. In his formulation of culture change both progress and decline are inherent to the processes of development of culture, and development is presented as cyclical.

Eicher and Roach-Higgins note that outside his evolutionary scheme Spencer's "observations on dress foreshadowed those of later social scientists, particularly Goffman" (1992: 24, n.6). Spencer dealt with the relationship between dress and patterns of authority and deference in social interaction and with how "various types of dress serve as guides to interpersonal conduct within the daily and special ceremonies of life" (1992: 24, n. 6).[71] He gave numerous examples of how different types of men's dress reinforce these patterns. Women's dress, on the other hand, did not receive any attention in his formulation.

Like Spencer, Westermarck in his *History of Human Marriage* (1922 [1891]) made extensive use of dress in his study. But by contrast with Spencer's treatment, Westermarck focused on the use of self-decoration by "primitive" people as a way to enhance "sexual attractiveness." Eicher and Roach-Higgins noted that "he used, and perhaps helped set, a pattern that anthropologists generally still follow: the practice of separating dress into the two categories of *ornament* and *clothing*" (1992: 25, n.10).

Crawley sometimes uses the term dress literally to mean clothing; but he also discusses body decoration. So he seems to have accepted the common division between clothing and ornament, even placing them occasionally on a social evolutionary scale of development, although with an awareness of its limitations: "It is difficult to say where clothing ends and ornament begins" (1931: 8).

Boucher (1966) accepts this division and puts it in an evolutionary paradigm. For Boucher, woven ornaments were considered part of an earlier phase in evolution: "[in the] primitive state of humanity, the first men seem initially to have worn, before or for lack of true 'garments', only ornaments such as necklaces and arm or ankle bracelets" (1966: 17). He also included hair and hairdresses. "Ornaments identify the wearer with animals, gods, heroes or other men" (1966: 17). But he considered this identification to be real for primitive people and symbolic for sophisticated societies.

Beginning in the 1960s Joanne Eicher, (henceforth referred to as Eicher), in collaboration with a number of other scholars, began a research project in which they studied what they called "dress" (see Roach and Eicher 1965, 1973, 1979; Barnes and Eicher 1992a, b; Eicher and Roach-Higgins 1992; Roach 1979; Roach-Higgins and Eicher 1992; Eicher 1995a, b; Eicher and Sumberg 1995). Their exploration of dress gave coherence to the data scattered throughout the literature and order to the various attempts to include dress in conceptualizations of culture and society. Covering nineteenth-century evolutionary theorizing in anthropology until the present, they also note examples when dress was excluded in studies. In the course of developing a sociocultural approach – comprehensive, cross-cultural, and grounded in ethnography – they articulated premises that established a foundation upon which others can build further understandings of dress.

The topic had by then accumulated a plethora of overlapping terms, such as clothing, costume, ornament, adornment, fashion, apparel, garment, among many others, which were assigned ambiguous meanings, adding to the confusion in the field. In 1966 Boucher distinguished between clothing and costume, the former functioning to cover one's body, the latter being "the choice of a particular form of garment for a particular use" (1966: 9). To Boucher, for example, "clothing depends primarily on such physical conditions as climate and health, and on textile manufacture, whereas costume reflects social factors such as religious beliefs, magic, aesthetics, personal status, the wish to be distinguished from or to emulate one's fellows" (1966: 9). He raised the question: "Must we envisage a process of emergence, which might place clothing before costume or costume before clothing?" (1966: 9).

Roche, to give another example, prefers "clothes" to "costume": "clothes is the word best suited to a social and cultural history of appearances at a time when practices, like social status, were in turmoil. The *Encyclopédie* understood by the word "everything which serves to cover the body, decorate it, or protect it from harm from the atmosphere." Costume, a word of Italian origin, is too ambiguous in its double meaning of custom and dress or way of dressing" (1994: 4). To examine the extent of the common use of the term "costume" versus "dress" in English, let us consider the entry "dress" in the *The New Columbia Encyclopedia* published in 1975. "Dress" (*The New Columbia Encyclopedia* 1975: 795) has "see COSTUME". Under "costume" (1975: 666) an article about 1,500 words long gives an overview of the history of clothing, citing a number of classic (nonanthropological) works on the subject such as Davenport (1948). Costume is used to denote a material form, particularly in Western styles of clothing (and fashion).

"Costume" is a restrictive term, as "demonstrated in Barnes' discussion of the writings of scholars who used the Royal Anthropological Society's

Notes and Queries as a guide for their investigations. In this case, which deals with several societies from the Naga Hills of northeast India, the result reveals astonishing discrepancies between the ethnographic report and the tangible, visible evidence" (Barnes and Eicher 1992a: 3–4).

Where in this terminology does "body art" or "body embroidery" fit? Can we include it along with clothing? The case of the Nuba in Africa raises the question of whether such a distinction is valuable for analysis or accurate ethnographically. In their view of clothed versus naked bodies, the Nuba provide a case that challenges the evolutionary scheme as a way to describe clothings and the classification that distinguishes clothing from body ornament. Among the Southeastern Nuba studied by Faris, "body art" is a celebration of the strong and healthy body" (1972: 8). This ethos encourages exposure of the attractive body, a premise that pervades the entire society. It is only those, according to Faris, "who are sick or injured, or whose bodies are otherwise incapacitated, [who] will wear clothing or some type of cover" (1972: 54).

We know in anthropology that humans have been altering their bodies and appearance across cultures and throughout the ages. Recently this became called body modification. Body modification "is a phenomenon possibly as old as genus *Homo*, or at least as ancient as when an intelligent being looked down at some clay on the ground, daubed a patch of it on each cheek, and caught the pleasing reflection on the surface of a pond" wrote Myers in his ethnographic study on "nonmainstream body modification" in several West Coast cities in contemporary United States (Myers 1992: 267; see also Sault 1994). According to Myers (1992), it includes "cosmetics, coiffure, ornament-ation, adornment, tattooing, scarification, piercing, cutting, branding and other procedures done mostly for aesthetic reasons" (1992: 267).

Roach and Eicher put body modification in cross-cultural perspective: "A displayer of scars within one culture and a person with a face lift in another may each undergo risk in order to achieve social approval. Thus scars and face-lifts are more alike than different; a search for beauty and a general disregard for risks to health or body functioning is indicated by each" (1973: 14).

In his examination of what he refers to as the "adornment theory" (reasons for the claim that in nonliterate societies the (natural) naked body is modified and adorned), Rubinstein, drawing upon existing ethnographic accounts, identifies and discusses eight distinct purposes (1986: 245–53). They are:

- to separate group members from nonmembers
- to place the individual in the social organization
- to place the individual in a gender category

- to indicate desired social conduct
- to indicate high status or rank
- to control sexual activity
- to enhance role performance
- to give the individual a sense of activity.

Eicher and Roach-Higgins (1992) show that the historical and anthropological record is replete with examples of human groups engaging in some kind or form of body modification or alteration which are used in various societies as marks of personal and social status. They identify related terms that exclude many or all body modifications – *apparel*, *garb*, *attire*, and *costume* – and consider the two commonly referred to categories of clothing and ornament to be overlapping. Alternatively, they formulated an approach that transcends these divisions by proposing a comprehensive sociocultural notion of *dress*. In Roach-Higgins and Eicher (1992) and Eicher and Roach-Higgins (1992) the notion of dress was extended beyond apparel to include "modifications and supplements to the body . . . body and hair conformation, texture and color, scent and sound" (Eicher 1995a: ix). Dress[72] is not only garments and accessories but also hairstyles and cosmetics,[73] and, like language or culinary and religious traditions, it marks what groups share and the boundary among them. Eicher observed that "a definition must allow room for all types of body supplements and modifications" (Barnes and Eicher 1992a: 4). "The analysis of dress needs to place the complete *objet d'art* into the context of a total cognitive structure" (1992a: 3; see also Barthes 1957).

They propose two general functions – communication and the alteration of body processes (Eicher and Roach-Higgins 1992). "Dress," they note, "may be a direct alterant of body processes in the case of some body modifications, such as tooth filing or cutting body tissues to introduce lip plugs. It can also be an alterant as it serves (as a cloak may) as a microenvironment and an interface between body and macroenvironment" (1992: 26, n.16). This contemporary approach to dress takes the subject in new directions. Clearly, as has been shown in this chapter, prior explanatory frameworks that have been developed in anthropological theorizing for dealing with dress are inadequate. This is notwithstanding the fact that some elements in them are supported by cross-cultural ethnographic observations about dress. The next section, *Dress As Framework*, discusses more fully the contemporary concept of dress and presents descriptions of women's dress from ethnographies on Arab society: Palestinian, rural Iraqi, Nubian, and Rashayda bedouin. A framework is developed for the study of Arab dress, including veiling, that lies, I argue, at the intersection of cultural notions of body and space, and social aspects of gender and the group.

Dress As Framework

Studies of traditional Palestinian apparel show how Palestinian dress communicates a general Palestinian identity that embraces an exact identification with a specific Palestinian region and even specifically with a (pre-1948) local village (see for example Weir 1989). One can view dress, in the light of a case such as this, to communicate identity within concentric circles of specificity and inclusiveness. In the current geopolitical situation, some of these early Palestinian villages are identifiable by apparel having elaborate embroidery, which is worn to this day by Palestinians and is displayed in exhibits, museums and photographic collections. These forms of costume are being revived nowadays to communicate a distinct Palestinian Arab identity. This feature of heterogeneity within homogeneity of ethnic identity is not uncommon. Noteworthy here is how dress survives destabilized geography and borders to communicate messages about identity and to serve as an embodiment of a group's memory. This can be seen in current Arab-American group events in Los Angeles, for example, when Palestinian men and women, particularly older immigrants, do often wear traditional apparel to communicate both their unity as a people and their spatial roots in a particular location in Palestine. Younger men and women wear other articles, such as the *kufiyya* worn as a neck scarf, bearing Palestinian colors.

In the numerous studies by Eicher an emergent, non-evolutionary approach shifted the subject of dress from the question of origins and originary functions to an emphasis on social meaning. "Textiles or skins as dress may be fundamentally protective," Barnes and Eicher write, "but they also have social meaning" (1992: 1). In other words, the strictly materialist orientation of the "protection hypothesis" identified by Crawley, which states that clothing originated in order to protect the body, was replaced in the studies by Eicher by a more comprehensive approach (Barnes and Eicher 1992: 1–7; Eicher and Roach-Higgins 1992: 8–28) that is supported by ethnography and utilizes a cross-cultural perspective. In so doing they admitted dress as a focal subject of study in anthropology, perhaps for the first time, and drew attention to the study of dress after a long absence.[74] Terms got sorted out and their focus on the more general subject, "dress," gave coherence to the subject, reducing the confusing proliferation of terms. Tools were borrowed from the study of other spheres of human and primate life, such as codes and principles of verbal and nonverbal communication, to approach dress as "a coded sensory system of non-verbal communication that aids human interaction in space and time" (Eicher 1995a: 1). Eicher proposed that "the codes of dress include visual as well as other sensory modifications (taste, smell, sound, and feel) and supplements (garments, jewelry, and accessories) to the body which set off either or both cognitive and affective processes that result in recognition or lack of recognition by the viewer. As a system, dressing the body by modifications and supplements often does facilitate or hinder consequent verbal or other communication" (Eicher 1995a: 1: see also Fred Davis 1986).

In Eicher's framework the emphasis is on the social aspects of dress, defined comprehensively, as a communication code with meaning. The reference to cognitive and affective processes is on the receiver's side of the communication. The cultural dimension of dress is not a salient component in their conceptualization of dress. To determine the social meaning of dress, Barnes and Eicher propose several essential attributes. One of these is marking identity. Dress "serves as a sign that the individual belongs to a certain group" (1992a: 1). And just as I demonstrated earlier in the case of Palestinian dress, they observe that "[a] person's identity is defined geographically and historically, and the individual is linked to a specific community. They also point out that it ". . . simultaneously differentiates the same individual from all others; it includes and excludes" (1992a: 1). This property – inclusion and exclusion – applies to the group as well.

In a study on women carried out in an Iraqi Shi'a village, Fernea (1965) describes the everyday black garments as consisting of *foota* (chin scarf), *asha* (headscarf) and a black *'abayah* (an all enveloping outer garment) over a black dress (1965: 128). On ceremonial occasions, as in *krayas* (*Qur'an* reading sessions for women led by women *mullahs)* young and old don "their best black *abayahs* [made out] of heavy silk crêpe, and a few of the black head scarves heavily fringed . . . [while] many wore a wide-sleeved full net or sheer black dress, called *hashimiya*, the ceremonial gown worn for *krayas* and similar religious services" (1965: 108–9). *Kraya* is a dialectic variant of the Arabic word *Qira'ah* (meaning reading or recitation), which is based in the time-honored Arab tradition of oral performance by men and women, often in the form of chant, of poetry, *Qur'an*, and narratives of ethnic origin. The *krayas* described in Fernea are religious gatherings of women from the village led by a woman *mullah*. Fernea describes the *mullah's* appearance. She wears a "sheer *hashimiya* of green and white over yellow, heavy make-up, bangles and necklaces" (1965: 109).

Whereas in the case of the Palestinian dress described earlier the marked attribute is one of embedded identities from village, to region, to a people, that of women in the Iraqi village communicates other social aspects. The outdoor black *'abayah* is quite commonly worn by women throughout the Arab world and is not dissimilar to the Iranian *chador* either, hence communicating a generalized gender and group identity of traditional Middle Eastern women. From Fernea's description we find that dress distinguishes daily wear from ceremonial wear and distinguishes rank – the female religious leadership from the other women. The two factors are the home versus the outside and religiously ranking women versus ordinary participants in religious gatherings.

Jennings (1995) describes women's dress in a Nubian village as a marker of a woman's Nubian identity. "She does not wear a face veil [but] she does wear distinctive garments that serve to identify her as a modest and respectable Nubian woman." She wears different clothing when indoors than when going out of the village, or even the hamlet. At home she wears a cotton *fustan* and a black *gallabiyyah sufra*. *Fustan* is a long-sleeved cotton dress in bright colors which "looks very much like a U.S. housedress of the 1940s, except that it is ankle-length" (1995: 47). Over it a woman wears another long-sleeved dress sewn locally in the village, called *gallabiyyah sufra*, "shaped like a smock, made of an opaque black fabric . . . sometimes it has a little bright trimming on the bodice" (1995: 47).

On ceremonial occasions a mature woman wears clothes made of silk, cut velvet or shimmering fabric from Saudi Arabia. Ceremonial clothing also marks a woman as adult. For trips outside her community she puts on another black covering called the *kumikol* – a "voluminous, square-shaped article worn by married, settled matrons [that] identifies the woman who wears it as a Nubian" (1995: 48). The *kumikol* has underarm gussets of contrasting fabric, but not bright trimming of any kind. She also wears a black kerchief, called a *mandil*, and a head veil, called a *tarhah,* which goes down over her shoulders. "[U]pon her head she carries a folded shawl, the *milaya*" (1995: 47).

The young woman dresses differently. When she leaves her home she does not wear the *gallebeya sufra* and *kumikol.* Like non-Nubian townswomen, she wears a *jarjar* – a loose overdress usually of semitransparent, lacy fabric, which reveals the dress underneath. It has "a large ruffle at the bottom that sways gracefully as she walks" (1995: 48). A young woman does go out with her head only covered by her *tarhah* (headveil). Sometimes she wears a bright-colored kerchief beneath it. In other words, while the adult Nubian woman does not face veil, as do some women from other groups, she wears multiple layers of headcovers, pre-dominantly in black. That is, dress in this case not only marks gender but becomes a vehicle through which adulthood is distinguished from youth and socially recognized maturation is expressed. Nubian dress, therefore, communicates both a woman's public persona and her social transitions. All the ethnographic records on different Arab communities share one common factor: women dress differently when they go outdoors than when they are in the privacy of their home. Public dressing is a traditional aspect of a woman's public persona in these communities (for diversity in Middle Eastern dress see Lindisfarne-Tapper and Ingham 1997b).

In addition to identity, Barnes and Eicher propose the attribute of status marker. Dress as described in the ethnographic cases above marks one's social, political and economic status. A crown, staff, or robe may communicate an emblem of power or one's position in society. "Textiles and jewelry, for example, can acquire great value as expressions of personal or communal well-being" (1992a: 1). To the ones proposed by Eicher I add the religious factor as an underlying marker of rank and special status. In my study of the 700-year-old annual religious festival – *Moulid Sayyid al-Badawi* – headdresses and colors mark different Sufi religious orders (see El Guindi 1995c). The festival (El Guindi 1990 (film)) is held in Tanta, Egypt in October to commemorate a thirteenth-century *wali* (holy man). At the culmination of a seven-day festival, a procession takes place to which the *khalifa*, a live successor believed to be a lineal descendant of the holy person, is completely focal, mounted on his horse with a red cloak, a white turban, and with an umbrella held over his head by another person throughout the processional parade around town. The color red represents the religious order that he belongs to, and the white turban is made of cloth that is purportedly from the "veil" of the holy person who seven centuries ago reportedly entered Tanta on horseback with his face double-veiled (*mutalathim*). Now the *Khalifa* turban embodies a sacred quality that draws believers to touch it for blessing. The umbrella is a symbol of rank that is not uncommon in Africa, and not a material object used solely for utilitarian reasons of protection from sun or rain. The umbrella held over the *Khalifa* throughout the procession marks his special religious status (for a filmic portrayal of these emblems in the context of the festival see the visual ethnography El Guindi 1990).

Finally, Barnes and Eicher (1992a) propose the factor of gender. "Gender distinctions are a crucial part of the construction of dress, whether they are made on biological or social grounds" (1992a: 2). In her ethnography on contemporary Moroccan women, Davis (S. Davis 1983) briefly discusses dress. *Jellabah* is a "long, hooded robe worn as outer garment by both sexes" (1983: 183). Women cover their bodies when they go out. They wear "either a *jellaba* (long robe) and veil, or a *haik*, a large piece of fabric which they wrap around themselves so just their hands, feet, and eyes remain visible" (1983: 61). The *haik* is a variation on the wrap worn in certain traditional circles by women in rural and urban areas of the Middle East. In that sense, it is both an ethnic and a gender marker. The hooded *jellabah*, or *burnus*, on the other hand, is worn by both sexes and is similar in appearance. As a clothing item it is dual-gendered, bringing out the nuanced variability of clothing as used by men and women.

Gendered Beginnings

My fieldwork-based visual study of a birth ceremony in Egypt revealed the significance of dress as both a key material object and also as a symbol for "beginnings" found in hidden sacred spheres that are not entirely religious. Traditionally, the beginning point of the individual Arab life cycle is marked by a particular ceremony, which is known in Egypt as *El-Sebou'*.

In this ceremony dress and the act of dressing are key symbols that relate to other ritual symbols to uncover a mythical realm of cosmological ideas about creation and birth – ideas prevailing in the region now called the Middle East since ancient times, predating and presumably influencing Biblical and Islamic bodies of thought.

El-Sebou' is an Arabic word deriving from the root (s-b-') which also yields *sab'a*, meaning seven. *El-Sebou'* is the name used for the traditional ceremony widely celebrated in rural and urban Egypt (and with some variation in ritual detail elsewhere in the Arabic-speaking region), by both Muslims and Copts, on the seventh[75] day after the physical birth of a child of either sex. It celebrates the occasion of a child's "coming out."

On the eve of the *El-Sebou'* ceremony, a special ceremonial clay pot is placed near the child. The *Sebou'* pot consists of a long neck[76] attached to the top of the base, and the top ridge, to which four candleholders are attached. The pot for a girl is adorned with a wavy rim encircling its upper neck, and is called *ollah*; for a boy the pot has one spout and one handle on each side and is called *abri'*. The gendered pot, which is placed close to the newborn on the eve of the ceremony, corresponds to the newborn's gender – *ollah* if the baby is a girl, *abri'* if the baby is a boy (see Figure 4).

In a special ceremony, women "dress up" a girl's pot with gold jewelry and/or the father "dresses up" a boy's pot with his prayer beads.[77] Recently, especially in urban centers, pots are especially purchased for the ceremony, already commercially painted and decorated with satin ribbons and bows, and some more elaborate, with battery-operated flashing lights. In the past the pot was purchased "naked" (natural), crafted out of clay, and in some instances painted deep red for girls and deep green[78] for boys. The pots were ceremonially "dressed" by the family, who gathered for the occasion in the newborn's house. They creatively decorated them with natural roses and other flowers tied decoratively with homemade ribbon bows – an activity collectively carried out by the family, who gather before the *Sebou'* in the newborn's home for the occasion.

In ancient Egyptian mythology, the gender-neutral creator Khnum is depicted "crafting" humankind by fashioning the child and "the other" out of clay shaped as an egg. Analogously, in the visual ethnography on the *Sebou'*

Figure 4 Gendered *Sebou'* pots drawn by Daphne Shuttleworth. Courtesy El Nil
Research, Los Angeles.

ceremony (see El Guindi 1986; see also El Guindi 1996b) a sequence shows
the modern potter crafting gendered *El-Sebou'* pots in the pottery village.[79]
The crafting of the *Sebou'* pot out of clay symbolizes creation, clay being
associated with human origins in the cosmological imagery of Egypt's past.

On the day of the main ceremony, and in preparation for it, the baby is
bathed[80] and "dressed" in *fustan*[81] *El-Sebou'* (the *Sebou'* dress), which is

especially home-sewn for the occasion and is identical in form and color for both sexes (see Figure 5). During the ceremony the family sing a special *El-Sebou'* folksong – *Hala'atak Birigalatak* ("earrings and anklets"). Its text is in gender-neutral language, and the same lyrics are sung by the family during the ceremony for babies of both sexes (El Guindi 1986 (film); 1996b).

The analysis of *El-Sebou'* ceremony and its symbolism utilizes the notion of dress in a way similar to that which has been developed by Eicher *et al.* – beyond concrete appearance. In *El-Sebou'*, dress is integral to identity and gender. It is embedded in the process of establishing the newborn's identity publicly and ceremonially – an identity shaped by the two most marked aspects of the culture: gender and family. The ceremony marks the first point in the ceremonialized life cycle of the individual, ending a liminal phase of gender neutrality and a natural state of "nakedness" (naturalness) spent in seclusion. Gender-neutrality of dress at birth is not unique to this Egyptian ceremony.

Eicher and Roach-Higgins observed that gender-neutral dress in the context of birth was widespread cross-culturally. They identified a few examples, which include: "hospital-provided diaper, long-sleeved undershirt, and knitted cap in the United States in the 1990s" (1992: 23, n.3); "a coating of oil and a touch of ochre around the fontanelle among the Nuba in the late 1960s" (Faris 1972, quoted in Eicher and Roach-Higgins 1992: 23, n. 2); "a paste of ground camwood applied to the head among the Tiv of the 1950s" (Bohannon 1956, quoted in Eicher and Roach-Higgins 1992: 23, n. 2).

"Dress," they argue, "is a powerful means of communication and makes statements about the gender role of a newborn child soon after birth . . . [s]pecific types of dress, or assemblages of types and their properties, communicate gender differentiations that have consequences for the behavior of females and males throughout their lives" (Eicher and Roach-Higgins 1992: 8). Crawley (1931) had observed that of the many possible social distinctions that can be communicated by dress the most important is gender. Other dress practices in the *Sebou'* are gender-linked – hair cutting and circumcision for boys and ear piercing for girls. Naming takes place for both sexes during the liminal period.

The theme of identification with gender and family appears throughout the ceremony. The shape of the key ritual object – the *El-Sebou'* clay pot – is linked to the gender of the baby and reflects an unambiguous gender marker (see Figure 4). During the ceremony the pots are "dressed up" – the male-representing pot by the father, the female-representing pot by women relatives on the mother's side. The objects used to "dress up" the clay pots are also consistent. The boy's pot is dressed with the father's prayer beads and the girl's pot is dressed with the mother's gold jewelry. This further establishes

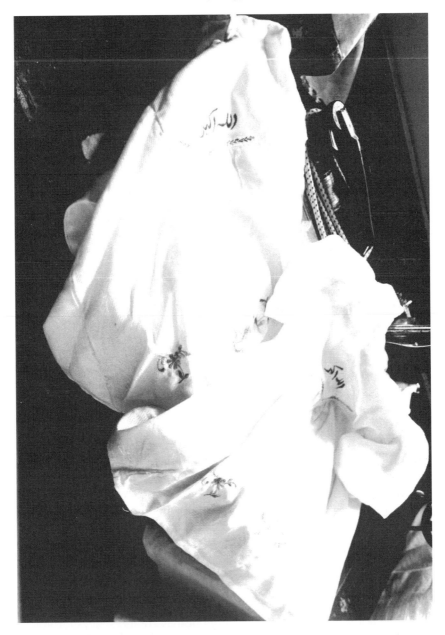

Figure 5 Ungendered *Sebou'* dress. Photo by Daphne Shuttleworth, 1985, of two identical dresses for the ceremony of newborn boy–girl twins filmed in *El Sebou': Egyptian Birth Ritual* (1986), a visual ethnography by anthropologist F. El Guindi. Courtesy of the Center for Folklife Programs and Cultural Studies, Smithsonian Institution.

the identification of the child with aspects of the cultural system that are most relevant to his/her gender identity.[82]

As the baby crosses the "threshold" on the seventh day of life, she/he formally enters the cultural world characterized primarily by identification with the family and a dual-gendered social sphere. Dressing pots and new-borns symbolizes the transitional process from a natural to a cultural world, a neutral-gendered to a dual-gendered social universe, a sole individual to a member of the family and community. The pots, like humans, are crafted naked and neutral-gendered. They remain in this state, symbolizing the baby's gender neutrality and aloneness (asociality), for the duration of the time/ space span of *seven*. On the seventh day the ceremony marks the end of seclusion. Both pot and baby, isomorphic forms of creative life, are ceremonially dressed (decorated/clothed), in a process of public gendering carried out by the family as it embraces the new member. To summarize the different dimensions of dress in this discussion: dress is a code of communication and a marker of a number of social domains – individual and group identity, social status, economic position, political power, gender, and religious role. Using dress comprehensively encompasses multiple aspects of dressing that are adequate to describing the social aspects. But as we examine next the notion in Arabic that is equivalent to dress, *libas*, the framework is accordingly expanded to include the cultural realm of the sacred by symbolic analysis.

Libas: Arab Dress

They [feminine gender] *are libas* [dress] *to you* [masculine plural] *and you* [masculine plural] *are libas* [dress] *to them* [feminine gender].

Qur'an 2: 187

In this work three modes of analysis are employed: the ethnographic, the visual, and the linguistic. These analytic modes apply to a number of bodies of data. They are: print ethnographic data, visual data (film and video, photos, picture postcards), historical records (primary or secondary), philosophical and theological materials (primary or secondary), and cultural knowledge. Beginning in this section three additional bodies are included: Qur'anic text as a primary source, *Hadith*[83] commentary and some *Tafsir* interpretations. The Islamic sources are examined in their original language, Arabic. In some instances, standard English translations are accepted or modified for use as needed. Otherwise translations are mine.

The Qur'anic text is considered sacred because of its quality in Islamic understandings of being divinely revealed. This quality, however, does not distance it from the believers. Rather, it is integrated in ordinary people's daily lives and engages them in discourse and debate, alongside other spheres of knowledge. I consider the *Qur'an* to be "living," not only in the sense used by Akbar Ahmed (in *Living Islam* 1993, the title for the six-part BBC television series and companion book), that is, Islam as lived by Muslims (see El Guindi 1995d; A. Ahmed 1988), but in the case of the *Qur'an*, also in the legal sense of a "living document." The polarity of "little" and "great" traditions previously used to describe Islamic society does not reflect the integrative quality characterizing the lived Islam in which multiple spheres of knowledge merge in their lives. Nor do I find useful discussions on "one Islam versus many Islams." A more extreme perspective is that which assumes that simply recording local voices is sufficient to produce meaning. It is not.

Perhaps such orientations account for the near-absence, in social science, particularly anthropological analysis, except for occasional referencing or quoting, of Islamic textual materials. Text is rarely (if at all) subjected to ethnographic analysis and integrated as a body of data in an anthropological study. This entails a particular perspective and specific methods. At the expense of stating the obvious, the same set of data can be interpreted quite differently by an Area Studies or Religious Studies scholar than by an anthropologist. That is because not only does anthropology generate a distinctive body of data of its own (ethnography, artefacts, etc.) that provides a primary cross-cultural, archeological and biological base, but its analytic tools enable it to analyze any body of data anthropologically.

In this study, the two methodological components – the data (whatever the source) and the analysis – are anthropological. My use of the various bodies of data in this work developed out of insights that emerged during my contemporary research projects about Arabo-Islamic society and culture, the anthropological study of the Islamic movement and the visual research project filming Hoksha, the Egyptian peasant master *ghurbal* craftsman. The film is about his making of the traditional sieve used for both winnowing wheat and ceremonially winnowing 7-days-old babies in their rite of passage to a gendered world. In both projects it was revealed that studying cultural systems of long historical, literate civilizational, and religious processes, such as the Arabo-Islamic culture, must draw upon the various interrelated bodies of knowledge to produce culturally significant meaning, because the local people themselves do.

This integrative approach captures better how people draw on Islam (as on other spheres of knowledge) in their daily lives. This was demonstrated in my fieldwork project for a visual ethnography called *Ghurbal*. During the interview (on camera), Hoksha (see Figure 6), who lives in a rural town in northern Egypt, fluidly drew upon several bodies of knowledge as he was

Figure 6   Anthropologist F. El Guindi interviewing Hoksha, the master craftsman, as he is being filmed. From El Guindi's visual ethnography, *Ghurbal*. Courtesy El Nil Research, Los Angeles.

describing his craft (see El Guindi (film)1995). Although it is often assumed that *Hadith* is the domain of Muslim experts, when referring to the use of the skin of dead animals for the crafting of the sieve, Hoksha drew upon the *Hadith* to support his observations of taboos against the use of certain skins. His information was accurate. During the three-hour interview Hoksha, who was stationary while crafting a sieve as we filmed (for the film *Ghurbal*), was "moving" in and out of sacred time and space by his words and behavior. Specifically, when the live call for prayer was heard from the nearby mosque ordinary conversation was seamlessly interrupted by appropriate remarks and gestures, and then resumed. This fluid but structured "movement" in and out of sacred space is a quality of Muslim people's life. Instead of predetermining which body of knowledge to cut out of the culture, the analysis reflects the multilayering of communication and bodies of knowledge ethnographically relevant to the understanding of dress.

My attention was first drawn to the centrality of dress in Middle Eastern socio-religious contexts during my field-based ethnographic study on the Islamic movement[84] carried out for a period of over two decades. The Islamic Movement began in the 1970s in Egypt and spread throughout the Arabic-speaking East, Islamic Asia and Islamic Africa (see Brenner 1996 on Islamic

Indonesia, and the earlier work by Nagata (1984), Zainah (1987), Ong (1990) and Wazir (1992) on Malaysia). A focal aspect of the Islamic trend was a new form of voluntary but standardized dress for men and women that was not prescribed by religious authorities, but was described by observers as conservative. Among the *Islamiyyin* (Arabic for men and women participants in the movement) the dress was known as *al-ziyy al-Islami* (Arabic) or "the Islamic dress." For women's dress the word *hijab* was often used.[85] Brenner (1996) explores veiling among Muslims in Java, Indonesia as a "conversion" from secular dress. She uses the term veiling as a "convenient shorthand" for "women's Islamic clothing," which refers to the practice in which a woman covers her head (usually also covering her hair and neck – although rarely her face) and all of her body except her hand (1996: 691, n.1; see also Hoffman-Ladd 1987). The similarity in Islamic dress among women in the different Arabic-speaking and Asian countries is striking.

In exploring various textual sources for the meaning and symbolism of *al-ziyy al-Islami* and the *hijab* the research led to another term – *libas*. The segment of Qur'anic text used as an introductory quote above, at the beginning of this section, states that men and women are *libas to* each other. *Tafsir* (Islamic Exegesis) sources state that Arabs refer to their "family" as their *libas*. A cursory look in *The Encyclopedia of Islam* and *A Dictionary of Islam* under the entry *libas* reveals extended listings of Arabic terms (also some in Turkish and Farsi) denoting diverse articles of apparel, clustered particularly around the complex phenomenon of the "the veil."

As has been discussed earlier, English-speaking contexts use the term "dress" restrictively to mean a concrete form of gender-specific clothing. The terms "clothing" or "costume" seem to have been more commonly used. After its reconceptualization in anthropology "dress" became a more general, comprehensive and inclusive concept. The Arabic usage *libas* shares with dress these qualities of comprehensiveness and inclusiveness. But, unlike "dress," my research shows that the Arabic word *libas* has always been widely used since the Pre-Islamic era in a general, comprehensive, and inclusive way, in oral and written text and by lay people, intellectuals and scholars alike.

Further examination suggested that the Arabic *libas* might be the closest equivalent in Arabic to the English notion of "dress." Instead of a socio-cultural framework that treats dress as a material phenomenon with meaning communicated at the social and cultural level, my analysis identified the realm of the invisible, intangible sacred domain, in which ideas and concepts can be made observable by symbolic analysis. Therefore, the approach developed for the subject of dress in Arab culture consists of a material/social analysis and a symbolic analysis, both the ordinary and the sacred realms, or the visible and the invisible domains. This brings out three important points.

First, the term *libas* is widely used in the *Qur'an*[86] and the *Hadith*, and it is used to denote dress. Second, its usage not only denotes material forms of clothing and ornament for women and men, but also includes diverse forms of the veil and veiling.[87] Third, it embodies an invisible, intangible realm of the sacred in which cultural ideas are relationally embedded.

A symbolic analysis of invisible aspects of the culture is added to the material aspect in a relational framework, in such a way that the study of dress in Arabo-Islamic culture is extended to connote family and gender as haven-shelter-sanctuary (all in one) – a protective shield, as it were. Demon-strating the basis for this idea begins with the analysis of the Islamic sacred origins of primordial humans.

Sacred Origins: Primordial Humans

To put the Islamic sacred origins in comparative perspective the Hebrew construction of human beginnings is presented first. Genesis (2: 8, Revised Standard Version) states: "And the Lord God planted a garden in Eden, in the east; and there he put the man whom he had formed." God made a command to him: "And the Lord God commanded the man, saying, 'you may freely eat of every tree of the garden; but of the tree of the knowledge of good and evil you shall not eat'. . ." (2: 16,17). Because the man was alone, "[T]hen the Lord God said, 'It is not good that the man should be alone; I will make him a helper fit for him'. . ." (2: 18) , so he "caused a deep sleep to fall upon the man, and while he slept took one of his ribs . . ." (2: 21), "and the rib which the Lord God had taken from the man he made into a woman and brought her to the man" (2: 22). "[Then] the man said, '. . . she shall be called Woman [Hebrew: *ishshah*] because she was taken out of Man [Hebrew: *ish*] . . . *And the man and his wife were both naked, and were not ashamed*" (2: 23,24, emphasis added). Spellberg observes that when Eve was formed from Adam's rib she had no name and that "the man named his wife Eve" [88] (1966: 312). Feminists also see that according to the Hebrew rendering a man is a whole missing one rib, and the woman – a rib – is a part of a whole, incomplete, and a relatively insignificant part of man.

Another aspect to the Hebrew story is revealed when the serpent tells Eve ". . . God knows that when you eat of it [the fruit of the trees of the garden] your eyes will be opened . . ." (3: 5). So the woman ate and gave some to her husband, and he ate: "[T]hen the *eyes of both were opened*; and *they knew that they were naked*; (3: 7, emphasis added). Then ". . . they heard the sound of the Lord God walking in the garden . . ." (2: 8), and they hid themselves. "But the Lord God called to the man . . . [who] said, . . . 'I was afraid, because

I was naked; and I hid myself . . . [T]he woman whom thou gavest to be with me, *she gave me fruit* of the tree, and I ate'" (2: 9,10,12, emphasis added). "The Man called his wife's name Eve (in Hebrew a word meaning 'living') because she was the mother of all living. And the Lord God made for Adam and for his wife garments of skin, and clothed them" (3: 20,21). The origin of clothing is linked to the development of a sense of shame about their bodies, nakedness, and sexuality.

Smith and Haddad summarized the theme thus: "the image of Eve as temptress and seductress of Adam is a familiar and pervasive one fully supported by Biblical reference" (1982: 135). Exploring the biblical text in English (Revised Standard Version) suggests a number of sub-themes and premises:

- God created the man first.
- The man was created as a complete living being.
- God commanded the man not to eat of the tree of knowledge (of good and evil).
- God wanted a companion and helper for the man.
- God took one of the man's ribs and created a female out of the man's anatomy.
- The man named the female Eve.
- The first name she was given in Hebrew is a linguistic extension of the referent "man."
- The man and the woman were both naked, but were not ashamed.
- The man blamed the woman, who had listened to the serpent, for their eating from the tree.
- Fruit from the tree of knowledge introduced consciousness needed to discern evil from good, hence producing shame in connection with nakedness (in the context of husband and wife).

The resemblance between the biblical and the Qur'anic renderings is striking. But the difference is even more striking. In the biblical construction the nature of the relationship of wife to husband is made explicit. Her name is given to her by him, she is physically and conceptually part of him, and he sees her as having led him to fall and sin. Also explicit is the fact that knowledge of good and evil (from eating the forbidden fruit) made them *ashamed* of their nakedness (sexuality).

"The Qur'an," write Smith and Haddad, "presents a somewhat different picture, one in which both members of the primordial pair are equally responsible in the sequence of events that resulted in the banishment of both from the Garden of Eden" (1982: 135). Smith and Haddad (1982) described this subject of human beginnings in an article, using an approach that is closer to social science analysis than most writings in Religious Studies on the same subject. "In the Qur'an the female partner of Adam is never mentioned by name. . . . both Adam and his wife are asked to dwell in the Garden and both are warned not to eat of the tree (of immortality) [2: 35, 7: 19]; Satan tempts them both and causes them to fall [2: 36, 7: 20] although in 2: 120 [my correction: 20: 120] Adam alone is tempted), and both eat of the tree and see their own nakedness [2: 121] [my correction: 20: 121]. Iblis for his perfidy is made to be the eternal enemy of both [2: 11], and both are expelled, with Iblis, from the Garden [2: 36, 20: 123, 7: 24] . . . In no instance is Adam's wife held responsible for his temptation" (1982: 136).

Let us explore themes identified in some of those passages referenced by Smith and Haddad and in a few additional *Suras* by examining the Arabic text directly. First, the "creation" of the first pair can be identified in the following two *Suras:*

Sura (51: 49) states:

All things we created in *zawjayn* [pairs] . . .

And *Sura* (49: 13) states:

. . . we have created you a *thakarun* [male] and *untha* [female] . . .[89]

From these two we can establish certain principles. The Arabic word *zawjayn* is the dual form (not the plural, which is *azwaj*) of the word *zawj*, an ungendered term commonly translated as "pair" in English. But it also connotes double, one of a pair, two as a pair, partner, and spouse. The use of "wife" in some English translations does not capture the nuance of the Arabic term, since the same word is used to refer to husband. Rather, it is a notion that linguistically encapsulates the "heterosexual complementarity of two autonomous persons," which is culturally considered the basis of society. Spellberg, in an article (1996) on Eve in Islamic conception (referring to her as *"nameless wife"*), misinterprets the notion "pair." She interprets *zawj* from an individualistic perspective to mean "half of the pair" (1996: 306,307). Looking at one of the pair as half rather than as "one of two" shifts the meaning from completeness to incompleteness, thus missing the nuance that is consistent in Arabo-Islamic constructions of gender complementarity. The very usage in the above context of the dual form (*zawjayn*) establishes the reference to two *zawj*, which further confirms the stress on completeness and complementarity. The term is used when there are two as a pair. Otherwise, another word meaning "one" would be used, such *fard, ahad, nafar,* etc. The reference to the creation of *Adam* states that out of the same single soul the *zawj* was created, hence stressing the wholeness of the pair.

Using symbolic analysis one can perhaps build an argument that Adam stands for humankind (rather than the First Man) as first created out of a single soul in the form of a heterosexual pair. Support for this neutral-gendered notion of "Adam" can be found in textual and contemporary linguistic usages. In most Qur'anic references "Adam" is not presented as masculine-gendered. In spoken and standard Arabic, women are referred to by a form of feminized Adam, as in *bani Admah*. In this view, the fact that the feminine part of the pair is not named can be support for a dual-gendered notion of Adam. Nonetheless, whether Adam is neutral-gendered, dual-gendered or single-gendered, the principle emerging from the two passages above (*Suras* 2: 35 and 7: 19) is that primordial humans had been created and formed as a pair. It is a simultaneous creation of both sexes.

The next theme considered here is the story of the Garden. *Sura* (2: 35) states:

> We said: O Adam, dwell with your *zawj* in Paradise; and eat whatever pleases you of its bounty; but approach not this tree . . .

In another *Sura* (7: 19) the same thought is conveyed:

> And O Adam, dwell with your *zawj* in Paradise; enjoy as you wish; but approach not this tree . . .

This sequence is about testing the human pair in obeying a clear and explicit divine order. Abundant bounty is available and accessible in the Garden, and they are welcome to everything but the tree. A divine test of their obedience to the deity is posed to them. But (2: 36) states:

> Then did Satan make them slip [from the Garden].

In the sequence on disobedience of God we encounter conceptualization about dress and body. This can be found in three segments of three *Suras*: 7: 20, 7: 22, and 20: 121, presented in order:

> Then Satan tempted them, only to reveal to them [unclothe] what was hidden – *saw'atihima* (genitals) . . . (7: 20)

> So Satan arrogantly deceived them and when they tasted from the tree, revealed to them both their *saw'atuhuma* (genitals), and they scrambled to cover their bodies with leaves from the Garden. *Iblis* (used interchangeably with Satan) was made to

be the eternal enemy of both, and both were expelled, along with *Iblis*, from the Garden (7: 21)

> ... They ate from the tree, revealed to both *saw'atuhuma* (genitals). Adam disobeyed God and desired ... (20: 121

Saw'at (pl. for *saw'ah*) does not mean nakedness or sex or sexuality. It means genitals. No "shame" is linked in these passages to Islamic human beginnings. When Spellberg translates/interprets (20: 121; 7: 22) as "both recognize *their shame*" (1996: 307, emphasis added), and "*shame . . . implies their joint nakedness (sexuality)*" (1996: 307, emphasis added) she is imposing Hebro-centrism on Arabo-Islamic constructions and imagery.

Smith and Haddad observe that twice [7: 189, 30: 21] the *Qur'an* mentions creation of mates "that you might find rest in them" (1982: 136). This interpretation "find rest in them" captures better the essence of the notion *yaskun* than "so that he might dwell with her" (see Spellberg 1996: 306). The reference here is to the Arabic term *yaskun*, a verb-derived noun from *s-k-n* that ranges in meaning from home, to sanctuary, to haven, and incorporates in the Arabic language connotations of serenity and peace. The emphasis of meaning is therefore on the heterosexual relation as a haven and woman as sanctuary, not simply on the literal rendition "to dwell."

The association of womanhood with home, privacy, and a safe haven is substantiated in various sources, ranging from ethnographic to textual. The emphasis is on gender mutuality and the completeness of a heterosexual pair that reproduces humankind. In the sacred Islamic imagination there is no shame in sexuality and no gender primacy communicated in the story of creation.

Dress is integral to these sacred beginnings in both Hebrew and Qur'anic constructions. Their meaning is different. In the Hebrew version, Adam and Eve were in shame-free nakedness until the "eating of the fruit," upon which they felt shame from their nakedness (sexuality). Dress is used after the "Fall" to clothe them in "garments of skin," an early human form of clothing used by pastoralists and their predecessors, prior to the advent of weaving. Dress is used in its material connotation.

In the Islamic construction, dress, in addition to its material connotation, links in metaphoric terms notions of gender, sexuality, sanctuary, and sacred privacy. These notions are manifested in culture. Abu-Lughod recounts comments by a woman of *Awlad 'Ali*: "You see, the male has no womb. He has nothing but a little penis, just like this finger of mine [laughingly wiggling her finger in a contemptuous gesture]. The male has no compassion. But the female is tender and compassionate [*idh-dhakar ma yirhamsh, l-antha thin wtirham*]. It is the daughter who will care for her mother, not the son" (1986: 129; the bracketed comment and the Arabic phrase are the original).

This comment leads to a closer examination of the Arabic notion *rahm* (both womb and uterine kin) and the related *rahma* (mercy or compassion), both derivatives of the root *r-h-m*. I interpret the ethnographic comments to mean that "womb" is central to *Awlad 'Ali* womanhood and provides a key entry into a rich cultural domain. Ahmed Abou-Zeid (1959, 1966, 1979), the first anthropologist to study the same group, applied a holistic search for meaning (what Mary Douglas calls "the coherence of culture" (1973: 249)) and explored the notion of "sanctuary," which laid out the path that oriented subsequent studies of bedouins (see Pitt-Rivers 1970: 862–75), and discovered its link to another key concept – *haram* (stress on the last syllable), which, as we see in this book, manifests itself in various domains of the culture. Along this line let us reconsider the notion of *rahm* brought to our attention by the woman of the Awlad 'Ali group who contrasted the womb with "men's little penis" (for more on *Awlad 'Ali* see Mohsen 1967, 1975).

My examination of ethnography on Arabs and my analysis of Islamic textual culture shows a connection between *r-h-m* and two spheres in Arabo-Islamic culture: womanhood on the worldly plane and God on the super-human plane. The word *rahm* (stress on the first syllable) connotes womb, but also is the term used in reference to uterine kin. At the level of the non-worldly, *rahman* (stress on the second syllable, "compassionate") and *rahim* (stress on the second syllable, "merciful"), which are derivatives of the same root, are prominent attributes of God in Islamic textual and lived culture.

I argue that the women of *Awlad 'Ali* seem to integrate this notion in their articulated self-image of womanhood. This observation finds support in Abou-Zeid's insight linking Arab womanhood to the notion of sanctuary, which is a productive line of inquiry. As a concept, sanctuary derives from analysis of the Arabic premises of *haram* (stress on the second syllable) and *hurma* (stress on the first syllable). Embedding the study of *Awlad 'Ali* in gender rather than in culture,[90] while reverting to universalist Western psychology (such as linking women's red belts to impurity, ascribing denial of sexuality to Islam, etc.), strips the people from their cultural identity. Culture becomes superficially the backdrop against which gender is written.

Evidence suggests that the Islamic primordial pair were clothed lavishly immediately after they first appeared. When they disobeyed the deity, parts of their bodies were exposed to themselves and each other. The penalty for disobedience was the descent from heaven to earth, a notion free from burdens of sin or curse for either sex. Their imperfection disqualified them from immortal life in heaven. Instead, they were to live a mortal (finite) life on earth. But the sign of divine displeasure was revealed in the revealing (exposing or declothing) of particular parts of their bodies. The reference is to the exposure of certain body parts, not to shame from the body or from sexuality. This was embarrassing (not shameful) to them; hence their scrambling for leaves to cover their naked bodies – a divine punishment for their disobedience and a message about human mortality and vulnerability.

There are explicit Qur'anic references about the role of *libas* (dress), as in the *Sura* (7), in two *ayahs* which state:

> O children of Adam! We have bestowed *libas* (dress) upon you to cover your genitals and serve as protection and adornment. *Libas* of piety is the best (7: 26)

> O ye children of Adam, let not Satan tempt you as he did your parents, causing their exit from Heaven, stripping them from their *libas* to reveal to them their genitals (7: 27)

Evident in the above passages is the use of *libas* in different senses: first, in the material sense in two ways: as clothing to cover the body for modesty and protection, and for aesthetic purposes as adornment and, second, in a metaphorical sense, as a code of morality, respect and humanness.

To sum up: in the analysis of sacred Islamic origins six premises emerge: (1) Both male and female, as a pair, were created (simultaneously) and treated equally in moral and behavioral responsibility; (2) neither female nor male was singled out in the disobedience, elsewhere known as the "fall," that was caused by Satan's deception – it is Satan who is sinful; (3) dress plays a fundamental role in their origins, their ultimate state of mortality and human morality; (4) dress is used in its material sense and in a symbolic sense; (5) *libas* in its material form functions for clothing, protection and adornment; and (6) *libas* is a symbol of interdependence between the sexes, gender mutuality, and a cultural notion of "respect" and privacy.

5

Sacred Privacy

Who could deny that privacy is a jewel? It has always been the mark of privilege, the distinguishing feature of a truly urbane culture.

Phyllis McGinley (1905–1978), US poet

It is certain that the "privacy" referred to in the above quote is a Western notion describing the right of the individual to non-intrusion. Use of "privacy" in the Arab and Islamic contexts is different. Both meanings, however, share the quality of privilege.

Arab privacy is based on a specific cultural construction of space and time central to the functioning of Islamic society in general, in the dynamics of Arab gender identity, and for direct unmediated individual or collective communication with God. Space in this construction is relational, active, charged and fluid, "insisting" on complementarities.[91]

"Space . . . is not a simple concept" writes Ardener (S. Ardener 1993: 4). She observes a connection between cultural notions of space and social life (S. Ardener 1993). Much earlier Durkheim and Mauss (1963 [1903]) wrote that much of social life is *given* shape, that there is a correspondence between the "real" physical world and its "social reality." "Cosmic space and tribal space are thus only very imperfectly distinguished and the mind," they wrote, "passes from one to the other without difficulty, almost without being aware of doing so" (Durkheim and Mauss 1963). Ardener finds that "*behavior and space are mutually dependent*" (1993: 2, emphasis in original); that people in space determine its nature (1993: 3).

Using the phrase "the court is where the king is" Ardener argues that people define space as seen when "the entry of a stranger may change a private area into a public one" (1993: 3). Edward Hall (1959) observes that "space speaks." What "it says" in Arab and Islamic cultural context is what concerns us here.

A distinctive quality of the Islamic construction of space is how it turns a public area into a private space, without the entry of a stranger. It enables ordinary Muslims temporarily to convert any worldly place (street, shop, aircraft aisle) into a sacred space set apart, simply by marking it and occupying it in a ritually pure state facing Makka. Gilsenan makes this point in his discussion of rural Lebanon (1982: 179). It also enables women and men to enjoy privacy and be in public.

Space conversion can be effected singly or collectively. The mosque during Friday noon prayer and the annual (traditionally once in a lifetime) pilgrimage to Makka represent collective sacred spaces activated by groups of Muslims. Both collective spaces, one activated once a week, the other once a year, provide a temporal rhythm to routine life. An ordinary faithful individual turns any worldly place into an individual sacred space by performing the five prescribed daily prayers.

During prayer a Muslim, stripped temporarily of worldly identity, is in a sacred state. Ritual purification is achieved by Muslim women or men through dress code, cleansing by *wudu'*, facing Makka, and performing prescribed rites of worship. Young describes in meticulous detail the rites involved in prayer among the Rashayda in his ethnography. While people stand, bow, prostrate themselves, and sit, they recite verses from the *Qur'an* and the various ritual formulae (1996: 73).

From Rashayda camps to the big city, a Muslim prays in a spot that he or she marks out, perhaps by spreading a mat or a carpet or newspapers. A merchant in his store can during business hours simply mark the spot where he is standing, thus converting it into a sacred space for worship. A buyer waits for the merchant to end his prayer before conducting transactions. The public call for prayer issued five times a day *(athan)* by human voice from the minarets of mosques reflects and establishes this rhythmic pattern (Dorsky 1986: 64–73).

Upon hearing the call, Muslims do not necessarily interrupt their routine activity, since there is a period of several hours during which a Muslim can perform each particular prayer. But even when engaged in ordinary conversation the instant the call chant is heard, a Muslim interactively recognizes the call by saying prescribed phrases in response to different segments of the call and then resuming ordinary conversation, saying, for example, "*Allah-u A'tham wal Izzatu lillah*" (*God is supreme, Glory be to him*) upon hearing "*Allah-u Akbar* (God is Great)." This and other phrases are spoken intermittently throughout the call in normal speech style, but with a different demeanor. This is visually demonstrated in the visual ethnography *Ghurbal* (see El Guindi 1995), in which I was watching Hoksha, the rural Egyptian master craftsman, craft a *ghurbal* (a traditional sieve made of animal skin) while interviewing him as filming was going on. Hoksha smoothly and spontaneously flowed in and out of ordinary space and time and sacred space and time.

This interweaving of space and time, as individuals move in and out during the course of the day between worldly and sacred spheres, is distinctly, perhaps uniquely, Islamic. What Ardener might call "spaces within spaces" or "overlapping universes" (1993: 3) is best described in the analysis of Arab culture as fluidity of space and rhythmic patterns of time. The two interweave throughout the ordinary day. Ardener discusses time as being "closely associated with space" (1993: 6), and quotes E. Ardener: "time-systems occupy spaces which are generated by and with the physical and social space" (E. Ardener 1975b: 11). In some cases space and time are homologous. Henrietta Moore (1986), in a study of the Endo of Kenya, recognizes the complexity in perceptions of time, the many ways of synthesizing experiences to the principal space/time orientations. Young notes how the Rashaayda's experience of prayer is integrated with their experience of time and space. Standing to pray facing the *gibla* (or *qibla*), i.e. towards Makka, "creates an altered experience of space" (1996: 74).

The paradigm public/private, and its corollary honor–shame, is the one most commonly imposed on Arab and Islamic cultural space to describe the division between the sexes. It has been argued that this paradigm is more appropriate to describe European Mediterranean and Balkan cultures (Campbell 1964; Hirschon 1981, 1993; Peristiany 1966: Pitt-Rivers 1963, 1965). And some do not even see such applicability to Mediterranean Europe, and find it more appropriate for describing Western culture (Sciama 1993).

The link between space and gender has long been observed in studies of dual classification and universal duality (Hertz 1973; Needham 1973,1979; S. Ardener 1993: 5). Cultural polarities, such as right/left, male/female, domestic/public, public/private have their roots in the studies of Durkheim and Mauss (1963), Hertz (1973 [1909]), Douglas (1970) and Needham (1969). These oppositions, early noted by Needham in his study of the Purum and other studies of symbolism, were universalized in early feminist anthropology in the form of private or domestic/public (Reiter 1975; Rosaldo 1974) among others. Sciama, after fieldwork in Italy, questions the value of the private/public paradigm, which she describes as "rigid private/public opposition itself reflect[ing] a bourgeois conception of society" (1993: 110, n. 2).

Sciama then concludes that "[n]either 'public' nor 'private' can be used as fixed analytical terms or readily be associated with negative or positive values" (1993: 110). Young also finds this paradigm questionable in the case of Rashayda ethnography: "it would be misleading to characterize the men's work as 'public' and the women's work as 'private' or 'domestic' " (1993: 54). He points out that the decorated products of women's work – tent cloths, camel covers, and women's veils – are always displayed publicly; hence one could say that women's work is "public" (see Figure 7). Young finds the dichotomy to be grounded in Western European formations and history

Figure 7 A Rashidi adult woman posing for the anthropologist William C. Young, displaying clothing items, jewelry, saddle bag, and tent cloth – the group's woven identity, as it were. Photo by W. Young, reprinted by permission.

(Roman *res publica*, the "public thing"), and one that should not be imposed on the Middle East (1996: 55).

Herzfeld raises the question of whether "reports of sexual stereotyping, of constricting role-structures, and of the control of women, [are more due to] an underlying tendency to view those societies as less civilized 'others' and at the same time obscure realities much closer to home" (1987: 59–61). These realities are discussed by Davidoff (1979), who locates the sharp differentiation between the domestic sphere and the workplace as a pattern that was most strongly developed in Victorian England, and that he sees as being a strong feature of nineteenth-century Northern European thinking (Davidoff 1979: 64–5). Sciama raises critical questions: "Might the opposition of private/public, then, have been transposed on to Mediterranean [mostly village] societies without sufficient attention being given to nuances in the use of space and in attribution of value? And might not accounts of the superiority of public male spheres in the European Mediterranean be partly a projection of Anglo-Saxon attitudes? . . . " (1993: 109). Evidently the culture of exclusion of women from male spheres is rooted in Western European traditions, and so is the correlate notion of female domesticity subsumed under the idealized concept of the *hausfrau*.

Ardener brings out the factor of color as sometimes associated with space in certain societies[92] (1993: 4). In the Arab cultural context space is not colored, but it is nuanced and dynamic, so much so as to accommodate privacy in public. This polarity is too rigid and static to apply particularly to Arab and Islamic space, which is characterized by the spatial and temporal interweaving pattern – the moving between sacred space and time and ordinary worldly space and time throughout the day every day. Sacred space and rhythmic time are both public and private.

Instead of the polarity, this study proposes "privacy" as the notion that, in its transformational fluid form, embraces the Arab cultural construction of space that connects space to time and gender. Sciama defines privacy as "the need for individuals, families or other social groups, to separate themselves from others at various times, for certain well-defined activities" (Sciama 1993: 87).

According to Sciama (1993), privacy derives from the Latin verb *privare* (adjective form *privus*, later *privatus*). She observes that "[t]he most important, and socially revealing, aspect of the word's development in English is the formation of the noun 'privacy'" (1993: 91).

She points out that "privacy" as a noun has no parallel in Latin or "other neo-Latin languages." Interestingly, while Latin has no equivalent noun-form (only verb and adjectival forms) for the word privacy, Arabic has no equivalent word at all, in any form. Sciama notes that by the sixteenth century the term "privacy" in English became widely used in literary contexts, eventually becoming a common usage. As an abstract notion, Sciama finds privacy to be indefinite, problematic and contradictory, just like the Latin *privatus* and *privare*.

The American Heritage Dictionary of the English Language (1991) defines privacy as the quality or condition of being secluded and the state of being free from unsanctioned intrusion. Based on English common-law traditions (which has had legal recognition in the United States since as early as 1890), the term "privacy" is used with reference to an individual's right to be left alone and in contexts of trespassing on private property. So the Western usage of the term is linked to the Western notion of individualism and individual rights to property (1993: 90–1).

Despite this inherent Western signification of the term, privacy is commonly presumed, even in anthropological work, to be a universal notion with universal meaning. As pointed above, it is rather interesting that the term "privacy'" has no equivalent in the Arabic language. Accordingly, the Arabic-English dictionary translates privacy in terms that correspond with the Western notion, such as "personal," "secluded," "secrecy," and "solitary," further supporting its non-indigenous linguistic origins.

The absence of a linguistic referent of some form does not necessarily mean that the manifestation of a notion of privacy is also absent. It does mean that its observability is less accessible and less obvious. I searched for the conceptual equivalent of privacy in Arab culture. Indeed, a notion of privacy in Arab culture was revealed in analysis. Its content and meaning, however, differ from their Western counterparts. Arab privacy does not connote the "personal," the "secret" or the "individuated space." It concerns two core spheres – women and the family. For both, privacy is sacred and carefully guarded. For women it is both a right and an exclusive privilege, and is reflected in dress, space, architecture and proxemic behavior. Their economic and marital autonomous identity is not connected to domesticity. A woman is guardian of the sanctity that is fundamental to the community. Upon marriage the Arab woman becomes *sitt el-bait,* or "the lady of the home" – a term that stresses an autonomous managerial role, not domesticity (El Guindi 1985b; 1986b). In his study of the Arab Rashayda of the Sudan, Young (1996) finds a similar notion, *ra'iyat el-bayt,* or the female guardian of the tent. She is the senior woman of a household. This further supports the premise of an adult woman's role of guardianship. Arab privacy is about neither individualism nor seclusion. It is relational and public.

Sanctity–Reserve–Respect

Haram and Hishma Revisited

Drawing upon various bodies of knowledge, the analysis of the veil reveals a fundamental code underlying many aspects of Arabo-Islamic culture, which embodies related concepts that are meaningful in textual and social contexts.

Although the term "modesty" is used in this book's title for the reason that Muslims have adopted it to describe the code underlying their practices, I contend that the modesty-based code – modesty–shame–seclusion – represents an ethnocentric imposition on Arabo-Islamic culture.[93] It makes more sense in Christian Mediterranean societies and, without shame, the Hindu-based societies of south Asia. This cluster of concepts is inaccurately ethnocentric; but, more importantly, it obscures the nuanced difference that is characteristic of Arabo-Islamic culture.[94] The "modesty–honor" gendered opposition is equally inappropriate (see also Herzfeld 1980).

To escape the trap of resorting first to familiar English terms to communicate cultural ideas from the non-English-speaking world, I devised a procedure by which I first identify the various possible culturally-derived terms to denote concepts that together (relationally) constitute the code that underlies patterns of behavior. I analyze these terms etymologically, ethnographically, visually and textually. They are grouped on the basis of shared qualities and linguistic and social uses. After examining their ethnographic context I search for the most appropriate (least ethnocentric) English term to represent them, while using the original Arabic terms whenever possible. It was not a terminological equivalence I sought, but a term contextualized in cultural meaning.

On the basis of my analysis, some of these term-concepts are *hurma* (h-r-m), *hishma* (h-sh-m), *sutra* (s-t-r), and related variants such as *tahashshud* (h-sh-d), and *haya'* (h-y-y), among others. These have their dialectical variants as well. They constitute a cultural code of sanctity–reserve–respect. This replaces the commonly used complex of the seclusion–shame–modesty code. And it does not, as Antoun proposes, inhere "in the women's physiology" (1968: 680). Neither is it true that "many quranic references are literally references to the protection of female genitalia" (1968: 679). Of the only three mentioned by Antoun as referring to women (23: 5; 24: 31: 70: 29) only one refers to women, and that is not about protecting genitalia. According to Abu-Zahra (1970), the first *sura* (23: 5) refers to men, who are enjoined to be "modest" and to "protect" their genital organs and not to have sexual intercourse except with their wives or their women slaves. In the second *sura* (24: 31), the rules of modesty and the covering of the genital organs are enjoined on women. In the third (70: 29) the same rules recommended in the first are again enjoined, this time once again on men (1970: 1081).

Antoun's approach is to be commended for seeking a complex cultural pattern and attempting to locate an accommodation between the Islamic norms and actual behavior. More studies should integrate scriptural text, provided that this is done by systematic examination. He rightly criticizes Abu-Zahra for her claim of a methodological problem in interpreting Qur'anic text in order to understand the code of modesty in "illiterate Arab Muslim villages" (Abu-Zahra 1970: 1079; see the exchange between Antoun (1970) and Abu-Zahra (1970) over this and other points). Antoun rejects her view that description and analysis should be confined to the single community studied, since the discipline of anthropology is comparative (cross-culturally and across historical periods) (Antoun1970: 1092).[95]

A key concept in the sanctity–reserve–respect code is the notion of *haram*. The root *h-r-m* "is among the most important Arabic roots in the vocabulary of Islamic practice" (Reinhart 1995: 101). According to Reinhart, it means something like "forbidden" or "taboo," and evokes constraint and heightened sanctity. *Haram*[96] means "forbidden, prohibited, unlawful, taboo, sacred." It is a word widely used in the Arabic vocabulary. It refers to all that is prohibited by divine authority. The derivative *muharramat* is a plural term that denotes all that it is forbidden to eat or to do. In legal thought an act deemed *haram* is one forbidden. Usually the term is synonymous with "proscribed," but it is sometimes used to denote the negative side of the legal scale of value, incorporating both the proscribed and the "reprehensible" (*makruh*). The continuum lies between what is *haram* (stress on the second syllable; "forbidden") and what is *halal* (stress on the second syllable; "permissible"):

> But say not – for any false thing that your tongues may put forth: "This is lawful [*halal*], and this is forbidden [*haram*]" so as to ascribe false things to Allah. For those who ascribe false things to Allah will never prosper. (16: 116)

According to Reinhart, "the term is used to refer to the area around the three holy cities of Islam – Mecca, Medina, and Jerusalem. Within the precincts of these cities, which are defined with considerable precision . . . certain restrictions apply that both reflect and define their sanctity. Hunting is forbidden, as is uprooting any tree or harvesting grain. Violence toward humans is proscribed. . . . The sanctity of the place is protected, and it protects those who flee to it" (Reinhart 1995: 101). The term used for this sanctuary, in which violence and the spilling of blood is prohibited, is *al-haram al-sharif* (the noble sanctuary). Other usages include *al-masjid al-haram* (the holy mosque) or *al-bayt al-haram* (the holy house) or *bayt-allah al-haram* (the holy house of god), which are used interchangeably to refer to Makka's Grand Mosque (El Guindi 1985a). *Al-shahr al-haram* (the holy month) refers to Ramadan, the month of fasting.

The same root also yields the word *ihram*, which means the state of ritual purity for pilgrims on the *hajj* (pilgrimage) (Reinhart 1995: 101), and involves "a special dress consisting of two seamless wrappers, one passed round the loins, the other over the shoulders, leaving the head uncovered" (Crawley 1931: 159) and ritual ablution and other prohibitions, which can only be undone by *fakk-il-ihram* ("untying" or "breaking" from the state), or the oppositional but equivalent phrase *ihlal* (making *halal*, or lawful).

In the context of gender, men in a relationship to a woman defined and bound by the incest taboo are her *maharim* (pl. for *mahram*). The following passage from the Qur'anic text is specific:

> That they [feminine gender] should not display their beauty and ornaments except what [must ordinarily] appear thereof; that they should draw their *khimar* [headveil]over their bosoms and not display their beauty except to their husbands, their fathers, their husbands' fathers, their sons, their husbands' sons, their brothers or their brothers' sons, or their sisters' sons, or their women, or the slaves whom their right hands possess, or male servants free of physical needs, or underage children. (24: 31)

With the woman as the frame of reference, the passage identifies those for whom the incest taboo is applicable, i.e. *maharim* (see Figure 8). It also refers to others for whom the taboo is unnecessary because of their disqualifying status, asexualized condition, or sexual immaturity. The reference "or their women" is the subject of analysis in a work in progress.

"*Haram* so-and-so" (stress on the first syllable) means the wife of so-and-so. In the Islamic cultural construction, *harim* becomes the part of the home in which women are both privileged and protected from encounters with non-*mahram* men (Graham-Brown 1988: 71–2). Women are the center of the family and its sanctity, and hence the term extends to the family in general, as commonly used in verbal greetings and inquiries about health.

Hurma, best translated as "sanctity" in English, denotes the concept that is closest to the notion of privacy in Arab culture. Its linguistic root *h-r-m* yields many other derivatives, such as *harim* and *haram*, that link women, religious space, family and community. *Hurma* refers to a woman or wife, and is used as well to refer to the sanctity of the home, as in "*al-bayt lahu-hurma*" (a home has its sanctity). Other derivatives refer to religious sanctuaries, such as mosques and pilgrimage sites. Women and men guard and respect this sanctity. It is common in traditional circles for a man, upon entering a home, to "*yihamhim*" (a throat-clearing sound), clap, or call out "*ya sattar*" (*s-t-r*) ("O Protector of Privacy," an attribute of God) to announce his imminent entry upon women's, or a home's, privacy.

Early describes the Egyptian "baladi" woman in her managerial role in the household. She tells this story "The fact that the home is the woman's castle was dramatized for me one morning when a husband returned home

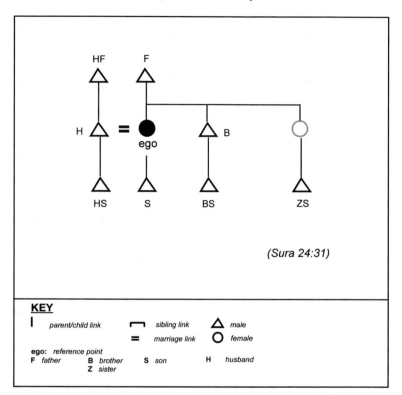

Figure 8 Kinship chart showing the relations specified in a passage in *Sura al-Nur*. Using a female point of reference, the relations of those in whose physical presence she can loosen her reserve and guard are charted. They include her *maharim,* slaves, eunuchs, and underage boys. Concept by F. El Guindi, computer graphics by D. W. Read. Courtesy El Nil Research.

unexpectedly from work to find his wife and her friends cooking. He paused to knock, not daring to enter without alerting the women within" (Early 1993: 68). Similarly in the Rashidi camp, according to the ethnography by Young (1996), Rashidi men who "see the end of the loom protruding from the western side of the tent, do not push aside the curtain to enter without first calling to the women and giving them time to veil" (1996: 52) (see Figure 9).

Antoun (1968) observes that one other meaning of the term *hurma* is "respectable woman," a connotation supported by the fact that the variant *ihtiram* (respect) is another derivative of the same root (*h-r-m*), connecting "respect" with *haram*. Respect, achieved by behavior and personal qualities and acquired by social or kinship status, is a key factor in the reputation of an individual and the group. Reputation is a carefully cultivated cultural investment.

Lancaster (1981) discusses the role of reputation for the Rwala Bedouin as being based on "how closely a person demonstrates Bedu virtues – honour, bravery, generosity, political acumen and mediatory abilities. In the past when all men were economically equal . . . the only way to distinguish one man from another in terms of worth was by his reputation. Wealth had little meaning as the only wealth was camels, which were acquired, over and above subsistence needs, simply to gain a reputation as a successful raider and then given away to demonstrate the raider's generosity – success in raiding and generosity were the main features in building a reputation" (1981: 43). Lancaster observes that reputation is equally important for men and women, and is carefully built and guarded since childhood. Socialization and up-bringing, particularly by the mother, includes ways to reinforce it. For a woman, reputation is based on qualities like competence, efficiency, maternal care, managing the household, generosity and bravery. "Quite apart from personal generosity a girl should materially aid her father's brother's or husband's reputation for generosity and hospitality" (1981: 44). It must be

Figure 9 Rashidi women working inside a tent and using a loom, displaying undecorated married and unmarried women's dress items. Photo by W. Young, reprinted by permission.

noted that this combination of qualities for women does not in any simple way correspond to perceived characterizations of Arab women. Their sharing with the men of reputation-building through culturally valued behaviors is far from insignificant.

Gilsenan, in his study on rural Lebanon, observes that "women are the center of a family's sacred identity" (1982: 171), for they embody the central values prized by the family that are key to their reputation and their status. Again the point is revealed in a different ethnographic case that there is interdependence between the sexes in building and guarding reputation. Reputation shapes Arab and Muslim community self-image. Women and men are entrusted with guarding the sanctity of the family and the reputation of the community.

Satr is a related Arabic term, a derivative of another root (*s-t-r*). It refers to the veil, curtains and sanctity. The verb means "to shield, to guard, to cover, to protect, to veil." In the Arabic–English dictionary synonyms for *satr* include *hijab, niqab, khimar, tarhah, burqu', litham, ghita'* – all terms of dress denoting head or face cover. The derivative term *sitara* (noun) means veil, curtain, and screen, and, like *hijab*, is used in spoken dialects and in Islamic text. It is another concept that relates to core concepts and to dress. *Satr* relates to *haram* and to *hijab* – a core concept of the veil discussed in Chapter 13.

The quality *hurma* (which centers womanhood and home in the culture) embodies a pervasive complex of values that identifies primary social and religious spheres as sanctuaries – sacred and inviolable.

The next concept is *hishma* (from *h-sh-m*). To capture the underlying meaning that *hishma* yields, I shall explore ethnography. The Rashayda use the two interrelated concepts *hishma* and *tahashshud* [97] to mean polite reserve, self-restraint, good judgment and respect. Young demonstrates how avenues that also recognize individual achievements are provided by the culture to achieve these qualities for both sexes. But ultimately what is protected is group reputation and identity. Like men, women are rewarded for competent skills and industriousness. They take pride in the appearance of the tent cloth or veils that they weave or decorate. The patterns woven on tent cloth are markers of tribal identity and a reflection of women's skill and talent (Young 1996: 50). A Rashidi woman "weaves" her community's identity, as it were.

Young's photos and ethnography provide systematic ethnographic detail about Rashayda dress. The data clearly illustrate that dress is a language that communicates multiple layers of messages. A visual analysis of the photo (Figure 7 above) shows "the borders of the rectangle below the woman's face . . . filled with lacy network of beads. The designs that flare out from the sides of this rectangle are called *jinah il-ghurab* (wings of the crow/raven). Sleeves trail on the ground. On the top of her head is the *marbata* (hair binding) – a flat square of black cloth decorated with lead beads and laid atop her head. Its left and right edges are equipped with ribbons for tying up her hair, to keep it standing out from the contours of her temples, which is bordered with beadwork and stretched across her crown and attached to the rolls of hair above each ear. It . . . hold[s] the rolls of hair up. The hair, although completely covered by the *gina'* (elsewhere *qina'*) appears bulky, thick and plentiful" (personal communication.)

Young points out that "she is wearing all of her jewelry: (a) a large silver *lawh* which projects from beneath the lower edge of her mask; (b) wide silver bracelets (*sa'af*) of the kind which are given to a bride as *sigha* (jewelry wealth) when she is married; and (c) silver rings, worn by married women when they dance at weddings. A collection of handicrafts are hung behind her. To the left is a saddlebag woven out of commercial, colored yarns; on the far left is the edge of an ornamental belt *sirdag* (belt)" (personal communication). The belt is "heavily encrusted with silvery lead beads, to the point where the black cloth of which it is made is almost covered over. It is tied securely to the woman's waist. The upper part of the belt, which fits her body closely, is seldom seen" (Young 1994: 66). "The top part is concealed by pulling up the loose cloth of the dress and letting it fall over the tight band around the waist. The belt has two large rectangular panels in front that hang well below the waist and are designed to be seen. Behind her to the right is an adult woman's *milayah*, a decorated piece of cloth that falls from the back of the head and covers the back. It is worn with the "married woman's ritual veil" (*burga'*, elsewhere *burqu'*) when women dance" (Young, personal communication).

In another photo (see Figure 10) two Rashayda women in profile are dancing at a wedding. One woman "has laid a *milaya* over her head and back and is wearing a richly decorated 'married woman's mask' but has not put on a 'married woman's ritual veil'" (personal communication). "Hence she is not competing for the 'dancer's prize' *(as-sagala)* that is given to the best dancers at a wedding or an Islamic holiday. The two little girls who stand next to her, facing the camera, are wearing the decorated 'virgin's veil' and *gargush*. The other woman . . . at the far right has 'taken the prize' *(akhadhat as-sagala)* – paper currency pinned to the side of her *milaya*" (see also Figure 11). The dancers' loose sleeves and skirts flare out as they turn; these parts of their clothing are called *il-bala*. The tight-fitting parts of their clothing, which are decorated with silvery lead beads, are called *il-wani*" (1998 personal written communication; see also Young 1993, 1996).

The related concept *Haya'* (*h-y-y*) is embedded in the notion of life itself.

Figure 10 Rashidi women dancing at a wedding. Photo by W. Young, reprinted by permission.

It is repeatedly mentioned in the *Hadith* as a quality central to the faith. *Hadith* (1406) states that "each religion has its moral character and the moral character of Islam is *haya'* ." Abu-Zahra (1970) mentions that the Prophet Muhammad is reported to have said: "If you do not have *haya'*, you can do what you want" (1080, 1087 – perhaps better translated: "If you do not have *haya'*, what does it matter what you do?") However, the present analysis shows that *haya'* shares core connotations with *hishma*, although the former is not as widely used in spoken form. Still, parents often use the phrase "*qalil al-haya*" punitively, to mean "lacking in decorum," when socializing their children. The range of referents in dictionaries and other reference sources (see *Lisan al-'Arab* [under Ibn Manzur 1883–90]; and Mawdudi (1985)) is very similar to those given for *hishma*.

The Awlad 'Ali of North Africa share the same conceptualization. The man from Awlad 'Ali quoted in Abu-Lughod, captures the cultural essence. He said that women *tahashsham* (verb from *hishma*) "from respect for their tribe, their husband, and themselves" (1986: 156). If we disregard Abu-Lughod's focus on modesty, which distorts cultural identity, and her reductionist readings[98] – "deference and sexual denial" or "women as closer to nature or natural sexuality," "sexual shame" and "sexual immodesty" (1986: 152, 154, 157, 162, 163) – the resemblance between the bedouin groups of the Awlad 'Ali, the Rashayda, and the Rwala becomes evident. All put a high value on the quality of reserve. Young (1996) adds to these the emphasis by the Rashayda on the individual woman's identity as an individual, and as a member of family and tribe.

This view builds on the notion of "woman as sanctuary" proposed decades ago by Abou-Zeid (1959, 1966, 1979), the first anthropologist to study the Awlad 'Ali. Pitt-Rivers (1954), who studied the Spanish peasants of Alcala, observed that the woman, particularly as wife and mother, represents the family as a moral corporation through her reputation. The challenge is to establish cultural measures for reputation. Translating the notions of *hishma* and *tahashshud* (in their dialect variants) as "modesty" stresses the wrong quality. Reducing it to sexuality diverts analysis away from the central cultural

Figure 11 A Rashidi woman dancing with her prize. Photo by W. Young, reprinted by permission.

notions of respect, privacy and identity. Anderson is right to observe that "veiling refers actions to a paradigm of comportment in general rather than to chastity in particular," challenging reductionism to nature and sexuality (1982: 403).

Analysis of veiling in social space reveals a communicative function in relation to social and kinship status and identity. Yalman's analysis (1963) focuses on the caste status and purity that is achieved through women's endogamy. The notion of "the purity of blood" is pertinent to the Arab system as well at the ideological level; in concrete terms Arabs were not exclusionist in their marital or descent affiliation. Islam further challenged exclusivist concrete blood purity as a basis for its community. It could not have succeeded in the Arab system otherwise (see Wolf 1951 on the formation of the seventh-century Islamic community). Pertinent here is Abu-Zahra's insightful remark (1970) that the Arabic word *sharaf (sh-r-f)*[99] refers to noble descent, which underlies isogamy (*kafa'ah* or the principle of equal status in marriage) and endogamy (which is formulated in ideal terms as patrilateral parallel-cousin marriage, but in fact is a broader endogamy) in Arab systems. I note that a *sharif (sh-r-f)* is one who traces descent (real or ideological) lineally in ancestry that is claimed to go back to the Prophet Muhammad himself, the ultimate expression of "blood purity."

The Arabic notion of *hasham (h-sh-m)* stands for ideas linked with culturally defined status as well as cultural notions of maturity in the individual life cycle. The Awlad 'Ali observe (Abu-Lughod 1986) that "virgins do not veil," that "veiling starts at marriage" and that "it occurs in interaction with senior kin and nonkin." This is similar to what Young (1996) discovered among the Rashayda. Veiling by women among the Awlad 'Ali, therefore, is not dissimilar to that by Tuareg men, and by rural women in North India and elsewhere, where it formalizes status, establishes identity and marks the life cycle. The whole tenor in the analysis of Arabo-Islamic culture must shift its emphasis from an overstated "moral purity" to "blood purity" (which centers women through metaphors of dress in the culture) as it translates into cultural notions of respect, identity, and space.

Gilsenan (1982) explores "the sacred" in the collective public social sense. He observes that the nature of the public zone is such that by definition "everything is visible" and that "it is within the sphere of men" (1982: 167). Women are excluded: "Women do not gather at the spring, nor do they enter the mosque or cross the area in front of it" (1982: 167). They remain within "the closed and nonvisible space to which no stranger may penetrate" (1982: 183). This is overstated since "[i]n fact, women engage in an enormous amount of visiting to and fro and are quite central in the exchange of information, arrangement of marriages, and so forth" (1982: 172, emphasis mine). He also mentions how the water well is an important meeting-place (1982: 167).

Gilsenan's notion of "seeing" goes beyond arguments of invisibility and anonymity and is not based on the linkage between public space, the sacred, men's sphere, and visibility – a linkage assumed in many works (Badran 1995a), but easily challenged by ethnography. Makhlouf (1979) observes that veiling in Yemen is not simply a device to reduce "all women to anonymous figures," but that in fact "[t]he veil does not prevent women from recognizing friends and relatives in the street or from chatting together when they meet" (1979: 32). Fernea (1965) makes a similar point about women in the Shi'a Iraqi village. But she had to learn these hidden signs after an extended stay in the village and immersion in the lives of the women. At the beginning she was anxious: "How will I remember who they were? They looked . . . so remarkably alike in their identical black head scarves, black chin scarves, and black *abayahs*" (1965: 29). But, as Makhlouf points out, women do recognize each other by identifying alternative signs, such as stature, mannerisms, etc. (1979: 32).

Gilsenan defines "seeing" as a "socially determined act, not a question merely of images on the retina and physiological process" (1982: 171). The question of *who "sees" whom* is focal in Arab society. Space is a highly structured relationship in which open (undefined) spaces are rare. When Gilsenan distinguishes "being seen" from "being visible" he is making a meaningful statement about Arab culture, which considers "seeing" a marked activity and cross-sex "seeing" as closely linked to respect and privacy. Because seeing is important it must be regulated.

Among the Rashayda an elaborate culture of dressing and veiling serves to establish a woman's identity, mark her status and earn her the respect of the community. Here women share public space with men, competing equally for rewards for competence and skills. A woman's identity and reputation are "seen," and are publicly recognized, in her material artistic achievements.

Young describes the Islamic holidays celebrated by the Rashayda as follows: every adult (married) woman stands right outside the tent by the pegs, her head covered by her sleeves and wearing a "long, richly decorated, thick veil called a *burga'*" that extends from her forehead to her waist, leaving only her eyes uncovered" (1996: 79). "This veil is worn only by married women and only on special occasions (such as weddings and Islamic holidays). When the men pass by as they return to their tents they give holiday greetings to each married woman . . . and [the man touches the woman] gently on one shoulder in a light embrace" (Young 1996: 80).

The Rashidi woman is thereby displaying her group's identity and defining her place in social space as she establishes her status as owner of the tent and guardian of the household. Dress (for women, shelter, or transport) encodes and communicates a message. It is a marker of both the individual's group status and the group's identity. The prize that the best woman dancer receives is symbolic of the value attached to the skill, competence, and artistic talent that are woven into the representation of tribal identity. Her clothes, movement and behavior are measured, because she holds the key to the group's identity[100] and reputation.

Privacy is active when a woman, who owns and is guardian of the tent, sits in her section and shuts out intrusions, while she skillfully "weaves community identity" and marks her position in it. In ceremonial time, as for example during Islamic annual celebrations of the 'Eid or in life cycle ceremonies such as a wedding, she becomes "seen" publicly by displaying her "woven representations" of her position and status in the group and her people's identity. She displays her skills when she performs the wedding dance or when she stands outside the tent by the pegs "receiving" men and exchanging 'Eid greetings. Public display does not violate privacy, since privacy is not about seclusion, exclusion or invisibility.

Mashrabiyya (lattice woodwork screens and windows) in urban Arabesque architecture serve to guard families' and women's right to privacy – that is the right "to see" but not "be seen" – and are not about seclusion or invisibility. Related to "who sees whom" is "who chooses whom." In an interview with a prospective urban Egyptian groom, he relates a story about his trip to Damascus in search of a bride – an encounter with privacy – describing his feelings, reactions and perspective. A visit was prearranged by acquaintances. He enthusiastically went to the prospective bride's home – a big two-story Arab-style home with *mashrabiyya* screens on the second floor overlooking the *majlis* (reception area) below. He was asked to sit in the *majlis* in the center of the house on the ground floor where he entered. He relates the following:

> I sat and waited. It seemed like a very long time. But somehow I had the feeling I was not alone even though I saw no one else around. [In fact, he heard female voices and murmurs coming from upstairs behind the *mashrabiyya*.] I felt self-conscious, nervous, embarrassed and awkward, with my legs tightly closed together, sweating as I listened to my heartbeat in between the murmurs and giggles from the women above.

He knew he was being "seen" and scrutinized. While he was the one who sought a bride, he found himself instead invisibly gazed at for approval or rejection. She was choosing a groom.

Mashrabiyya embodies the essence of traditional notions of Arab privacy – who has the *"right to see whom,"* who has the *"right not to be seen by whom,"* and *"who chooses not to 'see' whom."* In the case of the traditional rural community studied by Gilsenan (1982) he puts it this way: "because of the powerful convention, sanctioned ultimately by violence, . . . none 'see' them. They are publicly 'not there' *because* they are so significant" (1982: 172, emphasis in original). Makhlouf tries to make this point as well when she states that veiling functions "as much to exclude men" (1979: 34). But the emphasis on inclusion and exclusion is the wrong emphasis. In many ways, veiling resembles a *mashrabiyya*; but whereas *mashrabiyya* is stationary, veiling is mobile, carrying women's privacy to public spaces. A woman carries "her" privacy and sanctity with her, much the same way as when a Muslim worships in any space, converting it to sacred and private.

The link between dress, women and sanctity of space is also reflected in the Islamic rituals of "dressing" the *Ka'ba*, the center of the holy site of pilgrimage in Makka. Richard Burton (1964 [1855]) is perhaps the first Western observer to see a relation between key elements in the rites of preparation of the *Ka'ba* for the annual pilgrimage and metaphorically "dressing" the *Ka'ba* like a bride (Young 1993: 288). Young analyzes the *kiswa* as a central element in the rites of preparation surrounding the sanctuary. He observes how in the past the *Ka'ba* was the center of a number of annual rites: the transport of the *mahmal* and *kiswa* from Cairo, the replacement of the old *kiswa* with a new one, and the *ihram* of the *Ka'ba* (Young 1993: 287). Burton identified *ahzima* (belts) and *burqu'* (veil) as parts of the *kiswa*.

Kiswa is an Arabic derivative from the root that means "to cover," and is used in contexts of clothes supplied to the bride or new clothes for Islamic holidays. It is also used to connote "provide for" by the provider in the family. And the same term is used for the cloth that covers holy tombs. Each year, some forty days before the *hajj* (pilgrimage), an elaborate procession through the streets of Cairo was organized, which began the transfer of the *kiswa* (garment) from Cairo to Makka (Basha 1925: 1, 5, 9–12; 1925: 2, 304).[101] It consists of eight panels, two on each side of the *Ka'ba*. These are made out of silk. Long, narrow strips of cloth were sewn together. These are called *athwab* (sing. *thob*, a word used for a dress). Encircling the *ka'ba* there is a large decorative band made out of gold brocade, which consisted of eight *ahzima* (sing. *hizam*, or "belt"), each mounted on one of the supporting panels. Qur'anic verses were sewn with gold thread onto the belts. Then there is the *burqu'* (married woman's veil), embroidered with gold and silver thread and made of black silk and red and green satin, which was placed directly over the door of the *Ka'ba* (Young 1993: 292).

As Young demonstrates through his description, there is a striking analogy between the terms used to "dress" the sacred sanctuary, the *Ka'ba*, and Arab women's traditional dress in general. The correspondence between the sanctuary of the *Ka'ba* and the home (as sanctuary) is exemplified in the measures for protection and attitudes of protectiveness in both spheres. Young observes that in the past eunuchs (*aghas*) guarded this pilgrimage center (*haram*), as they also have women's quarters (*harim*) among the wealthy and the aristocracy in urban centers.

Young's analysis goes further, to show that in terminological vocabulary and ritual language there is analogy to a bridal procession. He sees a similarity in appearance and processional quality with the "litter" transported by camels: both are transported publicly and ceremonially – *hawdaj* in the case of a bride, *mahmal* in the case of the *kiswa* carried in procession (Young 1993: 286–300).

The terminology deriving from *h-r-m,* and relating the notion of *haram* to other similar concepts, was presented earlier to demonstrate connections among various aspects of Arab-Islamic culture that these usages underlie. The concept of sanctuary that connects sacred places, like mosques and pilgrimage centers, also applies to women, women's quarters, and family – a connection that brings out the significance of the idea of sanctity in these contexts. The veil, veiling patterns and veiling behavior are therefore, according to my analysis of Arab culture, about sacred privacy, sanctity and the rhythmic interweaving of patterns of worldly and sacred life, linking women as the guardians of family sanctuaries and the realm of the sacred in this world. I argue for the centrality of the cultural notion of privacy, as one that embodies the qualities of reserve, respect and restraint as these are played out in fluid transformational bi-rhythmic space. Dress in general, but particularly veiling, is privacy's visual metaphor.

6

The Veil in Social Space

A survey of dress styles among Arabs shows enormous variability in properties, shape and terminology. Yet an emerging pattern reveals shared qualities, common elements and overlapping usage, and reduces this apparently endless variability. Broadly, Arab dress can be distinguished in material terms on the basis of two usages: dress items that cover the head and the hair (such as *khimar*), or wrap/cover the body (such as *milayah, 'aba* or *izar*), on the one hand, and those that are explicitly and exclusively used to cover the face, partially or completely (such as *burqu', qina',* or *lithma*).

Makhlouf discusses kinds of headcover as indicators of the social condition of individuals in society and social status (1979: 32). She distinguishes different headcovers worn by women in Yemen. Two types of headcovers are worn indoors. First, there is the *lithma* (see Figure 19). It is a "brightly-coloured thin material or muslin draped around the head in such a way as to cover the hair and the forehead, while the lower part of it can be pulled down to uncover or pulled up to cover the whole face except the eyes" (1979: 30). It is worn by unmarried girls at all times and by married women in daily routines of housework or for informal morning visits. Converted to adjectival form, *mutalaththim(a)* denotes the state of having a *lithma* on. Other similar terms used in different Arab communities include *burqu'* and *qina'*. Derivative terms for *qina'* are *muqanna'* or *mutaqanna'*; and for *burqu'* there are *mubarqa'* or *mutabarqa'*, all used for women and men with changes of gendering markers. These usages can be found in the Prophetic Traditions or the *Hadith*, but pertain mostly to men. For dual-gendered usages of the veil and cross-gender usages during the period from about the fifth century to the beginning of Islamic society in the seventh century, see the discussion of dress styles and names as found in Arab poetry by Jubouri (1989). As to diverse forms of women's *burqu'* among the various contemporary groups in the southeastern Gulf coast of Arabia see the ethnographic materials by Wikan (1982) and Chatty (1997).

One property of the veil is its dynamic flexibility, which allows for spontaneous manipulation and instant changing of form. The quality of *pull down to uncover or pull up to cover* provides the wearer with the advantage of instant maneuvering. Makhlouf demonstrates this point when she relates instances when a man unexpectedly comes into a house, *after signaling his entry*, and how women rush to pull up their *lithmas*. The difficulty exists for those who have taken it off altogether and who are unable to drape it back quickly enough, so that they first try to drape it, or grab another piece of cloth, or hide their faces behind others (Makhlouf 1979: 33–4).

This veiling behavior is similar to that of Indian women as observed by Sharma. There is elsewhere the use of sleeves to cover or uncover head or face and the use of the loose hanging ends from the *'imamah* (turban) or *kufiyya* (headcloth) worn by men. The evidence found in *Jahiliyya* poetry indicates that there was once much more fluidity of headcover, even across gender, in which the head cover worn by men is referred to as *khimar* and in which certain *'imamah* forms were worn by women from pre-Islamic times and into the period of the Prophet (Jubouri 1989: 119).

In the ethnography by Makhlouf she describes the situation as that in which women relax their veiling when alone or with men of *mahram*. In some, particularly urban, contexts where women face veil, they do so in the presence of "strange men," defined as those who are not her *maharim* (male kin who are bound by the incest taboo, that is, in a relationship of unmarriagiability to the women) (see El Guindi 1981a, 1986b; Makhlouf 1979). This aspect finds support in the *Qur'an*, where relations are explicitly identified:

> Prohibited to you [male gender] are your mothers, daughters, sisters; father's sisters, mother's sisters; brother's daughters, sister's daughters; "suckling"mothers, suckling sisters; your wives' mothers; your step-daughters under your guardianship, born of your wives, wives of your biological sons.
>
> (Sura 4: 23)

These kin are in a relation in which the incest taboo applies, and they are prohibited from sexual and marital relations. To a woman her *maharim* comprise father, brother, son, father's brother, mother's brother, brother's son, sister's son, and suckling brother (see Figure 12).

The manipulation of dress "to face-veil" is noted in the ethnography. "Thus Papanek [1973] also notes that Muslim women in Pakistan who do not wear the *burqah* [henceforth *burqu'*] can manipulate their dress, chiefly through the positioning of the veil, according to the social situation. The same may be said of women in Ghanyari [in North India], who know how to draw the veil across the face in a dozen different ways to denote a dozen different degrees of respect or disrespect. I have seen the veil used insolently," writes Sharma (1978: 224). (See Figure 13.)

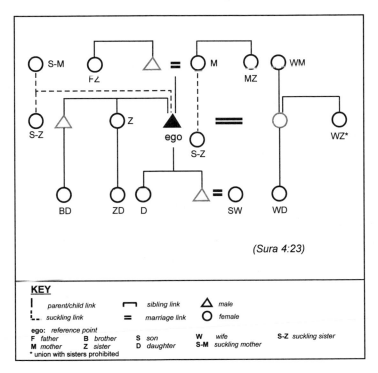

(Sura 4:23)

KEY

⏐ parent/child link	⎴ sibling link	△ male
⌐⌐ suckling link	= marriage link	○ female

ego: reference point
F father   **B** brother   **S** son   **W** wife   **S-Z** suckling sister
M mother   **Z** sister   **D** daughter   **S-M** suckling mother
* union with sisters prohibited

Figure 12   Kinship chart showing the relations specified in a passage in *Sura al-Nisa'*. Using a male point of reference, the relations of sex and marital taboo are charted. Gray symbols denote linking positions only. Note the relations of suckling kinship. Concept by F. El Guindi, computer graphics by D. W. Read. Courtesy El Nil Research.

The second type of Yemeni women's headcover worn indoors does not conceal the face, but only the hair, and is worn for purposes of fashion and elegance. "It is a long square or rectangular scarf of brightly-colored, sometimes printed muslin, worn over the head and shoulders, with a band of brocade tied around the forehead. This type of headscarf is worn by married women on afternoon visits" (Makhlouf 1979: 30).

For outdoors there are two "veils": the *sitara* and the *sharshaf*: "[T]he *sitara*, [is] a large piece of cotton material printed in red, blue and green, and covering the head and the body. To this is added a piece of black batik ornamented with large red and white circles covering the face and transparent enough to let the women see through" (1979: 30–1). (See Figure 14.) *Sitara* is a term used culturally and textually in the original Islamic sources. Here the analogy with the lattice screen of houses, *mashrabiyya*, is striking. (See Figure 15.)

Figure 13 Indian woman drawing her headcover over her mouth: an example of veiling proxemics. *Human Nature Magazine*, Vol. 2, No. 1, January 1979. Human Nature (now discontinued). Photo by Bill Cadge.

Figure 14 A modelled display of an urban Yemeni woman's dress. *Human Nature Magazine*, Vol. 2, No. 1, January 1979. Human Nature (now discontinued). Photo by George Holan Photo Researchers.

Figure 15 A traditional Afghan veil next to *mashrabiyya* architecture of Arabo-
Islamic style. Concept by F. El Guindi and composite computer graphics
by D. W. Read.

Sharma (1978) makes a similar point for North Indian rural women. She
says that "the veil which women in Ghanyari wear can also be used in a
similar way to the *burqah* as a kind of 'shutter' from the gaze of the public
in general, and is sometimes used by village women when they travel outside
their own neighborhood" (Sharma 1978: 223–4). While all face veils have
the same property – "transparency" for the wearer – the one that makes the
point dramatically is the Afghan form. A veil – *mashrabiyya* visual comparison makes the point (see Figure 15).

The other Yemeni outdoor item considered a veil is the *sharshaf*. It "consists
of three parts: a long pleated skirt worn over the dress and a waist-length
cape covering the head and shoulders, both made of black silk-like material . . ."
(Makhlouf 1979: 31). Then there is the *khunna*: a piece of thin black muslin
to cover the face. According to Makhlouf, "women of the lower socio-

economic status tend to wear the *sitara* while those of higher rank wear the black *sharshaf* "(1979: 34). Interestingly, women in the middle rank tend to "alternate between the two, wearing the *sitara* for casual occasions such as morning errands and visits to immediate neighbors, and wearing the *sharshaf* for afternoon visits" (1979: 34). All girls above ten and all women wear either one or the other when they go out of the house. The only unveiled women in the streets are non-Yemenis and women from the class of *akhdam* (servants).

This use of women's veiling is consistent with the use of the veil as a status symbol reported in stratified urban societies, as in Mesopotamia, and in the modern era in most Arab urban centers. The *gargush* is a little hood made of brocade and worn mostly by girls below the age of ten. The relationship between the form of veil used and the individual life cycle was shown in a case that Makhlouf considered an anomaly. An adult but unmarried woman was observed wearing the *gargush*. She also saw contradictory aspects to veiling. She states that "the veil, though it is obviously a restriction on communication . . . [is also a symbolic] communicative device . . . [and] veiling certainly constitutes an obstacle to the free expression of women as persons. . . [yet it enhances] the expression of self and femininity" (Makhlouf 1979: 32).

In Mamluk[102] Egypt, a dynastic rule of about two and a half centuries between 1250 and 1517, women were quite prominent and visible in many domains of public life (ar-Raziq 1975, 1923; Lane 1883; Ibn Khaldun 1867-1868 ; Fawwaz 1896; al-Hajj 1929). Chroniclers of this era describe it as an era of enormous material luxury, and one in which women were held in high regard. It is reported that common Muslim women participated on councils of education, learning and orthodox religion and were active in Sufi activities. For Sufi sessions they wore woolen rags (as a sign of self-denial and renouncement of worldly material pleasures) and formed orders under the leadership of women *shaykhas*. Even women of high rank joined, such as Khawnad[103] Shukr Bey the wife of Sultan al-Thahir Khashqadam, who wore the Ahmadiyya rags (ar-Raziq 1975: 30–2). She was pious and charitable and believed in Shaykh Ahmad al-Badawi and visited his tomb (in Tanta) often (El Guindi 1990 (film)). Women were active in public in other capacities as well. According to al-Hajj (1929) and al-Maqrizi (1972) women went to the market and even did all the clothes shopping for their husbands. They also went regularly to the public baths – social events in which vital family information is exchanged – and returned not only clean and refreshed but dressed in the most luxurious of clothes, body decoration and ornamentation (al-Hajj 1960: iii, 173).

Sayyid-Marsot discusses how "women showed entrepreneurial talents to the extent that they amassed more property and wealth than many males roaming freely in the marketplace" (1995: 40). From her study of deeds and endowments of the period, it was revealed that women invested in houses for rent, in shops of various kinds, and in tax-farms. They founded trusts and endowed charities, from which the men of religion (the *'ulama*) stood to benefit materially. They are the largest group to register trusts. Powerful women had a role in the political life of their men. It is an accepted fact that women have important intercessionary functions as wives of powerful men. Also learned women were brought into the Mamluk "harem" to teach young female Mamluks. Archival documents indicate that Mamluk women bought and sold and invested funds on their own in their own natal family name. Women had taken over the management of property since before the eighteenth century. When the French under Bonaparte landed in Egypt in 1798, they asked about administrative matters and were told "in recent times, most of the tax-farms went to the women" (Sayyid-Marsot 1995: 26). The Ottomans in Egypt made attempts at controlling Egyptian women's mobility but could not stop them from going about the marketplace. Soon the Ottomans sent out a public crier to declare that women who went out in public should be modestly dressed and "were not to wear a headgear known as the *qazdaghliyya*, described as a circle of multicolored muslin tipped onto the forehead" (al-Jabarti 1882: 2: 140). Women of the middle and working classes were not veiled.

During this period in urban centers, veiling the face and covering the body in public was considered a mark of a woman's high rank, respectability and inaccessibility. Among a number of honorific titles to address women two are of special interest, because they explicitly use terms of dress, and specifically the veil: *al-satr al-rafi'* (aloof protection) and *al-hijab al-mani'* (inaccessible partition) (ar-Raziq 1975: 359; Hamdy 1959: 64). Both titles use metaphorical dress vocabulary, *satr* and *hijab*, to describe the valued privacy attached by the culture to women and the family. Only servants and slaves did not, indeed were not allowed to, cover the face. Common women in public covered their face with a variety of *manadil* (pl.(, (kerchiefs). It was said that Omar Ibn al-Khattab[104] once saw a slave girl wearing a *qina'* (face mask), and he beat her and said: "Are you trying to imitate a free woman?" (al-Hajj 1929: i., 145). Interestingly a woman who was a *muqanna'a* (wearing *qina'*) was given the title *al-qina'*. It was made out of muslin and was worn on the woman's face underneath the *izar*. There was also the head veil, which hung loosely over the face down to the shoulders. Wearing these veils was an innovation in Egypt during the reign of the Mamluk Sultan Ibn Qalawun. The prices reported for these veils indicate that only women of high rank could afford to wear them. Also worn by high-ranking women was the black net that covered the entire face (ar-Raziq 1975: 188–97).

As for commoners, Abd ar-Raziq describes other veils: a black and white *mandil* (sing.) called *al-burqu'* that cover the face right below the eyes. Another that was commonly used was *al-niqab*, a black mask with two slits for the eyes. Evidence for these veil forms, which were referred to in Arabic sources, came from Orientalist paintings and the writings of travelers. It was suggested that the *niqab* gradually spread from that period of Mamluk rule to Bedouin women.

Crawley argued that "dress is the most distinctive expression in a material form of the various grades of social life. The biological period thus becomes a social period of existence, and the individual is merged in a functional section of the community" (1931: 117). It seems that Crawley accepted the stages in van Gennep's formulation of rites of passage, but may have assumed that they universally coincide with biological changes, so that social actions related to them are "laid over" these phases, as it were. In fact, rites of passage mark transitions as culturally defined. So cultural contexts are important. Birth may be marked by the actual physical birth or on the day a baby is baptized or on its seventh day of life, as in the *El-Sebou'* ceremony in Arab culture. We know, however, that transitions are marked and that in many societies they are marked by dress. As Eicher and Roach-Higgins (1992) point out, prescriptions for dress according to gender and age can become complex as individuals progress through various life stages. In each of these stages differences in form of dress for women and men can define, support, and reinforce relative power and influence, while, as the case of the Rashayda demonstrates, they also define expectations of ability and participation in the work necessary for group survival.

Young concludes in his ethnography that the Rashayda's most visible signs of cultural identity are their clothes – in particular the men's turban (*'imamah*) and the married women's mask (*gina'*). The turban is a quite common headgear for men in the Arab region. Moving from Islamic sources to literature and poetry of the *Jahiliyya* period (pre-Islamic) as a source of ethnographic data leads us to interesting information. "*al-'Imamah*", writes Jubouri, is "'*libas*' wrapped around [a man's] head . . .[,] . . . one or several times" (1989: 196, my translation). It is reported that Omar Ibn al-Khattab (Companion of the Prophet and second Khalifa succeeding him) said: "*al-'Ama'im* (pl. *'imamah*) *tijan* [crowns] *al-'Arab* [of the Arabs]." Jubouri mentions that the same saying was attributed to the Prophet himself (1989: 197). Examining what is said in poetry and other sources on the headgear it becomes evident that this is a dress article that is highly differentiated in symbol and use, with elaborate terminology and shifting meanings over the eras. It is clear, however, that it did exist among Arabs before Islam and into Islam until it flourished as of the tenth century. It was worn in a range of colors, particularly white, black, yellow and red. But after the Crusades it was used in Arab communities to distinguish Muslims from Christians and Jews. Christians were to wear blue and Jews yellow, while Muslims wore black or white. There are some indications that green became a desirable color at the time of the Prophet. Jubouri describes the place of the turban among Arabs before Islam as "the pride of the Arabs and the emblem of their prestige" (1989: 117, my translation). He points out that it plays a symbolic role like the flag, and in fact it has been used as a flag waved around to mark the identity of a group in times of battles. "It is the *libas* of the *ashraf* (nobility)," he writes (1989: 201). At times when Persians wore *qulunsuwa* and pre-Muslim Arabs who ruled over certain principalities wore "royal crowns" the turban became a symbol of identity and modesty. It has also been associated with gentleness in character. With the emergence of the Islamic Umma, the Prophet Muhammad gradually began to institute it as the headgear to identify Muslims. In the *Hadith*

> the Prophet was said to have been on the *minbar* (pulpit) wearing a black *'imama* (turban). In another segment (3556) the Prophet was heard to have said: the difference between us (Muslim faithful) and *al-mushrikin* (the idolatrous poly-theists)[105] is that we wear turbans and they wear *qalanis* (sing. *qalansuwa*, tall headgear).
>
> (Abu Dawoud: 3511)

And, in the same *Hadith*, a man was heard to have said:

> the Prophet *'ammamani* (put *'imama* on my head), and he let the ends hang from behind and down my chest
>
> (*Hadith* Abu Dawoud: 3557).

Turbans worn by contemporary Rashidi men (see Figure 16) are often three meters long or even longer – much longer than those worn by other Arab groups. Young examined photographs from the 1920s which show that this style is not recent. According to Jubouri there is evidence of extremely long turbans (much longer than three meters), which even got longer into the tenth century, as length acquired prestige. Many terms were use to refer to the turban in pre-Islamic poetry and multiple ways to wear it. They were worn in several colors by choice. The most common were black or white. When a man dies, his turban dresses the raised head of the cofffin lid in the funeral procession, and marks his tomb (or a substitute sculpture of a turban is placed at the head of his tomb) (see Jubouri 1989: 208)

"In recent years," wrote Young, "most Rashayda have added to the distinct-iveness of their turbans by wrapping them around colored felt caps that they

Figure 16 Rashidi man wearing turban. Photo by W. Young, reprinted by permission.

import from Saudi Arabia" (1996: 28). The turban distinguishes Rashidi men from the neighboring Hadendowa (a non-Arab group) and other Sudanese Arabs (Young 1996).

Young describes the Rashidi married women's mask in detail. The *gina*'[106] "consists of a tube of black cloth which is flared at the lower end, to cover the shoulders, chest, and back, and is narrowed at the upper end, to fit snugly around the face. The lower opening is so much larger than the upper opening that the garment resembles a hollow cone with the top end cut off. After slipping this conical tube over her head, the woman who wears it lays the posterior edge of its uppermost opening over the crown of her head. Then she pulls the opposite edge of this opening down across her face until it is almost taut against her chin. Some of the loose cloth below her chin can be pulled through the opening, resulting in a semicircle stretched tightly across her nose and mouth. Once put in place, the mask is so tight that the wearer cannot open her mouth widely. Almost all Rashidi women wear both plain and decorated versions of this mask. The decorated version is covered with hundreds of tiny lead beads that frame the wearer's face" (Young 1996: 28–9; see also Young 1994: 66).

Young noted that maturity is not expressed through calendrical age and birthdays.[107] As do some other groups across cultures, Young shows in his ethnography that the Rashayda divide the life-span into phases, each marked by specific clothing. "Infants (*bizran*, literally seedlings) are dressed in a loose, gownlike garment called a *thawb* for as long as they are unable to speak and walk properly and are not toilet-trained" (1996: 45). After toilet training, they wear longer clothes that cover their legs more and are tied at the waist – girls wear a long skirt (*tichcha*), boys a shirt and a pair of long, loose pants (*sirwal*) (1996: 45).

The next phase identified by Young consists of adding head coverings – girls wear a large black or colored cloth (*gargush*) over their heads and shoulders, with the edges fastened by a pin. This goes over their heads down their shoulders and chests. In the case of boys the head covering is a knitted cap (*tagiya*). As individuals advance along the scale of maturity more clothing items are added. The older, the more clothing. Further stages of maturity are marked by the addition of still more articles of clothing. "Girls first add a 'virgin's veil' (*mungab*)[108] to their wardrobe and then a black gown (*thawb*) that covers them from neck to ankle. Boys add a white *thawb* to their costume first then follow it with a long white turban (*'imaama)*, that they wrap around their knit caps" (1996: 46). Note that *thawb* is the Rashidi Arabic word used for both genders.

Young observes that the Rashayda themselves explicitly recognize the link between clothing and maturation. This "knowledge" is revealed in their discussions of aging and in contexts of arranging marriages for their children. For example, when a mother is considering potential wives for her son she inquires about their age, not in calendar years, but in terms of the clothing that they wear. "A *bint umtachchich* 'virgin wearing a skirt' is quite young, a *bint umgargash* 'virgin wearing a *garguush*' is more mature, and a *bint umnaggab* 'virgin wearing a *mungab*' is close to adolescence; her breasts have started to develop and must be covered by both the *garguush* and the lower part of the *mungab*. A *bint umthawwab* 'virgin wearing a *thawb*' is ready for marriage" (1996: 46). I find it interesting how the Rashayda manipulate language, by making verbs out of nouns that in common usage denote specific articles of clothing. This points to a clear "markedness" of the processual quality embedded in the developmental phases of individual maturation, and of how these levels of maturation are accompanied by patterned dress change, and, as Young points out, of expectations about levels of skill and ability, participation in work, and behaviors (Young 1996: 45–7).

Clearly in the Rashayda case veiling (and weaving dress as shelter, for camels or for people) is a language that communicates levels of maturity in the life cycle of individuals that determine their status and expresses group identity, since different groups have different patterns woven on their tents and clothes. For contrast and clarity, a non-Arab culture of Muslims that shares the practice of women's veiling can provide insights as to what "the veil" symbolizes and what "veiling language" explicitly communicates given the different cultural context.

In a study on South Asia in the Himalayan village of Ghanyari, Sharma (1978) describes a particular practice, namely *ghungat,* in which "veiling" behavior is also detailed and explicitly communicates, in this case, kinship relationships and behavioral restrictions instead of levels of maturation, as in the case of the Rashayda. The term *ghungat* refers to the practice whereby a woman veils her face from all male affines senior to her own husband. She states that *"ghungat* limits the interaction of junior women with senior males, especially high caste senior males i.e., those who may be expected to wield most power in the community" (1978: 218). It is interesting that in the Ghanyari case, veiling behavior that includes fluid manipulation of the veil, and not simply the veil *per se,* has a term. *"Ghungat nikalna"* writes Sharma, "means to draw the edge of the scarf over one's face so as to veil it completely" (1978: 218). Sharma specifies the kinship contexts in which a married woman practices *ghungat* – "before her husband's father, elder brother and uncles and indeed before most of the older men of the village where she is married" (1978: 218). This fluid manipulation has been mentioned in some ethnographies elsewhere, but no particular local term was identified in ethnographies as a reference to that behavior. This fact suggests that studying the veil as fixed material covers of certain parts of head and body is not sufficient for understanding the phenomenon.

As in the case of the Yemeni women studied by Makhlouf and described earlier, Sharma describes the common occurrence of a sudden stop during informal conversations among women, and a scurrying to veil themselves when an older man passed by the courtyard where they were sitting. Sharma interprets this behavior as an example of the "silencing" and "restraining" of women (1978: 218). I find the stress to lie elsewhere. The critical ethnographic questions are: Who is the older man? Is he a consanguine or an affine and what status is his caste *vis-à-vis* that of the women? Is he from her natal village or her husband's village? The answer is communicated by veiling[109] and is about respect and authority in the affinal setting and kinship status and relations.

Sharma notes that other accounts – Hitchcock and Minturn (1963); Jacobson (1970) – give a good deal of useful information about veiling practices and reveal some variations in the way in which *ghungat* is practiced in different regions of north India, but rejects their analyses of veiling as "avoidance behavior" or "distance technique." She sees these notions as influenced by social anthropological contributions made by Radcliffe-Brown and Murphy (Radcliffe-Brown 1952; Murphy 1964). Yet Sharma is rightly concerned about the neglect in most existing ethnography on South Asian society in reporting this central institution, which connects clothing behavior, kinship positions and caste status. She observes how the position of the woman shifts upon marriage and is reflected in her "veiling" behavior to her affines. Her ethnographic example of how "a woman does not veil herself before her *peke*, men of her natal village" (1978: 251) is not trivial. It is important that a single term is assigned to a category of people to mark a significant differentiation, namely "men of her natal village." The practice (veiling) constitutes, as it were, village exogamy. Veiling is clearly a correlate of kinship behavior. The differentiation is further expressed in her observation that upon marriage a woman's personal name becomes "so-and so's wife," which is no different from the practice of Western women, who become "Mrs so and so" after marriage. But whereas in the Western case name-merging is an expression of the emphasis on the union, which gives a woman her husband's identity, in the Indian case the naming shift is consistent with the sharp boundary marking natal relatives from affinal relatives. Veiling is a central ritual behavior in weddings, which bring together the two sides. "[I]n the wedding rites the bride's veil is tied to the groom's scarf as they pace around the nuptial fire. When they reach the entrance to the husband's courtyard after the ceremony is over, they enter with his scarf tied to her veil, having 'tied the knot' "(1978: 231). Here the veil and the scarf symbolize the new union and her new identification as part of the husband's group.

Cultural context is relevant. In the Rashayda case, the camp is not internally stratified, and clothing patterns and behavior do not reflect in-camp stratification. Rather they distinguish the Rashayda in general from other people and one group of Rashayda from another. In the North Indian case, as revealed in the ethnography by Sharma, veiling distinguishes consanguinity from affinity, men from women, and caste from caste. For example, Sharma writes that a woman in her husband's village must veil to a category of men – all those with whom sexual relations are forbidden. However, men of lower castes may see her face, yet must definitely not have sexual relations with her for reasons of ascribed social status. "A Brahman woman in Ghanyari will not veil herself before a man of lower caste in her husband's village, even though he be older than her husband and treats her husband as 'nephew'. But a woman of barber caste will veil herself before a Brahman man of the same age as or senior to her husband" (1978: 224). In cases of equal caste status in the same village there would be mutual veiling. Chamar women from the leather worker caste, the lowest in Ghanyari and regarded as untouchable by other castes, who "married in Ghanyari without exception veil themselves from older men of other castes in the village . . . [and] their behavior is very deferential" (1978: 224–5). Three forms of subordination operate simultaneously here: impure to pure, junior to senior, female to male.

Ghungat also stresses that a woman's relation to the village is through her husband, and her status is defined through her husband – the categories of men she must veil to are determined by her relationship to him (1978: 230). So veiling communicates various cross-cutting strata of relations[110] that characterize the society as well as the cultural construction of women's natal and marital identity.

In contrast the identity of the Rashayda woman, like that of Arab women in general, is economically and maritally autonomous. She continues to be identified as member of her natal group after marriage, and has the right to have an autonomous "credit" line in her maiden name that does not merge with her conjugal "household purse." She is the owner of the conjugal tent and the guardian of the conjugal household. Clothing behavior reflects these cultural features.

The existing evidence is clear neither on when Arabian women adopted veiling nor on the extent to which the practice obtained at the rise of Islam. There are scattered references to individual women in the pre-Islamic period, such as the one to Hind, wife of an-Nu'man of Hirah (Stern 1939a: 109). The reference makes comparisons with the women of Hums in Syria, who purportedly veiled in public. In both contexts the word *nasif* (a term that is not common nor to my knowledge used much elsewhere) is used for veil, and in Hind's case it is clear from the text that it was some form of head veil or garment with which she veiled herself. The women of Hums were considered of high social standing, as was Hind. Stern (1939a) mentions the lack of evidence regarding when Arabian women adopted veiling and the extent of the practice at the rise of Islam. She observes that the custom "most likely was restricted to women of a certain social status" (1939a: 109). However, references in *Jahiliyya* (pre-Islamic) poetry indicate that terms for face-veiling existed with reference to bedouin women at least three or four centuries before Islam.

One factor clearly associated with veiling is status differentiation, as was shown in the Muslim North Indian rural community examined by Sharma (1978). It is a community that is highly stratified and differentiated by caste, affines versus consanguines, men versus women, etc. This factor was also revealed in the study of the Muslim Tuareg Berbers, another highly stratified group.

There are other aspects to the veil. Sharma reports that many women began to wear a *dupatta* – a narrow strip of transparent colored cloth draped about the neck – and that one form of "teasing" of girls that strongly irritates and insults them is snatching their *dupatta*s (Sharma 1978: 232). "In Ghanyari, married women often touch their elders' feet with the ends of the shawl as a respectful greeting" (1978: 232). Sharma mentions that in his early study of the *Holi*, a festival held in the north Indian village, Oscar Lewis described the women in a role-reversal joking ritual in which they beat their husbands and elder brothers-in-law with sticks, but that in the past "they used to *beat their husbands not with sticks, but with their veils*" (1978: 232, referencing Lewis 1956: 233, emphasis mine). Here we have an example that shows the veil as interchangeable with a beating stick.

Stern relates an account mentioned in *Kitab al-Aghani* (1285H: 19, 74 (see Asbahani 1927)) of an incident that took place at the famous open market of *Ukaz* concerning a woman who wore a veil. The veil "was torn from her by a trick played on her by a party of young men of Quraish and Kinanah. This incident was said to have caused one of the outbreaks of the wars of the Fijar" (1939a: 109).

This incident suggests that veiling by Arabian women in public was uncommon and that the oddity of this veiled woman's presence in the market may have provoked the teasing. But it also indicates that there was considerable cross-sex contact during public events. There is another dimension to veiling. According to Abbott (1942), after the death of Prophet Muhammad, 'Aisha, his widow, became even more active in public and political affairs. It is reported that she had just left Makka on one of her trips, when, about twelve miles out of Makka, she was given the news of the murder of Uthman, a companion of the prophet in his lifetime, and one of his successors. She turned around immediately and went back to Makka. The sources cited (Yaqut, Geog., II, 208) relate how she went to the mosque and took her stand at the sacred spot of Hijr, the ancient foundation of the sanctuary in Makka, purportedly laid by Abraham. Ceremoniously she veiled. The people then gathered around her and she gave a public address about Uthman's murder (Abbott 1942: 130-131). It is interesting to note the analogy between 'Aisha's use of the veil to ceremonialize publicly her political position and the Prophet's reported entry into Makka in victory wearing a black *'imamah* (*Sahih al-Bukhari* 5361), described as having loose ends hanging down around his face. Is this not veiling of power?

Face veiling is not permissible in Islam for either sex during worship in prayer or on pilgrimage – two core pillars of Islamic ritual prescribed to Muslim bellievers. The premise for the prescribed dress code derives from the Islamic textual construction of the notion of bodily privacy and moral reserve. Private parts (genitals) for both sexes are referred to as *saw'at* (the singular is *saw'ah*). A more controversial notion is *'awrah*. It is noteworthy that *'awrah* is used only three times in the Qur'an, in three different contexts: one in reference to men intruding on women's privacy at times of exposure of women's bodies (*Qur'an* 24: 31), and another referring to "homes" being exposed to theft and intrusion mentioned in the context of a battle (*Qur'an* 33: 13), while the third is a reference to sexual privacy in which three specific moments are identified and referred as *'awrat* (plural for *'awrah*). The contexts comprise three moments during the day in which persons must seek permission to enter upon sleeping quarters (*Qur'an* 24: 58). This notion of *'awrah* has been a subject of heated discourse and reactions as a result of much misleading reference to it in the literature, which seems to come from secondary and later sources. It must be noted that characterizing a woman's body as *'awrah* does not come from the *Qur'an,* and "vulnerable" is a connotation closer to its multi-context usage, and hence more accurate, than the commonly used "blemish."

In Islam neither gender is characterized as being pure or impure. These characterizations, which in other cultures are rigid dualities, are not so in Islam. Instead, bodies (of men and women) are fluidly characterized as being in states of purity or impurity. These are temporary states. The state of impurity ends with the ceasing of the discharge of bodily fluids, which is marked by ritual washing. Bodily discharges from both sexes temporarily put the person in a state of impurity. The fixed opposition of pure versus impure, particularly as it links women to impurity, is neither Arab nor Islamic.[111]

As was discussed in the section on Sacred Origins, the primordial human pair were created from one self, and from them the rest of humankind came forth. After their disobedience of God they were both "declothed," and their *saw'at* (private parts) were "seen" by both. Hence their subsequent exit from heaven for a lifetime on earth. Through these originary events, Islam weaves notions of bodily privacy, human sexuality and divine authority.

The divine realm of a de-anthropomorphized and omnipotent God is separate and apart from the mortal world of human beings, as it is expressed in the Qur'anic statement (112: 2). *Shirk* is unacceptable in Islam. From the root *sh-r-k* (share), it means to share authority or divine power. Sharing divine authority is considered idolatry. This undivided, unshared authority establishes order in the world of mortals. There can be a representative on earth [such as a *khalifa*] to enact this authority, but not to legislate or share it. God communicates his message to mortals through one or a combination of three means: apparition (through angels), a messenger, or from behind a veil (*Qur'an* 42: 51). In a Qur'anic statement God says to Prophet Muhammad:

ya ayyuha an-nabi, lima tuharrim ma ahhalla allahu lak'? ("Why do you forbid what god permits?").

This passage establishes the ultimate source of authority.

In solitary or collective worship, in prayer or pilgrimage, there is a code of cleansing, orientation, concealment of certain body parts, and *Qur'an* recitation followed equally by both sexes. The genital area is to be concealed by both sexes. Significantly, there is more reference in the *Hadith* to the proper dress for men than for women, both in general and particularly during prayer, to prevent the exposure of their genital areas (*Sahih al-Bukhari* 5372, 5373). The color white is the preferred color for both. For women, covering is from head to toe, but the face and hands are left uncovered. There is no ambiguity with regard to this.

For Muslim men in worship, it is minimally prescribed that they should cover themselves from the navel to the knees. To worship, a Muslim (man and woman alike) must be in a state of purity – cleansed and temporarily desexualized. Sexual and other bodily discharge ends the state of purity for both sexes. In pilgrimage one is in a state of *ihram* after ritual cleansing, dressing according to code and following prescribed rites and recitations. In *Hadith* (*Sahih al-Bukhari* 5356, 5358) in *ihram* men are not to wear *kamis* (upper shirt), *sirwal* (pantaloons), *'imma, burnus* (hooded cloak), or *khuff* (sewn footwear). The dress code in *hajj* for men involved replacing their ordinary clothing with two unsewn wraps, the *izar*, which fell from the waist to the feet, and the *rida'*, which covered one shoulder and the upper body. A woman also replaces her ordinary clothing. If she usually wore a face veil (*niqab, lithma, burqu'*), she removed it, but covered her head and hair. Both wear white, remove jewelry and refrain from using perfume.

Performing the *hajj* is special for Muslim individuals. They are publicly celebrated by their families and in their communities with much festivity. Their status is altered for ever. A man acquires the title *hajj*, a woman the title *hajja*. After fulfilling the last of the five pillars, usually in old age, these titles and the status attached to them are irreversible. Women dress differently – austerely and modestly – in daily life after performing the *hajj*. Figure 17 shows the image that used to be that of every Muslim's grandmother, wearing a white headcover, no makeup, and a black overcoat (see Figure 17). It is as if having ascended to this state one does not "move in and out" any more from worldly space to ordinary space. Having become a *hajja*, which in the past used to be in old age, a Muslim woman, while engaged in worldly affairs, is permanently in sacred space on earth.

Figure 17 A *hajja* in dress connoting her change of status after a pilgrimage to Makka. Courtesy of El Nil Research.

7

The Veil of Masculinity

The subject of the veil has been approached in the scholarly literature almost entirely from one of three perspectives: Religious Studies, Area Studies and Women's Studies. These perspectives have situated the veil respectively in textual sources, the Middle East area, and gender. The anthropological approach used in this study re-framed both the context in which the veil and veiling are examined and the questions formulated to direct the research investigation.

One outcome of re-framing is extending the study to include the veil's material aspects (Part I) as well as its symbolic meanings. Another result, in Part II, is situating the veil in the context of the study of dress anthropologically (i.e. cross-culturally and holistically) and culturally (*Libas*). As a material object, the veil, as a head- or head-and-face-cover, was extended to include men's head- or head-and-face-covers. This is a significant shift that derives from the methodological notion of adequacy and from the ethnographic data.

A crucial, neglected and overlooked fact about veiling is the clear evidence that men in Arab society veil. More productive is to examine the head- or head/face-covers for both sexes, rather than to look at the veil as a unique or isolated woman's phenomenon, which misdirects analysis. The approach established here integrates the veil in the study of society and integrates men's veiling in the study of the veil. For at least several centuries before Islam, evidence shows that Arab men veiled. We are aware in anthropology that Berber men in North Africa veiled; but veiling by Arab men in Arabia was overlooked. Even less known are the reported incidents that the Prophet Muhammad himself face-veiled on certain occasions. This leads to the questions of what is a veil and what does veiling mean? Is veiling by women the same as the veiling by men? The Women's Studies approach confined the veil to women's clothing and behavior, invariably presented as reflecting women's invisibility, women's anonymity, female subordination, women's oppression in "patriarchal" societies, or a function of Islam. These gender-specific explanations for veiling cannot account for veiling by men. Men's veiling, an ethnographic fact, becomes an anomaly, particularly against the common misunderstanding that only women veil. How can these approaches accommodate veiling by men? We cannot comprehend a phenomenon by leaving out an entire sex. Nor is it, as in the case of women in culture, a matter of "add men and stir." Resolving the anomaly can only be achieved through analytic re-framing of the problem and conceptualizing the phenomenon under study in a holistic, relational framework.

My realization of the insufficiency of focusing on women's veiling began when I started the ethnographic field project in Egypt in the 1970s to study the Islamic movement. The entire focus then was on the fact that young secular college women had turned to conservative veiling. My exploratory field research immediately revealed that it is not the veil *per se,* but the code underlying the veil that should be the focus of research attention. Once the focus shifts it becomes clear that men (college and secular youths) were also "veiling" as it were. In one sense they veiled materially by wearing *kufiyya*(s) as head cover, which they used to cover part of their face in specific situations. One of these situations, which I personally observed and wrote about, was on one of the secular campuses of the secular university in Cairo called 'Ain Shams University.

It was during the semester when college lectures were in session, and I was engaged in fieldwork, that is, spending time on campus observing and talking with students in and outside the movement. While I was with women students in the women's lounge, a man knocked on the door. The women scrambled for their *hijabs* and *qina's.* Moments of confusion and tension passed, after which the man knocked again on the door. Finally, although still unsettled, the women leaders among them invited him in. I looked out of the door and saw a man in a *gallabiyyah* (an ankle-length white, unfitted gown with long sleeves). He pulled his *kufiyya* (head shawl) over his face and entered very cautiously, literally rubbing against the wall trying not to look in the direction of the women until he reached a curtain diagonally hung in the corner of the room. He went behind it and sat facing the women from behind the curtain. That is, it was the man who both face-veiled when with women and sat behind the *hijab* (curtain). His shadow showed him lifting the *kufiyya* off his face and letting it down to his shoulders, but keeping it on his head. He proceeded to discuss Qur'anic *suras*, particularly those pertaining to the *hijab*, according to the interpretation by Mawdudi (1972, 1985; see note 119). The women asked him questions, and mildly challenged some of his comments, but all in all did not seem to be awed by or subservient to his performance. They were abiding by their own self-imposed rules of ritualized cross-sex encounters in public space. After about thirty-five minutes, he excused himself, and went through a ritualized exit, similar to his entry.

As he closed the door behind him, the women started to relax their head- and face-covers and proceeded with the activities they were engaged in before his "interruption." Some ate, some talked and laughed, some changed, some cleansed and prayed individually, and others prayed behind a woman Imam, as others rushed to class. A few were reading *Sura-t al-Nur* in groups of two or three and discussed the basis of the *hijab* in the originary Islamic community.

Through this incident, along with observations of other behavior of these college students, it became evident that in order to understand the phenomenon the study cannot be restricted to the superficially obvious or the obviously visible (women veiling), but rather it must seek in intangible spheres an underlying code. This revealed the "dress" movement to be practiced by men and by women, and similar in manifestation among both.

The inclusion of men was a significant discovery for the understanding of the overall phenomenon. It was extended to examining the notion of the veil and veiling historically, ethnographically, and cross-culturally, using the premise of the inclusion of both sexes and the intangible dimension. Exploring the Islamic textual data led to more discoveries. For example, some references mentioned the Prophet as having veiled his face on some occasions. In the *Hadith* (*Sahih al-Bukhari* 5360; Abu Dawoud 3561) it was reported that in one instance he had approached the house of Abu Bakr *mutaqanni'an* (face-veiled). Another instance is mentioned in the *Hadith* source (*Sahih al-Bukhari*: 934), in which the Prophet is reported to have entered upon 'Aisha, *with his face covered with his garment*, and found two slaves beating drums and dancing. Her father Abu Bakr was there.

While much space was given to men's dress in *Hadith* sources, only limited mention is made of men's face-covering. In Ibn al-Hajj (1960: 1,134) it is reported that Imam al-Tartoushi reported that a rare *Hadith* was related in which "Prophet Muhammad ordered *tallahhi* and prohibited *al-Iqti'at*." This is with reference to men's *'imamah*. *Talahhi* (which derives from a root meaning "beard") means to be bearded by the hanging ends of the *'imamah*, and *iqti'at* (which derives from a root meaning "cut") means to wrap all the cloth into a headdress, without leaving loose ends hanging down over the sides of the face. This suggests, as has been observed in different references elsewhere in this work, that Prophet Muhammad was in favor of some face draping for men.

However, Ibn al-Hajj takes a very strong position against actual face covering by men. He was critical of men who wore large sleeves and very large and loose clothes and those who wrap the *'imamah* "as if to strangle on it," preoccupied with arranging its ends, which tumble in the wind and uncover the face, "just like veiled (the terms used here are both *qina'* and *khimar*) women who fear the revealing of their heads and faces" (Hajj1960: 1, 134).

As evidenced in Arab poetry, the *khimar* (woman's headcover) seems to have been in existence for a few centuries at least before the formation of the Islamic community. The phrase *'takhammarat almar'ah bil-khimar wa-khtamarat'* means the woman wore the *khimar*. Jubouri mentions that in pre-Islamic Arabia the men's *'imamah* was sometimes referred to as *khimar* (the term for a woman's headveil), and that a man can *takhammur bil-'imamah* (which uses *khimar* in verb form so that it means "he veils with the turban"). These are cases in which men cover their mouth and face with the ends of the *'imamah*, and hence face-veil. "It has been reported that some Arab warriors," writes Jubouri (1989: 223), "used to attend the *mawasim* (public celebrations) and *aswaq* (public market fairs) *mutaqanni'in* ("face-veiled"; verb from *qina'* or "mask") or *mutalaththimin* (verb from *lithma*)."

Clearly, men's veiling is not confined to the Berbers studied in anthropology, although these were also ignored in studies of veiling. There are reports on Arab *Jahiliyya* poets such as 'Abdul Rahman, known as Waddah, Abu Zaid al-Ta'i, and al-Makri'a al-Kindi as having "veiled themselves, when present at festivals" (Stern 1939a: 108). A good source is the original Arabic multi-volume work, known as *al-Aghani* ("The Songs"), compiled in 976 AD, which recounts tales and is a record of poems and songs performed and told in Arabia since before Islam. It contains evidence, albeit scattered and indirect, of veiling by women *and* men. "Ubayy, a poet at the court of Hirah, was known as *al-Munakhkhal* (Stern 1939a: 109, citing *Kitab al-Aghani* 1285H: 9, 166 (see Asbahani 1927)). He "was said to have acquired this title by wearing [across his face] a *munkhal*, which literally means a sieve, but must, in this instance, have applied to a coarse net" (Stern 1939a: 109, n.1).

The explanation given for the practice is "protection against the evil eye" (*Kitab al-Aghani* 1285H: 6, 33 (see Asbahani 1927)). Westermarck (1926) also adopted the view that men's veiling is due to fear of the evil eye (i, 427). Crawley noted that "in early Arabia handsome men veiled their faces to preserve themselves from the evil eye" (1931: 76; see also Wellhausen 1897: 196). But there is no indication in the *Hadith* of this theory's having any bearing on the veiling of women either in pre-Islamic times or in the following era. The theory of the evil eye seems to have been advanced only with regard to men's veiling.

The explanation given in Jubouri is different from the ones proposed by Crawley, Wellhausen and Stern about men veiling as protection from the evil eye, which seem to derive from the same source. Jubouri, who is an expert on *Jahiliyya* poetry, connects men's veiling in public fairs with tribal battles and the presence of persons from the enemy camp in the same public spaces. The use of *mutalaththim* (the state of having a *lithma* on) is also reported in an incident when, during his conversion to Islam, the man *Ka'b bin Zuhair* saw the Prophet Muhammad arrive at the mosque for morning prayer *mutalaththim bil-'imamah* (wearing the ends of the turban as a *lithma*, or face-cover).

According to Jubouri (1989: 119) a number of pre-Islamic Arab men were known by the title *thu khimar* (the veiled ones). He specifically mentions al-Aswad al'Ansi ('Ablahah ibn Ka'b) and 'Awf ibn al-Rabi' ibn thi al-Ramahayn (who reportedly is known as "the veiled one" because he fought in battle wearing his wife's veil) and was victorious; so that when a fallen man in battle was asked "Who stabbed you?" the answer was "The veiled one."

There are insufficient systematic data to establish all the situations in which men veil and their different meanings. But enough evidence shows that men did veil, and do in contemporary situations as well. The Tuareg,[112] a Muslim Berber Hamitic-speaking group, are a known case in anthropology. The French called them "les hommes bleus," and Hollywood immortalized them as "the blue-veiled men." In his classic article on the Tuareg, Robert Murphy (1964) describes their social organization. They are traditionally matrilineal, organized into a number of major tribal confederations based on regional continuity. The component tribes are territory-holding units under a chief whose powers are kept in check by Tuareg egalitarianism and the power of the notables of the tribe. Tribes are divided into subtribes, conceived as descent groups whose members acknowledge common ancestry. "[T]he fundamental unit of Tuareg society, the *iriwan*, or house, consists of some 50 to several hundred people who reside about a water well to which they hold rights and who pasture their herds in the surrounding land" (1964: 1261). Their traditional system was differentiated on the basis of descent and in terms of three endogamous classes: nobles, vassals, and slaves. The noble tribes are politically dominant. They are called "*imajaren.*" Each noble tribe exacts tribute from one or more vassal tribes, with both noble and vassal tribes acting as corporate entities in their interrelations. Vassals are called "*imrad.*" Members of noble and vassal tribes individually hold property in slaves, who work as herdsmen. These are called "*iklen*" (1964: 1261).

In determining the origin of slaves, Murphy realizes the difficulty in tracing precise ancestry but notes that they share the language and the culture of the Tuareg. Gradually, the rigid stratification has broken down and their populations have been reduced in size, which has affected their lifestyle. Yet, as Murphy notes, even after slavery was abolished the status groups remained (Murphy 1964: 1263).

The most distinguishing and visible feature of the Tuareg is the men's veil. In the Air Tuareg dialect it is called *tegelmoust.* (See Figures18 and 19.) The

Figure 18 *Tegelmoust* (Berber) and *lithma* (Arabic), here worn by a Tuareg
nobleman to mark his status. © Victor Englebert 1970.

Figure 19 A Yemeni woman's *lithma*. Compare with the men's face veiling shown in Figure 18. By permission from *Women of 'Amran* by Susan Dorsky. University of Utah Press, Salt Lake City, UT, 1986.

Tuareg dress consists of "an underrobe and a flowing outer garment that extends from shoulders to ankles. The underrobe is sleeveless, but the outer garb has loose wide sleeves ideal for carrying the long daggers that are worn in sheaths strapped to the arm. These robes are either blue or white" (1964: 1263). Murphy observes that the blue cloth, which is made and dyed in Nigeria, is more expensive, which makes the blue turban and veil special items of dress, used on festive occasions.

There is skill in mastering putting on the veil. "[T]he cloth is wrapped about the head to form a low turban and the end is then brought across the face, the top of the cloth falling across the nose and the bottom hanging well below the chin" (1964: 1263). As a result only part of the face shows, particularly when worn higher and tighter, in which case "only a narrow slit is left open and even the eyes can barely be seen. There are situational differences in the actual attitude of the veil and the amount of face that the wearer exposes" (1964: 1263).

The veil is worn continually by men – at home, travelling, during the evening or day, eating or smoking, sleeping and even, according to some sources, during sexual intercourse. To eat, a Tuareg "carefully raises the veil enough to enable him to eat but not far enough for his mouth to be seen [for if he] . . . lowers his veil to eat [he] reveals his low status" (1964: 1263). A noble, explains Murphy, does not expose his mouth (1964: 1263). And again, the pattern connecting the veil (or other items of dress) and maturation, which has been described among a number of groups, exists among the Tuareg. The veil is a mark of maturity. Only as a youth approaches maturity, at about the age of seventeen, does he wear a veil. Unveiled youths and slaves do much of the menial work and the herding. Tuareg women are not face-veiled at all, but they do pull their shawls across the lower parts of their faces when expressing reserve – a behavioral pattern that re-emerges in the ethnography of veiling.

Explanations of this practice were of either the "origin" type or the utilitarian type about protection from the elements. Neither explanation holds – the origin theories are circular and easily refuted in ethnography, and the utilitarian ones are not sufficient. They do not explain why the practice does not exist among other groups having similar conditions. In other words, why the veil and not something else? Why do not the Tuareg women, who share the same material environment, veil? Then there is another theory that claims veiling results in invisibility and anonymity for the wearer. Ethnography shows that, just as in the case of women's veiling elsewhere in the Arab world, the Tuareg recognize each other despite concealing their faces. Veiling does not conceal identity. Crawley mentions how Socrates and Julius Caesar veiled their faces "at the moment of death," as a typical Greek and Italian national custom (1931: 76). The identity of a veiled individual is revealed through proxemics and gestures and via other body parts. As Murphy suggests, reading the face and mouth, which are used in communication by other groups, shifts to the reading of eyes in the Tuareg case. In interaction, the Tuareg focus on the eyes.

Among the Tuareg the veil becomes a vehicle of elaborate communication. It is worn highest and conceals the face most strictly when a Tuareg man is among men who are closest to him, and it is worn loosely and slacker when among more distant persons, and particularly non-Tuareg (Murphy 1964: 1264).

According to Henri Lhote (1955), the veil "is brought up to the eyes before women or prestigeful persons, while it is a sign of familiarity when it is lowered" (Lhote 1955: 308–9, as quoted in Murphy 1964). Nicolaisen (1961) argues that a proper understanding of the veil must be sought in the social system. He notes how the veil is always worn high and tightly below the eyes when interacting with a stranger (or a socially distant individual), and especially a woman. This status is distinguished in Tuareg society from that of a friend or acquaintance who is not as formally involved in the dynamics of the social system. Murphy (1964) concurs. Many of those who were most lax in their veiling were members of the inferior vassal tribes or of the slave class. Slaves also go unveiled. "Among all segments of the Tuareg population, the veil is worn higher when confronting a person of power and influence. The Tuareg do not prostrate themselves before a chief, as is the custom among their Hausa neighbors, but they do elevate their veils to the bridge of the nose" (1964: 1267).

As was shown above regarding women's veiling, the men's veil is not a static or fixed article either. The Tuareg "are continually adjusting and readjusting the veil, changing the height at which it is worn, tugging on the lower part of it, tightening its ends beneath the turban and straightening its folds" (1964: 1266).

The imagery projected from men's veiling is that of virility and masculinity for these men and Arabs in North Africa and Arabia who wore turbans and veils as they rode camels or horses. According to legend, in the twelfth century Sayyid Ahmad al-Badawi went on a voyage from Morocco to Makka to Baghdad to Egypt. He journeyed to Egypt after experiencing a vision directing him to go. He rode into Tanta – a northern Egyptian Delta town that was a commercial center – on horseback, his face double-veiled or *mutalaththim* (from root *l-th-m*), that is with loose cloth hanging down from both sides of his turban tied cross-wise over the nose. He lived in seclusion meditating on top of a roof of a house, and followers gathered around him.

Eventually the Sufi order *al-Ahmadiyya* was formed. He had become venerated as a holy man. After his death a mosque was built over his tomb and the town had become the site of a very popular annual pilgrimage during which about two million pilgrims visit from all over Egypt and the Arab region for the duration of a week. The imagery connected to him remains that of virile masculinity, piety, and Sufi meditation. Every year the successor (*Khalifa*), a lineal descendant of his companion, heads a procession starting from the mosque built around the spot where Sayyid Ahmad first prayed when he entered Tanta and ending in the mosque that houses his tomb. The contemporary lineal successor ceremonially wears a turban that is otherwise kept in the tomb for the occasion. It is purportedly made out of the cloth that was Sayyid Ahmad's original veil. It has acquired a special sacredness, and pilgrims yearn to touch it for blessing. As Crawley puts it "often regalia is more sacred than the person officiate" (1931: 59). This is presented in a visual ethnography about him and the pilgrimage (El Guindi 1990 (film); see Figure 20).

Among the Tuareg it is disrespectful for a high-ranking member to show his mouth among his people. There are restrictions surrounding the use of the veil that are rigid and highly formalized (Murphy 1964: 1266). Men wear the veil when courting – ceremonial avoidance but also dignity-and respect – courting is formalized and men are most dignified. There is name-avoidance of the father-in-law, whom he calls *amrar*, or leader, with reference to his being the head of a household. Conduct toward the senior affines is characterized by general restraint and self-effacement (1964: 1270). A Tuareg man covers his mouth to communicate his rank and his respectability. The two related Tuareg notions of *tekeraki* and *isimrarak* constitute the Tuareg notion of proper behavior and respect[113] (1964: 1267).

Among the Rashayda there is *hishma* and *tahashshud* (Young 1996), constituting the Rashidi sense of polite reserve, self-restraint and respect. Similar notions exist among the rural Jordanians (Antoun 1968; Abu Zahra 1970), the Moroccans (S. Davis 1983), the Arabians, the nomadic, and the urban. In rigidly stratified social systems, such as the Tuareg (Murphy 1964) and the North Indian village (Sharma 1978)[114] veiling by men in the first and by women in the second conveys a message about kinship distance and appropriate avoidance behavior toward spouses and elderly affines. In general, veiling by women or men communicates, not subordinate gender status or the shame of sexuality, but the group status of the individual, the identity of the group and the sacredness of privacy. Whether it is the Prophet entering Makka in victory or 'Aisha in a public political speech, veiling becomes a device to formalize communication and a means to ceremonialize one's status and one's group identity. But when the two sexes are together joined in sacred time and space to worship God the central spatial object of the pilgrimage, the *Ka'ba*, itself veiled, becomes the metaphor of sacred privacy in public.

In sum, the veil in social space is about privacy, identity, kinship status, rank, and class. And if we look at the veiling behavior patterns in the various ethnographic accounts and examples presented in this study, another theme emerges – the veil as a symbol of power. Among the Rashayda prize money is given to the woman who dances best in public at a wedding, and it is pinned to her *milayah*. In the past in Muslim India women ritually beat their husbands with their *veils*. In Bahrain, village women attach the key to the lock of the house to their headveils or hair. During Islamic holidays adult Rashidi women cover their heads with their sleeves, wear the *burqu'* and stand outside the tents, which they are the guardians of, to greet men. According to *Hadith*, 'Aisha, the Prophet's widow, went to the main public square, ceremonially veiled, and then gave an important public speech to

Figure 20 The *Khalifa* in spectacular procession during the *mulid* of Sayyid Badawi
in Tanta, Egypt, wearing the "sacred" turban. From F. El Guindi's visual
ethnography *El Moulid*. Courtesy El Nil Research.

the Muslim people. The Prophet Muhammad veiled his face as he approached the tent of his wife when her father, his father-in-law, was there. Tuareg men "pull rank" on commoners and slaves in their group by pulling the veil tighter. The ethnographic instances are many. The theme is that of the veil as a symbol of rank, power and authority. It is, as we shall see, also a vehicle of liberation and resistance (see Part III).

8

The Veil Becomes a Movement

In Egypt the contemporary veil represents a movement that has passed through several transitional phases since the 1970s, spreading all over the Arab world and among Muslims worldwide. Today the Islamic movement continues to grow strong as it enters its third decade. Dress has played a pivotal symbolic, ritual and political role in this dynamic phenomenon. The new vocabulary and dress style embodies a moral/behavioral code. Islam has struggled to position itself *vis-à-vis* the Islamic veil. The response of secularists and feminists shows how threatening this trend is to their ideological position.

But by 1997, a quarter of a century later, Egypt (and other Arab countries) had accommodated the new movement and put effort into integrating it politically, despite initial attempts by the state to suppress it. Nonetheless, the veiled and unveiled continue to interact normally in daily life. Some mothers who originally objected to the veil have adopted it. The Islamic *ziyy* (dress) goes almost unnoticed in Cairo by the local population.

Islamic veiling in Egypt is somewhat different from the situation of the *chador* in Iran. In Iran the *chador*, a black head-to-toe wrap, is the body cover worn by rural and urban traditional women before the Revolution. The Shah, to Westernize the country, banned it, and the Islamic Revolution, to indigenize tradition, enforced wearing it. In Egypt, the Islamic dress worn after the mid-1970s by women replaced modern secular clothes and is part of a grass-roots activist movement. Unlike Egypt, both Iran and Turkey have long traditions of State-legislated dress reform for both sexes. Although State-discouraged in Egypt, veiling initially met with phenomenal success and spread throughout the urban centers. The authorities of Al-Azhar were silent about it.

As some young Egyptian women took up veiling in the mid-1970s, the government increasingly felt the threat of Islamic militancy and looked for solutions. In 1993, the education minister (Husain Kamal Baha' al-Din) sought to combat the spread of Islamic activism by imposing changes in the area of education, such as the transfer or demotion of teachers with activist leanings, a revision of the curriculum, and restrictions on the wearing of the veil (Barraclough 1998: 246). However, a ban on wearing the veil at universities was thrown out by the courts. By 1994, attempts to limit the wearing of the veil in schools to students who had their parents' permission were receiving heavy criticism. The minister of education started back-pedaling – conceding that schoolgirls could wear the veil even without parental consent. State interference focusing on the veil remains controversial in Egypt.

In Turkey and Iran there is a history of State legislation of dress, in the past mostly for men, but recently regarding the *hijab*. In the Ottoman world there were deep roots to the tradition of clothing laws – extending to the beginning of the empire. And as elsewhere Ottoman clothing laws gave a particular emphasis to head coverings, which typically designated honor and rank. Turbans played a key role in mid-eighteenth century rituals surrounding the Ottoman coronation ceremonies in Istanbul. "In the procession, two horsemen each carried turbans of the monarch, tilting them to the right and to the left to receive the homage of the accompanying janissaries. The centrality of the headgear already was evident in the early 14th century" (Quataert 1997: 405).

According to Norton, Turks can judge people simply from appearances. They consider dress to be a marker of difference, devotion and defiance. "A glance at what a stranger is wearing is often enough to tell them that person's religious and political stance. Clothes can tell them the wearer's defiance of or devotion to the principles of Kemal Ataturk, the reformer who founded the Turkish Republic and banned the fez" (1997: 149). The present situation in Turkey, similar to that of most groups in the Islamic world, is such that dress has become the marker of "the front line" in the emergent battle between advocates of an Islamic society and extreme secularists. In secularist Turkey the women's veil had not been the subject of sartorial rules; the men's fez was. Norton observes that generally the veil was discouraged and in some places prohibited, but Turkey avoided an outright ban on the veil, the measure that the Shah took in Iran. "Forced unveiling of women in Iran [is comparable to] the shock that Westerners would experience if women of all ages were forced to go topless in public" (Norton 1997: 165, citing Goldschmidt 1983).

In the 1970s there was a one-party effort to create "indigenous dress styles for Muslim women and to legitimize traditional Islamic dress" (Norton 1997: 165). Turkish women began to wear long coats and headscarves. Deep divisions formed between secularists and Muslim advocates (Olson 1985). The word *turban* began to appear during the "headscarf issue" and was then ruled to be worn instead of a headscarf.

Interestingly, by the mid-1980s in Egypt some of the women who were reluctant at first to wear the *khimar* (a headcover that covers the hair and extends low to the forehead, comes under the chin to conceal the neck, and falls down over the chest and back) began to wear a turban-like headcover that had Turkish origins. It was seen as more chic.

Roots of Islamic Resistance

At some point the characteristically Islamic rhythm of daily life in Egypt by which Muslims weave ordinary moments with sacred time and space tipped toward a mode of permanent religiousness. Some observers referred to this state as escapist religiosity. It was not confined to Muslims – Copts had a similar experience.

This general mood in Egypt can be traced to two sociopolitical events: the 1967 defeat in the Six Day War, in which Israel attacked Egypt and swiftly destroyed its air force on the ground, and the 1973 victory in the Ramadan (or October) War, in which Egypt attacked Israel and swiftly destroyed the Bar Lev Line, until then mythologized as invincible. Between 1967 and 1973 Egypt passed through several stages that, across cultures, typically characterize religious revival (Wallace 1956; El Guindi 1980, 1981a: 469, 1998a).

In the aftermath of the 1967 defeat a climate of intense religiousness developed in Egypt among the urban population in general, both Muslim and Coptic. People's faith in Nasser, then Egypt's President and until then an unshakeable symbol of pride, dignity, power and strength, shattered and was replaced by feelings of doubt, insecurity and diminished self-esteem. Confusion and gloom loomed over Egypt, a demoralized nation. Fantasy mixed with fact as war stories in graphic detail, real or imagined, circulated among the people. Egyptians at all levels and of all persuasions felt humiliated, betrayed and threatened by the destruction from the technological and military powers and threat from Zionist and Imperialist forces. No rhetoric could mask the profound impact of this defeat on the psyche and lives of Egyptians at that time.

Disbelief gradually turned to disillusion, anger to depression, and discontent to resignation. Defeat became interpreted as God's will to punish Egypt for the increasing decline in people's morals. Many joined Sufi orders during this period. And an image in light of the Virgin Mary allegedly appeared publicly in Zeitun, Cairo several months after the war and continued to reappear for several months afterward. El Guindi (1981a) describes the apparition as related by a college student[115] in a taped interview:

We heard from many people; many were saying the Virgin appeared in Zeitun, near the Coptic church of Zeitun, the church is where the tree is, the tree under which Virgin Mary sat with Jesus in the same place a church was built. For a long time we hear the Virgin appears at night. So we went, we spent the evening: thousands and thousands went; important personalities also went. So we spent the night there once. It was like daytime – chanting and tunes, much activity there. It was 2.00 a.m. at dawn when the image of the Virgin appeared with lots of white pigeons around her. One person saw it first and got up. Everybody stood up then, stretching on tiptoes, standing on chairs. I only went once. My father went there daily. It is like a passing light, a flashing light.

Thousands of Muslims and Copts – men and women, young and old, from all strata – flocked to the spot where the Virgin Mary is purported to have once sat to rest with Jesus and Joseph under the tree and where her image was appearing in light. People waited hours and days to catch a glimpse of the "miracle".[116] Men sat in coffeehouses listening to Umm Kulthum[117] between prayers.

In October of 1973, the surprise Ramadan war brought about victory over Israel in the name of Islam (El Guindi 1980, 1981a, b, 1982c). The Egyptian army destroyed the Bar-Lev line and with it the myth of the invincible Israel. Many Islamic signs and metaphors marked the military event. It took place during the holy month of Ramadan. The army troops roared "Allah Akbar" in unison at the moment of the attack, and the phrase "God is Great" was said to be scrolled across the sky as the troops crossed the Suez Canal.[118]

From that moment an Islamic Movement was born, and evolved through various phases until the present time. Within the framework of Revitalization Movements, the religiousness of the 1960s represents a phase in the process. But there is no doubt that as an Islamic movement it began after the 1973 Ramadan war. Youth and college students began to dress differently in public from the majority of urban rising middle- and even upper-class Egyptians, who since the 1930s had worn modern Western clothing.

The Religious Movement

The term *mitdayyinin* (pl. form), which derives from the root *d-y-n* (religion), was coined in the context of this new visible trend and was used to refer to women and men who adopted a new austere appearance and behaved conservatively in public, in a near-ritualized manner different from the norm of most urban Egyptians. The word itself means "the state of being religious." Unrelated individuals who became *mitdayyinin* referred to each other as "brother" and "sister." They reached this state of religiousness by *iqtina'* (conviction). No overt pressure or force was exerted, only perhaps the indirect influence of a change in public moral climate in which some men and women became activist symbols of an "Islamic model" of comportment and dress. In general, they used no coercion to make others join. They themselves, small in number but strong in presence, became living models to emulate.

The dress adopted in the movement was distinctively austere in style and color, unfamiliar in historical and contemporary terms. Accompanying this dress, particularly during the movement's first decade, was a conservative comportment, what anthropologists would call cross-sex avoidance behavior. This does not mean that men and women stopped interacting in public, since the university campuses are co-educational and most public places in Egypt are shared. Rather, interaction was marked by reserve and austerity, almost ritualized. They were neither formally organized in associations nor were they secluded in one area or place. It did not take the form of a "cult-like" seclusion that physically separated them from mainstream society. They shared the bond of *iltizam* (discipline, compliance and commitment) after switching out of the ordinary secular way of life and into their innovated Islamic way of life,[119] but they continued to live in their homes with their parents, dispersed among the many secular and religious university campuses and schools. They articulated and became exemplars of a shared behavioral, moral and dress code.

In the early phase of the movement, college students made up the core of its "informal membership." They described themselves as *mitdayyinin*. At the university they did not form their own separate organizations. Instead they continued as assimilated students interacting with the rest of the students and participating in university activities, although they were distinguishable by dress, manner, and public comportment. It was common at the time to find a secularly dressed student discussing how, slowly, she was becoming convinced of the new trend and how she was considering making the commitment. Friendships between the secularly dressed and the Islamically dressed continued as usual.

To participate in campus functions the *mitdayyinin* joined the student organizational structure already in existence. This provided a mainstream framework for campus politics and a base from which to organize among the rest of the students. The existing structure comprised the Student Union for governance and the *Osrah* (family) – clubs for various social and recreational activities. They successfully ran in student elections for governing offices. Their Islamic-based ideology countered that of Nasserite-leaning students. Through the *osrah* organization they formed clubs dedicated to religious activities to counter the recreational and social clubs. They slowly gained popularity, and Nasserite students were beginning to find an appeal in the new Islamic ideology, perhaps through its quality of resistance. As it grew stronger it spread beyond the campuses and penetrated the various sectors of society in Egypt. By the mid-1980s the word *mitdayyinin* was replaced by *Islamiyyin*, and it had become a major oppositional political force.

But there is more to it. This movement represented a major shift in the bi-rhythmic balance, the moving in and out from ordinary space to sacred space, from ordinary time to sacred time, that characterized public street life and the social and cultural landscape of contemporary Islamic Egypt. The code embodied in the new movement was unidimensional – adopting it meant you were permanently in sacred time and space even when performing worldly activities. The balance tipped and the rhythmic pattern was challenged. Many Egyptians reacted against it. The sacred appearance that was reserved for the special status attained after pilgrimage in old age became standard and ordinary. It was no more a status enjoyed by one's grandmother or grandfather in their later years. Rather, these young college men and women forged their own permanent status of sacredness, thus challenging the Islamic life-cycle rhythm. Many of them, still in their twenties and thirties, performed *hajj* (pilgrimage) not once but several times. But even without the pilgrimage they had adopted a code in symbol and ritual that positioned them in this state of sacredness without any rite of passage, without the pilgrimage. Al-Azhar, the Islamic seat of learning and scholarship in Cairo and the university that produces the scholars of Islam, was not ready or prepared for an innovation of that magnitude and impact to emerge from below.[120] And as much as the State wished it, al-Azhar could not condemn the new appearance. It was particularly difficult since the *mitdayyinin*, while maintaining their distinct appearance and a general aura of reserve and austerity, were assimilated into mainstream society. And although the dress, which men and women called *al-ziyy al-Islami* (the Islamic dress), was new to Egypt, it embodied a code they all equally shared with devout Muslims.

Al-Ziyy Al-Islami (The Islamic Dress)

The Code

Women's Islamic dress, known as *al-ziyy al-Islami*, is an innovative construction that was first worn in the mid-1970s by activists. It does not represent a return to any traditional dress form and has no tangible precedent. There was no industry behind it in Egypt – not one store carried such an outfit. Based on an idealized Islamic vision gradually constructed for the early Islamic community in the seventh century,[121] it was made in their homes by the activists themselves. Privacy, humility, piety and moderation are cornerstones of the Islamic belief system. Luxury and leisure await Muslims in the next world. Some elements of this vision can be supported by reference to the *Qur'an*, others find support in the secondary source of Islamic information, the *Sunna,*[122] through the *Hadith*. The "Prophetic vision" had become idealized through the ages, developing into a model to be emulated via recurring revivalist purifying movements within Islam, just as in the Islamic movement of Egypt in the 1970s.

In the *Qur'an* (considered the primary and divinely revealed source), but mostly according to the *Hadith* (a worldly source), evidence suggests that the Prophet Muhammad had paid much attention to a dress code for Muslims in the emerging community, with a specific focus on Muslim men's clothing and bodily modesty during prayer (al-Hajj 1960; al-Bukhari 1996). By comparison, reference to women's body cover is negligible.

In the *Sura al-Ahzab* one *ayah* (33: 53) protects the privacy of the Prophet's wives from growing intrusions by male visitors and another (33: 59) distinguishes their status and that of all believers from all others.

Men and women in the contemporary Islamic movement read works by the ideologues Sayyid Qutb and Abu al-'Ala al-Mawdudi. They argue for the Islamic dress and behavioral code, using as support for their argument two specific *Suras* in the *Qur'an* – *al-Nur* and *al-Ahzab*. The two *ayah*s of concern in the *Sura al-Nur* (24: 30, 31) translate as follows:

> The believing men are enjoined to lower their gaze and conceal their genitals [30] and the believing women are enjoined to lower their gaze and conceal their genitals, draw their *khimar* to cover their cleavage [breasts], and not display their beauty, except that which has to be revealed, except to their husbands, their fathers, their husbands' fathers, their sons, their husbands' sons, their brothers or their brothers' sons, or their sister's sons, or their women, or the slaves, or eunuchs or children under age; and they should not strike their feet to draw attention to their hidden beauty. O believers turn to God, that you may attain bliss.
>
> (*Qur'an* 24: 30,31)

These kinship and social positions are diagrammed using the tools of genealogical analysis (see Figure 8).

Islam links socio-moral behavior, sacred space and sartorial preferences. Two points can be drawn from the text mentioned above: (1) the Arabic notions of *ghadd al-basar* (lower the gaze) and *hifth al-furuj* (guard or cover the genitals) are central to the code; and (2) men are first mentioned as having to abide by these two premises, to control their gaze at women and suppress their passion and forwardness when interacting with "strange" women. Likewise, in the *Hadith* men especially are enjoined to cover their genitals. The phrase *hifth al-furuj* is used often in the *Hadith* regarding men's dress and bodily modesty during worship. Next, the text similarly enjoins women to lower their gaze and conceal their genitals. The significance of the specific message communicated in this text lies in this relational context addressing men and women, and in the fact that men are addressed first, and then women. To understand the message both text and context must be considered.

Unlike other religions, orthodox Islam accepts sexuality as a normative aspect of both ordinary and religious life (Mernissi 1975; Marsot 1979; Nelson 1974) and fluidly accommodates both sacred and worldly activity in the same bi-rhythmic space. There is no contradiction between being religious and being sexual. Sex is to be enjoyed in matrimony. However, outside marriage, behavior between men and women must be desexualized. Both body and interactive space need to be regulated and controlled and both men and women are required to abide by this temporary desexualization to make public interaction between them possible. This presumes that cross-sex interaction would potentially be sexually charged. Islam accepts sexualized, reproductive men and women and guides them to regulate their public behavior. Having chosen not to sublimate sexuality theologically or ideologically (as have, for example, some major trends in Christian theology) Islam poses the opposite challenge to individual Muslims, that is to accommodate both human qualities – sexuality and religiousness[123] – as normative while they strive to fulfill the ultimate ideal of sociomoral behavior.

Three other aspects in the same *Sura (al-Nur)* show how concealing and revealing are very much tied to cultural notions of respectability, sexuality, eroticism and privacy. One segment enjoins women to draw their *khimar* (head veil) over their *juyub* (breast cleavage). *Khimar* is one of two clothing items for women referenced in Qur'anic text. The other is *jilbab* (long shirtdress). Also *zina* (pronounced *zeena*), which means both beauty and ornament, is integral to references about women's dress and comportment.

Sayyid-Marsot observes that the particular "passage in the Quran which tells women to use the head covering (*khimar*) to cover their cleavage has been interpreted as a total covering of the body" (1995: 11). She points out that "[i]t is men from the eighth century onward who interpreted the passage in the Quran which enjoins men and women to dress modestly to mean that women should be totally covered and segregated, neither seen nor heard" (1995: 11). These are the learned men, the *Ulama*, who are the interpreters of the *Qur'an* and the Islamic teachings. In fact, there were also learned women, who were referred to as *alimat* (sing. *alima* or "woman Islamic scholar"), who never, according to Sayyid-Marsot, "acquired the status and degree of authority of a *alim* [male Islamic scholar]" (1995: 11).

I contend that the reference to drawing the headveil to cover a woman's cleavage may have been in reaction to the way contemporary women in the region (Arabia–Africa) seem to have worn clothes that exposed their bodies.[124] A visual analysis of images from modern Yemen, for example, shows women from the low-status group of *al-akhdam (servants)* wearing clothing that reveals the breasts. The image evokes, not seductive sexuality, but slovenliness[125] (see Figure 21). Another prohibition concerns anklets. The admonition "that they should not strike their feet" is a reference to the practice in which women wore decorative jingling anklets[126] made of heavy metal (silver or gold). It is not the anklet *per se* that is erotic, but the jingling that evokes erotic passions.[127]

Early (1993) in her ethnography on *baladi* (local traditional urban) life in Cairo describes the traditional *baladi* dress, *milayah laff* (an overall black wrap) worn in public draped over a housedress to cover the hair and entire body, with the ends tucked under the arm. "From underneath, a tightly knotted scarf covers the hair" (1993: 70). El-Messiri notes the dimension of sensual playfulness: "walking coquettishly" in a manner that makes a woman's hips seem to "roll" to the rhythm of her "clicking high heeled sandals, tinkling anklets, and the little bursting noises of chewing gum bubbles," a dress that combines sexual glamour and modesty (1978: 526, 529).

Within Islam, a woman's sexuality does not diminish her respectability. Islam in fact supports this combined image in womanhood. The *Hadith* mentions an incident in which the Prophet Muhammad told a woman to color her fingernails with henna so that her hands were not like the hands of men. What Islamic morality forbids is the public flaunting of sexuality. In general, the Islamic code would consider the behavior of urban *Baladi* women in Egypt described in El-Messiri and Early's ethnographies as exhibitionist. Dressing and moving in a way that draws sexual attention to the body is *tabarruj* (exhibitionist dress and behavior). It is associated in Islamic perception with Arabian women of *al-Jahiliyya* (the "Days of Ignorance," or pre-Islamic days) and was frowned upon during the formative years of the Islamic community in the seventh century.

The third aspect in the *Sura* (*al-Nur*: 24: 31) deals with the context of heterosexuality, privacy and eroticism. It enjoins women not to reveal their *zina* (meaning "beauty" or "ornament") except in the presence of those who are in a position in which sexual relations are legitimate (such as their husbands), taboo or forbidden (culturally specified kin), or not possible (underage children or asexualized men). With a woman as the point of reference these relations, diagrammed in a genealogical chart form in Figure 8, are clearly specified: husband, father, husband's father, sons, husband's sons, brothers, brothers' sons, sisters' sons, brothers' wives' sons; or their wives' sons; slaves, eunuchs or underage boys. These constitute (except for

Figure 21 The dress of Yemeni women in domestic service and public
entertainment, illustrating the link between status and body exposure in
Arabia. From *World of Islam Festival Trust*, edited by R. B. Sergent and
Ronald Lewcock, 1983, plate 99, p. 413, photography by D. Hoppe. ©
R. Lewcock.

the spouse) kinfolk (consanguineal and affinal) or domestic personnel who share the private space with women.

As to the other relevant *Sura* (*al-Ahzab*) there is reference in two *ayah*s to the Prophet's wives. One (33: 53) enjoins strangers who wish to speak to any of the Mothers of the Believers to do so from behind a screen or curtain. The term used in this context is *hijab*. It is noteworthy that *hijab* is not used in the *Qur'an* in the literal sense of women's clothing.[128] The other reference (33: 59) enjoins the Prophet's wives, daughters, and all Muslim women, to don their *jilbab* for identification and protection from molestation. The other *ayah* (59) translates as follows:

> O Prophet tell your wives, daughters and believing women to put on their *jilbabs* so that they are recognized and thus not harmed.
>
> (33: 59)

Jilbab refers to a long loose shirtdress. It does not connote head or face cover, although, as the ethnography of bedouins and rural Muslim Indians shows, veiling is not always accomplished through a fixed item covering the face. Often *jilbab* sleeves or headcovers are used situationally for covering part of the face. This passage refers to women directly connected to the Prophet (wives and daughters) in order to distinguish their status, and it extends the enjoinder of wearing *al-jilbab* to all believing Muslim women. It is interesting in this regard that in the Islamic movement in Indonesia, *jilbab* is more commonly used to refer to women's Islamic-style clothing, although it has no consistent meaning – some use it to refer to the head covering itself (An Indonesian–English Dictionary (3rd ecn), ed. Echols and Shadily 1989: 24, cited in Brenner 1996: 692, n. 5), while others use it to refer to the complete outfit. Brenner observes that it is "generally understood as describing the newer style of Islamic clothing imported from the Middle East and worn mostly by younger women as opposed to the more traditional *sarong*, *kebaya*, and loose headscarf or woven cap worn by older Indonesian women" (1996: 692, n. 5). In the context of the early Islamic community I contend that the intent was to mark group identity (the community of believers), to achieve social distance for the Prophet's Wives, and to project an image of respect to avert harassment.

Significantly, in neither *Sura* referred to above, nor in any of their constituent segments, is there any explicit mention of face veiling or any cover solely for use as face cover for women. The two dress parts mentioned for women are *khimar* (the head veil) and *jilbab* (a long gown), which had not been newly introduced by Islam but were likely already to be part of the wardrobe of the time. Various forms of *jilbab* and head cover for men and women are items of Arab dress. Islam attached specific and characteristic meaning to their use, pertaining to privacy, respect and status.

Further support for aspects of the code can be found in the *Hadith*, although here most references pertain to men's dress code and comportment. The dress vocabulary used in *Hadith*, focusing on Sahih al-Bukhari and Sahih Muslim, comprises the following: *'izar* (cloth wrap from waist down), *qabba'* (shirt-dress), *sirwal* (pantaloons), *farruj* (wrap open at the back worn over other clothes), *jubba* (cloak). There are also *burdah, jummah, hibarah, mulabbada,* and *anbaganiyya,* all of which refer to various thick, solid-color cloaks approved of by Prophet Muhammad. Four themes can be identified from the various references in *Hadith* sources: (1) bodily modesty which pertains mostly to men in worship, (2) averting distraction in worship, (3) moderation in daily life and (4) distinguishing the identity of the Muslim through aversion from certain forms of dress (hair, color, etc.).

A general theme that recurs in *Hadith* references is about the distraction caused by clothing during worship. This is expressed in a number of contexts in which Prophet Muhammad shuns wearing colorful designs on clothes.[129] In this reference it is stated: the Prophet prayed in a *khamisa* [dress made out of fabric of silk or wool, striped and with decorative design], and then asked for its replacement with an *anbaganiyya* [opaque heavy cover without embroidery or decorative designs]. He also referred to other distractions during worship, such as "the sheer patterned cloth hanging from 'Aisha's quarters," which overlooked the worship area and was therefore within the view of worshippers. Prophet Muhammad found this distracting.

Another theme is about general austerity and moderation in lifestyle,[130] and it is suggested that men avoid wearing gold,[131] fabric made out of silk,[132] big rings, and colorful patterned fabric.[133] There is a recurring reference favoring thickness and opaqueness of fabric for clothing and shelter.[134]

The final recurring theme on the subject of dress is about dress as a marker of Islamic identity for men. Several references are made to hair pattern and the avoidance of fabric color in order not to have the same appearance as other groups, whether *mushrikun* (Arabian polytheists) or other mono-theists.[135]

The Notion of 'Awrah Reconsidered

'Awrah, a term mentioned a few times in the *Qur'an* and more in the *Hadith*, is among Islamic notions[136] subjected to lay and expert interpretations considered unfavorable to Muslim women. The term's most common English translation is "blemish," and the reference is to a woman's body, parts of which are characterized in these interpretations as a blemish that must be

concealed. Many publications on Muslim women in particular tend to use this connotation uncritically. Interestingly, major scholarly works on Islam do not address or critique the notion at all. The English translation "blemish" along with some other significations can be found in dictionary renditions. Etymologically, the term derives from the root *'a-w-r*. Consulting *Wehr's Arabic–English Dictionary* (1994) leads to two significations: (1) (sing.) defectiveness, imperfection, blemish, flaw; (2) (pl. *'awrat*) (a) pudenda, genitals; (b) weakness. Other derivatives range in meaning from blind in one eye, false or artificial (as in teeth or hair), and lending/borrowing, among others.

My anthropological analysis of the term as it is used in the Qur'anic text shows *'awrah* as neither confined to women nor to the body. Examining the primary source directly and in its original language, the Qur'anic text reveals the use of the term in the following passages: *Sura al-Nur*, 24: 31, 58 and *Sura al-Ahzab*, 33: 13. *Sura* 24: 31 refers in part to the males sharing the private space of women in whose presence women need not conceal certain parts of their bodies. The term *'awrat* is used as follows:

> . . . and male slaves or eunuchs or underage boys not yet sexually mature for contact with women's *'awrat* [genitals] in intercourse . . .
>
> (24: 31)

In the above text *'awrat* connotes women's genitals. No valuation is put on the term. There is no sense of imperfection or blemish inherent in this context. The next passage is about privacy (*al-Nur*, 24: 58) as the text states:

> O believers, eunuchs and underage boys should not intrude upon your privacy on three occasions [or at three times of day]: before *fajr* [dawn] prayer, when you are resting at noon, and after *'isha* [night] prayer.[137] These are three *'awrat*, outside of which interaction is not held against you or them . . .
>
> (24: 58)

The usage *'awrat* (pl.) in the above passage is interesting. It refers to a notion of privacy and private space and time, rather than a woman's body. The final passage in the *Qur'an* that uses the term is in the *Sura al-Ahzab*, in which the term is mentioned twice in the same segment. The context is a battle scene in which men joined the Prophet out of Yathrib (the seventh-century name for Madina). It states:

> . . . if a group of them ask the Prophet for leave saying "truly our homes are *'awrah*'," though they were not *'awrah*, then their intent was to flee the battle . . .
>
> (33: 13)

Again the term is not used in the sense of blemish or woman's body part. It connotes protection, safety, vulnerability, security, and privacy with regard to a home. There *is* a context in the *Qur'an* that is unambiguously about the genitals, which is in *Sura al-A'raf* (7: 26, 27), that relates the episode of creation and the first humans in the Garden. In these two instances the term used twice in two consecutive *ayah*s is not *'awrat* but *saw'at,* and it pertains to both sexes. The text states:

> O ye children of Adam! We have bestowed *libas* [dress] upon you to cover your *saw'at* [genitals] . . . [and] . . . stripping them of their raiment, to expose their *saw'at* [genitals].
>
> (7: 26, 27)

Taking all the Qur'anic text passages together, a range of contexts are revealed, all of which make sense if the meaning imbued to *'awrah* becomes "inviolate vulnerability" rather than the commonly assumed "blemish." Several contexts discerned are: women's genitals (sexuality), home, conjugal privacy, women's privacy. If we add *Hadith* text to the selected Qur'anic text we can further establish that the term *'awrah* (or *'awrat*) is often used with reference to men's immodesty when their genitals are exposed as they bend over during worship. Referentially, men's bodily immodesty during worship is in fact the most frequent context.

With regard to bodily modesty for men there are many references about clothing appropriate to ensure the concealment of men's genitals. First, there is bodily modesty for men during worship. One theme that re-emerges in different contexts is about layering clothes, or specifically "not wearing only a single item" that exposes men's genital area (men's *furuj* or *'awrah*) in certain reclining positions or while bending or crossing the legs.[138] It is in this context of the inappropriateness of clothing worn by men as they learn the new practices of Islamic praying – bowing, bending, prostrating themselves, kneeling, etc. – that in a reference[139] to worship women were told not to lift their heads until men had taken a "sitting position."

This leads us to two conclusions. First, that women and men shared space for worship during the Prophet's time. Secondly, owing to the inappropriateness of men's clothing for worship women were asked to avoid being in a position to "see" exposed men's body parts, or their *'awrah* (vulnerability). In other references women had complained to the Prophet about such awkward exposures on the part of men.

'Awrah, therefore, does not mean "a blemish on women's bodies," but rather the immodest exposure of men's genitals. It is better understood if situated in a more comprehensive paradigm that stresses its basic and original

connotation of weakness and vulnerability. A more comprehensive paradigm will reveal connections with the broader notions of the Arabo-Islamic sanctity and privacy of the home and the family.

The Dress

Beginning in Egypt, in the Arabic-speaking region, the subject of the *hijab* was revived in the 1970s in the context of an emergent Islamic consciousness and movement that spread steadily throughout the Islamic East (El Guindi 1980, 1981a, b, c, 1982a, b, c, d, 1983, 1984, 1985a, 1986a, 1987, 1995b, 1996a). The Qur'anic dress terms *khimar* and *jilbab,* and the notion of immoderate excess (*tabarruj*), and a contrasting opposition *tahajjub/sufur,* all reappeared as a revived contemporary vocabulary dominating daily discourse among the youth in the movement and around the nation (Hamza 1981; Sidque 1975).

This vocabulary framed the debate about Muslim women's and men's dress, conduct, morality and Islamic identity. *Hijab* became the object and the symbol for the new consciousness and a new activism (El Guindi 1982a, 1983). Arab dress again provided the conceptual and material tools for identity. This time, however, it was also for resistance; it was set forth in the name of Islam, and was born in a completely different historical context and sociocultural setting. The veil in resistance, for it or against it, is not new. It has recurrent precedents in Middle Eastern history.

In the contemporary revival, the dress code was translated this way: men and women wear full-length *gallabiyyas* (*jilbab* in standard Arabic), loose-fitting to conceal body contours, in solid austere colors made out of opaque fabric. They lower their gaze in cross-sex public interaction, and refrain from body or dress decoration or colors that draw attention to their bodies. The dress code for men consists of sandals, baggy trousers with loose-top shirts in off-white, or alternatively (and preferred) a long loose white *gallabiyya.* They grow a *lihya* (a full beard trimmed short), with an optional mustache. Hair is to be kept shoulder-length. (This last feature has not been sustained and was eventually dropped.) The general behavior code of austerity and restraint has support in Qur'anic segments that repeatedly stress the undesirability of arrogance and exhibitionist demeanor.[140]

In women's dress there is a gradation: A *muhajjaba* (a woman wearing *hijab*) wore *al-jilbab* – an unfitted, long-sleeved, ankle-length gown in austere solid colors and thick opaque fabric – and *al-khimar,* a headcover that covers the hair and extends low to the forehead, comes under the chin to conceal the neck, and falls down over the chest and back. The common colors used by women during the first decade of the movement were beige, brown, navy,

Figure 22 Contemporary veiling showing a *muhajjaba* (head-covered) woman and a *munaqqaba* (face-covered) woman as they cross paths on a street in Cairo 1995 on an ordinary day. Ethnographic photo by F. El Guindi. Courtesy El Nil Research.

deep wine, white and black (see Figure 22). This dress is worn while engaging fully in worldly affairs in public social space in which not only is her gender accepted, but also her sexual identity. Austere dress form and behavior are therefore not accompanied by withdrawal, seclusion, or segregation.

The voluntary informal dress code extends beyond clothing to a general demeanor characterized by serious behavior and an austere manner, an ideal applied to both sexes. A *munaqqabah* (a woman wearing the *niqab* or face veil) more conservatively adds *al-niqab*, which covers the entire face except for the eye slits; at the most extreme, she would also wear gloves and opaque socks to cover her hands and feet. This trend[141] has been spreading throughout the Arab world, particularly among university students. Chatty (1997) describes a similar pattern occurring in southeastern Arabia. Gradually, this Islamic dress code became standardized, its adherents continued to grow in number, and their presence in the midst of the urban public landscape became routinized (see Wallace 1956 on phases in Revitalization Movements crossculturally).

During the first decade of the movement in Egypt the dress code for women corresponded to the degree of Islamic knowledgeability and reading, as well as to a step on a scale of leadership among women. The more intensely covered the college woman, the more "serious" her public behavior, the more knowledgeable she was in Islamic sources, the higher she was on the scale of activist leadership among women. She would lead discussions, for example, in mosques and in women students' lounges between lectures. This correspondence dissolved as the movement spread outside the university campuses and as the *hijab* became part of normal life, mingling with secular life in Cairo and the other major cities (see Figure 23).

This Islamic dress was introduced by college women in the movement and was not imposed by the al-Azhar authorities, who ordinarily prescribe Islamic behavior by issuing decrees. Instead, this was a bottom-up movement. By dressing this way in public these young women translated their vision of Islamic ideals by becoming exemplary contemporary models. Encoded in the dress style is a new public appearance and demeanor that reaffirms an Islamic identity and morality and rejects Western materialism, consumerism, commercialism, and values. The vision behind the Islamic dress is rooted in these women's understanding of early Islam and, as earlier presented, in primary and secondary textual sources. But it is a contemporary movement about contemporary issues.

Clearly, the movement is not simply about a dress code. Like early Islam in Madina, this activism espouses egalitarianism, community, identity, privacy, and justice. It condemns exhibitionism in dress and behavior, which was also characteristic of *jahiliyya* (the pre-Islamic era). *Jahiliyya*, then, is not just a historical moment, but a state and a condition of society that can occur at any time. Reserve and restraint in behavior, voice and body movement are not restrictions. They symbolize a renewal of traditional cultural identity.

Figure 23 In contrast with the 1970s, now veiling does not attract attention. Scenes of ordinary daily life in the streets of Cairo, showing how "veiled" women are integrated with the rest of the population. Ethnographic photos by F. El Guindi, Cairo 1995. Courtesy El Nil Research.

9

The Sacred in the Veil: "Hijab"

> True meaning lies as if hidden behind a series of waxed seals . . . breaking one
> open only inspires the need to break open another . . . each meaning crumbles
> under the pressure of knowing . . . This is the principle of the veil well known
> to the Saracens [Sc. Arabs],[142]
>
> Fra Mauro, sixteenth-century monk cartographer to the Court of Venice,
> referring to al-Ghazali (Cowan 1996: 10).

There are two beginnings in Islam – that of the primordial pair and that of
the *Qur'an*. Both are about descent, and both use dress in their imagery, and
both yield meaning about integrating a sacred divide. Islamic imagery of
the primordial originary human cross-sex pair (Smith and Haddad 1975;
1982) shows them off as bedecked lavishly with *libas* (dress) and ornamentation for bodily privacy, luxury and comfort (*Sura* 7: 26). In their
beginnings, therefore, humans were not naked. Their private parts were
hidden from themselves and each other. They were granted access to the
whole Garden and its resources, except The Tree. Satan deceived them and
they disobeyed God and approached The Tree. After disobedience, their
private parts (*saw'atihim*) were revealed to them and to each other.

> Satan tempted them, so that he might reveal to them their private parts that had
> been hidden from each other.
>
> (7: 20)

In another passage:

> We have sent down to you clothing in order to cover the private parts of your
> body and serve as protection and decoration; and the best of all garments is the
> garment of piety.
>
> (7: 26)

In another context the text states:

> They [women] are a garment to you and you are a garment to them.
>
> (2: 187)

Here we discern the theme of an interdependent mutuality of the sexes. Adam and spouse/mate immediately recognized their wrongdoing, i.e. their disobedience of God. God sent them out of the Garden (Paradise) down to live on earth for their lifetime. On earth they will multiply and divide into groups, among whom will be friends and enemies.

But in Islam there is another sacred beginning – that of the revelation through oral tradition of the Divine Word that was subsequently put together in the form of the *Qur'an* now familiar to us. In the very first moments there was an encounter. Archangel Gabriel appeared to Prophet Muhammad in his seclusion. Prophet Muhammad was shaken and rushed to his wife Khadija, trembling and feverish: "Cover me, cover me with cloth." The voice of God then said:

> O you, enwrapped [in thy mantle], arise and spread the word, worship God and purify your clothes.
>
> (74: 1)

This incident is described in Qur'anic *Sura al-Muddathir*. The encounter marked the beginning of the revelation and the descent over an extended period of the *Suras* that together comprise the *Qur'an* – the most sacred and holy object and symbol of Islam. Again, here is a context of sacred beginnings connected with dress, or in which dress is a metaphor for a sacred divide.

Hijab was not mentioned in either, but the idea of a sacred divide was set forth. Here we have the separation of obedience from disobedience, God from Satan, immortal from mortal, heaven from earth. In this imagery there was no veiling and no seclusion and no sin. Privacy – moral and material – was violated. A connection was made between dress, privacy and sacred space.

Myths, Francis Ferguson tells us, have the power to "generate new forms . . . in the imaginations of those who try to grasp them" (1966: 140). In the Turkish and Persian sacred imagination, Prophet Muhammad is represented as face-veiled in white, with a nimbus of flame over his head. A Persian miniature of the sixteenth century depicts the first encounter between Prophet Muhammad and Khadija (see Figure 24). He is on a camel, his face is white-veiled, and a nimbus of flame over his head marks his special sacred status. He faces Khadija, who is inside a tall Arabian house, with lattice work decorating its front, looking from a window at Prophet Muhammad. Khadija's face is not veiled. Khadija was a prominent Makkan widow of wealth and power. She managed trade caravans. It is reported that she had employed Muhammad to manage her trade activities. She then proposed to marry him, and they were monogamously married for twenty-five years until her death.

Figure 24 An image of Prophet Muhammad on a camel, his face white-veiled, on first meeting Khadija, who became his monogamous wife of twenty-five years. Khadija's face is not veiled. Miniature from: Ishaq an-Nisapurai, Qisas al-Anbiya' , Iran, around 1560. Chester Beatty Library, Dublin. Reprinted by permission.

She was the first believer in his visions and revelations and became the first follower of Islam.

As far as is presently known, Islam did not invent or introduce the custom of veiling. Veiling for men and women had existed in the region prior to Islam – in Hellenic, Judaic, Byzantine, and Balkan cultures. Whether by adoption, reinvention or independent invention, veiling in Arab social systems has evolved a distinct function and characteristic meaning from that in the northern Mediterranean regions.

Stern (1939a) observes that the custom of veiling must have been in use in pre-Islamic times, particularly in towns and among certain classes. Greek and Roman women veiled themselves when appearing in public by drawing the upper garment over the head and across the face. She argues that veiling in Arabia did not seem to have had any connection with women's seclusion (1939a: 108).

Ahmed (L. Ahmed1982) was right when pointing to the absence of evidence for veiling among Egyptian women before Christianity, although according to one reference some women may have been using a head veil in public in the later period during the reign of Ramses III (20th dynasty). She was wrong in suggesting that Jewish women, too, did not veil. She wrote that the only exceptions to the otherwise very widespread practice of veiling throughout the region were "*the Jews* and the Egyptians" (1982: 523, my emphasis). But Jewish women at the time of Christ veiled (Stern 1939a: 109).

Biblical evidence of this can be found in *Genesis* 24.65: "And Rebekah lifted up her eyes and when she saw Isaac . . . she took her veil and covered herself"; in *Isaiah* 3.23: "In that day the Lord will take away the finery of the anklets . . . the headdresses . . . and the veils"; and in *Corinthians* I: 3–7: "Any woman who prays with her head unveiled dishonors her head – it is the same as if her head were shaven. For if a woman will not veil herself, then she should cut off her hair, but if it is disgraceful for a woman to be shorn or shaven, let her wear a veil. For a man ought not to cover his head, since he is the image and glory of God; but woman is the glory of man."

Evidence also suggests that Jewish women of the eleventh century veiled their faces. According to Goitein "[t]he meticulous covering of the head was motivated also by religious sentiment. In the Aramaic language . . . [the word] *bareheaded* meant *bold-faced*, defiant. But we should not be irreverent in the presence of God, who is constantly with and above us" (1978: 159). This is different from the conception of head cover in Islam.[143] Regarding Jewish women in the Geniza period, Goitein (1983) discusses Document I, "A Karaite Marriage Contract from Jerusalem", 26 January 1028 (1983: 314–16). The contract lists "the valuables brought in by Sarwa to the house of her husband Hezekiah" (1983: 315). Clothing items include a number of different kinds of veils and wimples (transparent and opaque) and face masks (*qina'*) and long gowns going down to the ground. In another document, "A Rabbanite Engagement Contract from Fustat (Old Cairo)," a *khimar* is listed (318–21).

It is evident that Jewish women's seclusionary/exclusionary quality was characteristic of society as reflected in the Geniza documents. Among Jews of medieval Egypt public segregation of the sexes was institutionalized. Women and men entered their temples from separate doors (Goitein 1983: 61). Goitein discusses how frequent the term *bab al-sirr*or, or "secret door," appears in the documents. He also points out that "doorways to the women's galleries of synagogues . . . were designated [by the same term] but also by *bab al-nisa*, women's entrance" (1983: 61). He adds "[b]oth in private and in public buildings the secret door opened out to a street different from that approached through the main doorway" (1983: 61). The secret door, as quoted by Goitein from the documents, is, "according to the best authorities, to enable a paramour to enter the *harim* [or women's quarters]" (1983: 60).

Goitein (1983: 64, 67) discovered two examples in the Geniza documents, one from Alexandria and one from Fustat, Islamic Cairo, that refer to women's *qa'a* or quarters: in the one case a Jew rented the place from a Christian, and in the other a Jewish doctor built it for his son. The document relating to the latter, according to Goitein, makes a connection between the "completeness" of the house, in this case his son's, and its having "a women's qa'a" (1983: 67).[144] Both cases provide evidence that during this period probably only Jews and Christians, like the Hellenic and Byzantine systems before them, secluded women.

Compelling evidence comes from the study by Nelly Hanna (1991: 42–3, 73–4, 75, 141) as discussed in Sayyid-Marsot (1995). Hanna conducted a systematic study on architectural patterns and function changes of habitations in Cairo. Her focus was the seventeenth and the eighteenth centuries. She noted changes in *mamluk* houses previously unknown, such as the division of the house into a male section and a female section. Using her findings, Sayyid-Marsot (1995) states that terms such as "the women's gate" (*bab al-harim*) and "the women's kitchen" (*matbakh al-harim*), which were previously unknown, begin to appear in the eighteenth century.

On the basis of Hanna's study, Sayyid-Marsot notes that "in the early eighteenth century only 2.5 percent of the houses had such elements as a gate for women . . . [and by] the middle of the century that number had risen to 40 percent, while by the end of the century the term appears in 84 percent of these houses along with terms such as 'the women's kitchen' and 'the women's garden'" (Sayyid-Marsot 1995: 38). If the division of homes into male and female sections is considered new for eighteenth-century Egypt, then most likely this division did not exist among the majority population during the Geniza period. "In the numerous documents from Fustat written by Muslim notaries no such division [male and female] is visible" (Goitein 1983: 64). In this case, only Jewish Egyptians may have instituted such a partition. This would have been consistent with the Jewish practice of the time of instituting separate street doors for women (Goitein 1983: 61).

There is a tradition of gender segregation and public seclusion of women in the Judaic and Christian traditions that is rooted in conceptions of the purity and impurity of women and connections between womanhood and nature. These conceptions have a bearing on individual self-image and the public and religious sense of self. On the basis of ethnographic and textual evidence this perspective that derives its meaning from Judaic roots, when uncritically applied to other groups, distorts and misrepresents cultural constructions of womanhood unique to these other groups. For example, these notions do not have an Arabo-Islamic basis. Gender separations in Arabo-Islamic societies must be examined in a different framework. A subtle and nuanced divide, but one that makes a difference, exists between religious cultures

We have seen evidence that women in Arabia prior to Islam occupied an important position and were active in the religious and social life of the community. Two clans (the Banu Isma'il and Banu Qahtan) may have practiced some form of female veiling in pre-Islamic times. There was much regional trade and political contact at the time, and it is unlikely that the custom of veiling was unknown in the region even in the societies that did not practice it. Evidently Arabian men veiled on some occasions, such as during the performance of poetry in markets (Stern 1939a: 111). And as was mentioned earlier, it has been reported that on a number of occasions Prophet Muhammad himself face-veiled, an image well depicted in Turkish and Persian miniatures.

But the fact must be emphasized that neither in the *Qur'an* nor in a reliable *Hadith* can be found any explicit ordinance promulgated by the Prophet Muhammad ordering either Muslim women in general or his own wives to veil themselves, or in particular to face-veil. Stern observes that "[t]he only ordinance that could possibly have any bearing on this subject is Sura 33, 59, which was addressed to his wives, his daughters, and the women of the believers enjoining that they should cover themselves with their *jilbabs* . . . [L]egists have never tried to support their theories of veiling on this verse, . . . [but] commentators such as al-Tabari, al-Baidawi, and as Suyuti do refer to veiling in their *Tafsir* [Interpretation] on this verse.[145] Al-Tabari includes in his commentary on this verse the tradition on Muhammad's wives going out at night, which is amongst those given as being the origin of Sura 33, 53" (Stern 1939a: 111).

Likewise, the *Tafsir* of *Sura* 24: 31 "merely prescribes modesty in comport-ment and dress" (Stern 1939a: 111). This does not directly relate to the actual content of the *Sura* nor discuss how much of the woman's person is to be covered. Plausibly, these commentaries were written long after the first days of Islam, after the custom had already established itself among Muslims (Stern 1939a: 111–12).

Hijab is not the Arabic word for "veil." It is not a recent term; but neither is it that old. It is a complex notion that has gradually developed a set of related meanings. Stern notes, on the basis of the sources explored, evidence that the term had a well-defined meaning by the ninth century AD (1939a: 108). The term *hijab* itself presents a number of interesting points. It had become part of the Arabian Arabic vocabulary in early Islam. Other terms were used to refer to the veil itself, but the phrase *darb* (adopting) *al-hijab* was used in Arabia in discourse about the seclusion of the wives of the Prophet. By the nineteenth century, upper-class urban Muslim and Christian women in Egypt wore the *habarah*, which consisted of a long skirt, a head cover, and a *burqu'*, a long rectangular cloth of white transparent muslin placed below the eyes, covering the lower nose and the mouth and falling to the chest. In mourning, a black muslin veil known as the *bisha* was substituted. Perhaps related to the origins of the practice among Jews and Christians, the word *habarah* itself derives from early Christian and Judaic religious vocabulary. When the veil became the center of feminist/nationalist discourse in Egypt during the British colonial occupation, *hijab* was the term used by feminists and nationalists and secularists. The phrase used for the removal of urban women's face/head cover was *raf'* (lifting) *al-hijab* (not *al-habarah*: the term used for cloak/veil among upper-class Egyptian women at the turn of the century (El Guindi 1996a: 110).

What does the *Qur'an* say about the *hijab*? The *Qur'an* has a number of references to *hijab*, only one of which concerns women's clothing. As Islam gradually established itself in the Madina community, what has come to be interpreted as "seclusion" for Muhammad's wives came from a reading of a Qur'anic verse:

> O believers, enter not the dwellings of the Prophet, unless invited . . . And when you ask of his wives anything, ask from behind a *hijab*. That is purer for your hearts and for their hearts.
>
> (33: 53)

Evidence suggests that this *Sura* concerning the *hijab* was revealed possibly before 5 AH. During that time, many people from the growing Islamic community were going to the homestead of the Prophet for queries, favors and requests. His wives resided in quarters surrounding the courtyard that became the first mosque the Prophet Muhammad founded for Muslims. This was in Madina. Stern describes the wives' quarters as huts "situated on one side of the *masjid* [mosque] with their entrances possibly on to its court . . . Aisha's hut had an entrance to the *masjid* . . . while Umm Salamah built some type of screen to her hut, in order to form a barrier between her and the people" (Stern 1939a: 116; n.2; see also Stern 1939b). After discussing the tradition, in Ibn Sa'd (1905–28) and the commentaries, relating to the events that are said to have occasioned this revelation (33: 53), she mentions that the passage has become known as "the verse of the veil." The events are summed up as follows: after the wedding feast some of the guests lingered on in Zainab's hut. The Prophet grew impatient and visited his other wives, waiting for their departure. Only after he went to Zainab's hut for the second time did they depart. Stern relates that the reason for this *Hadith*'s wide circulation is probably that Anas Ibn Malik lived till the year 90 AH or later, and thus came into contact with a generation that was unknown to many of the other Companions. This *Hadith* is told only on his authority, although it was transmitted by many well-known authorities. There are other Traditions that give alternative explanations for this ordinance. For instance, it is related that the hand of 'Umar (Prophet Muhammad's Companion) touched the hand of one of Prophet Muhammad's wives during a meal, and the *hijab* was then prescribed. According to another tradition, given on 'Aisha's authority, she and Saudah went out at night and the latter, being a tall woman, was recognized by 'Umar, who called out to her. As mentioned earlier, the ordinance is said to have been revealed at the time of Prophet Muhammad's marriage to Zainab bin Jahsh in the year 5 AH.

The Sura (33: 53) is ultimately about privacy of the Prophet's home and family and the special status of his wives in two ways – as Prophet's wives and as leaders with access to Islamic information and wisdom who are increasingly sought by community members. There was need to protect women's right to privacy by regulating the flow of visitors and the comport-ment of the men who entered upon the women's quarters. It is not about women's clothing. Men entering the wives' quarters are required to ask permission or enter only when invited and, even then, to talk to the Prophet's wives from behind a partition or curtain. The non-ordinary status of the Prophet's wives is evident in the passage:

> O, wives of the Prophet, you are not like other women (*Sura* 33: 31).

Other references further stress the separating aspect of *hijab*. For example, *al-hijab* is mentioned in nongendered contexts separating deity from mortals (42: 51), wrongdoers from the righteous (7: 46, 41–5), believers from un-believers (17: 45), light from darkness, and day from night (38: 32).

The *Sura* that is most subject to controversial understandings that is most cited is *Sura* 24: 31. The critical point to be made in this context is that by extracting the *ayah* number 31 out of its context in the *sura* number 24 the intended meaning is then lost. *Ayahs* 30 and 31 must both be read in sequence together. When *ayah* 31 is read in isolation it biases the reading against women, since it then implies that they are singled out for "reserve" and "restraint." The fact is that *ayah* 30, which immediately precedes it, addresses men first. The text of 24: 30 is translated below:

> Tell the believing men to lower their gaze and *conceal their genitals* ; for that is purer for them. God knoweth what *they do*.
>
> (24: 30, emphasis added).

Then *sura* 24: 31 continues on the same theme:

> And tell the believing women to lower their gaze and conceal their genitals, and not reveal their beauty, except what does show, and to draw their *khimar* over their bosoms, and not to reveal their beauty except to . . . (see page 85 and Figure 8 for the complete text and a schematic representation of the sense of the remaining text).
>
> (24: 31, emphasis added).

In terms of what the *sura* enjoins women to do, the text is clear. It does not use the term *hijab,* and it does not enjoin covering the face, and it does not use the terms *niqab* or *lithma,* which make unambiguous reference to face-masking. Rather, it mentions men first, and stresses the moral imperative of their behaving with restraint and covering their (men's) genitals. It then addresses women, and broadens the issue to their general comportment and the identification of relations sexually tabooed to them. In another passage the text states:

> O Prophet, tell thy wives and thy daughters, and the women of the believers to draw their *jilbab* close round them . . . so that they may be recognized and not molested.
>
> (33: 59)

The stress here is on the special status of the Prophet's wives. Here the reference to women's dress is confined to the *jilbab,* the long, loose garment. Again the terms *hijab* and *niqab* are not mentioned. In both passages the text uses *khimar* (head cover) and *jilbab* (body dress or cloak), and the focus of both verses is on restrained behavior and reserve in comportment, starting with men, who are enjoined to cover their genitals, as well as on the special status of the Prophet's wives and the special status of relations who are outside the pool of sexual and marital access for women.

In other words, to understand the comprehensive meaning of the *sura* both *ayah*s must be examined together and one must consider aspects of culture and society outside the single factor of gender. In addition to cultural notions of body and sexuality there are the factors of privacy, social and kinship relations, rank, and the elements of building a new community.

Stern examines the *Hadith* that was said to have been the grounds for arguing for the institution of the *hijab* and finds some credibility in the notion that certain *Hadith* did have influence on the development of this institution. In the above *sura* (33: 53) she gives two clarifications with regard to the ordinance addressed to men to talk to Prophet Muhammad's wives from behind a curtain, the first being that Muhammad had no definite plan for the seclusion of his wives at the time of this revelation, but that it was connected with annoying intrusions occurring during Zainab's wedding feast and a few other incidents.

The second, and the much better attested, is that he did have definite plans for giving his wives superior rank in the Muslim community, as is found in many ordinances. These are included in three chapters of Ibn Sa'd and must be considered alongside *Sura 53*. In these ordinances, Prophet Muhammad instructed his wives not to marry again after his death (*Sura 33: 53*), not to consider themselves to be like other women, and not to be too complaisant in their speech. They were to protect their privacy, go out only when necessary, not frivolously, and avoid exhibitionist dress resembling that of the women of the *Jahiliyya* (*Sura 33: 32*). He conferred upon each of them the title "Mother of the Believers" (*Sura 33: 6*) (Stern 1939a: 113).

The use of the veil to distinguish status and identity is quite common, but its use in Islam for this purpose must have been gradually developed and adopted, since at the time of the rise of Islam there was no substantial wealth within the emergent community of Muslims separating believers by class. Indeed, the premises underlying the *Umma* (the early Islamic community) stressed justice and the egalitarian sharing of wealth. They discouraged socioeconomic stratification or ranking by tribal identity.

The major transformation as the Islamic community developed was in the shift of loyalty and identity from tribe to faith, the basis of the *umma* (community), which included those of other related faiths with sacred books, namely Jews and Christians. As the community grew so did the challenges to the ideal.

Later references from Prophet Muhammad's life suggest that his wives began to desire material acquisitions and adopt a more leisurely and luxurious lifestyle, which became a cause of tensions with him (*Sura 33: 28–32*). Stern mentions al-Tabari as the source for the reference "that Prophet Muhammad secluded himself on account of his annoyance at his wives' request for more worldly goods" (1939a: 114). The desirability of moderation and modesty is further stressed by referring to the contrasting concept *tabarruj* (exhibitionist display of the body and flirtatious mannerisms):

> O wives of the Prophet! You are not like any other women. If you keep your duty, then be not soft of speech, lest he in whose heart is a disease aspire, but utter customary speech. And stay in your houses. Bedizen not yourselves with the bedizenment of the Time of Ignorance.
>
> (33: 32–3)

In none of these references is the word *hijab* used. When it is used elsewhere, it conveys more the sense of separation than of veiling. The three Arabic terms *khimar, jilbab,* and *tabarruj* are the ones used in the context of women's dress to stress the special status of the Prophet's wives. *Al-tabarruj* (exhibitionist display of dress, body and mannerisms) was used to describe women's public manners in the pre-Islamic "days of ignorance." The phrase stands in contrast with *al-tahajjub* (reserve in dress and manners), a term that derives from the same root as *hijab*. What did the term *hijab* mean in this particular revelation?

Hijab is derived from the root *h-j-b*; its verbal form *hajaba* translates as "to veil, to seclude, to screen, to conceal, to form a separation, to mask." *Hijab* translates as "cover, wrap, curtain, veil, screen, partition." The same word refers to amulets carried on one's person (particularly as a child) to protect against harm. Another derivative, *hajib*, means "eyebrow" (protector of the eye) and was also the word used during the caliphal periods for the official who screened applicants who wished for audience with the caliph. The European term "veil" (with its correlate "seclusion"), therefore, fails to capture these nuances, and oversimplifies a complex phenomenon. A closely related concept is *satr* (s-t-r), discussed above in Chapter 5. Furthermore, "veil" as commonly used gives the illusion of having a single referent, whereas it ambiguously refers at various times to a face cover for women, a transparent head cover, and an elaborate headdress. Limiting its reference obscures historical developments, cultural differentiations of social context, class, or special rank, and sociopolitical articulations. In Western feminist discourse "veil" is politically charged with connotations of the inferior "other," implying and assuming a subordination and inferiority of the Muslim woman.

Evidence from its usage in the *Qur'an* and from early Islamic feminist discourse, as well as anthropological analysis, supports the notion of *hijab* in Islam as referring to a sacred divide or separation between two worlds or two spaces: deity and mortals, good and evil, light and dark, believers and nonbelievers, or aristocracy and commoners. The phrase *min wara' al-hijab* (from behind the *hijab*) emphasizes the element of separation/partition, not, as is commonly proposed and frequently assumed, women's seclusion. Abu-Lughod asserts that "veiling is that which covers sexual shame [and that it] communicates deference, but its vocabulary is that of sexuality or chastity" (1986: 159). This is invalidated by the analysis of both ethnography and sacred Islamic text. When the reference is to women's dress, the pertinent meaning combines sanctity, reserve, and privacy.

Part 3

The Resistance of the Veil

10

Reactions to the New Trend

In the mid-seventies a phenomenon became noticeable in the streets of Cairo, Egypt that seemed incomprehensible to many observers of the Egyptian scene and bewildering even to the local people. This was the strong, visible and growing presence of a new Egyptian woman, with an appearance unfamiliar to contemporary urban Egypt and to her own parents. The new woman was a young urban college student completely "veiled" from head to toe, including the face. Confused at the thought of a future "veiled" doctor, engineer or pharmacist, many observers speculated as to the cause of this development. Was this an identity crisis, *our* version of America's hippie movement, a fad, youth protest, or ideological vacuum? An individual psychic disturbance, life-crisis, social dislocation, or protest against authority?

A rather trivial response to the contemporary veiling came from radical secularists, who ridiculed the trend using exclusivist, materialist language: "these women are covering their hair because they can't afford to go to the hairdresser!" Or "they are veiling to hide their ugliness." A common lay reaction was expressed in class/lifestyle terms: "students of peasant background coping with the big city" (for more responses see Williams 1979, 1980). Another response to the new trend was to attack the veiled women's morality: *they* are veiling to cover illicit sexual relations and immoral behavior. The irony of this latter observation is in how it exactly reproduces European women's attacks in the late nineteenth century in Egypt on the morality of prominent Egyptian women feminists such as the leading aristocratic feminist Huda Sha'rawi herself.

In her memoirs, Sha'rawi writes of the Frenchwoman Eugenie Le Brun, the first wife of Husain Rushdi Pasha. Mme Rushdi befriended Huda and became her confidante and mentor. One day Mme Rushdi told Huda, according to Sha'rawi's memoirs, that there had been some gossip about Huda that she had left her husband in order to find a younger man, because *"many secrets were hidden behind the veil "* and that Egyptian women, unlike European women,[146] who did things in the open, *"camouflage disreputable deeds behind a mask "* (Shaarawi 1987: 86–7, emphasis mine). Today, secularists, elitists and feminists are reproducing the same colonial accusations, but are now directing them at women who voluntarily choose a different appearance by adopting an Islamic identity.

Egyptian social scientists repetitiously claim social "class" to be the factor accounting for the Islamic trend – dispossession among youth of a rural background or from families of a rural background recently migrating to urban centers and turning to religion for solace or to erase class origins (Dessouki 1982). The first empirical study conducted by Egyptian social scientists[147] showed connections with variables of social background, parents' education, and type of employment, etc. (Radwan 1982). A sociologist on the project conducted interviews in prison with members of a fringe Islamic cult group arrested by the government. On the basis of these interviews observations were published about the various concrete Islamic groups, again with the emphasis on class background (Ibrahim 1980, 1982). Two primary factors were proposed: shock from a city lifestyle and socioeconomic dislocation and dispossession among the rising middle class.

First, there is tautology in such claims – the variable is both cause and effect. Secondly, to provide perspective for such observations we need to determine the proportion of Islamic activists with a rural background to Egyptians with a rural background in general. Also needed is the proportion of Egyptians who are of rural background and are recent migrants to urban centers who are not Islamic activists. The inclusion of these inquiries will probably challenge the initial observations made in these early studies.[148]

My field-based ethnographic study of this trend revealed certain patterns: Men and women are activists and initiators; activists were predominantly college-level youth; these college students were among the highest achievers; they tended to major in the professional subjects of human medicine, veterinary medicine, dentistry, engineering, and pharmaceutics – all requiring high scores ranging between 95per cent to 97 per cent by national competition (El Guindi 1981a, 1982a, 1983). The subsequent study by the National Center in Egypt confirmed the above observations (Radwan 1982). Ethnographic evidence shows that the factor of social class or rural/urban background cannot adequately account for a trend of such import. In addition to circularity of reasoning (youth turned activists because they are X, youth are X because they are activists) local sociological factors are insufficient to explain the phenomenon, which has been shown to be the outcome of an interplay of factors that include equally both regional and global developments.

Veiling, which is the most visible aspect of the trend, has been steadily spreading, and has penetrated not only the rising middle classes, but also the most exclusive environments, from the Gezira Club to the American University in Cairo, gradually reaching all sectors of urban society by the end of the 1980s. My own observations show Islam in its ordinary non-revivalist form as integral to most Muslim people's lives, outlooks, attitudes and behaviors (El Guindi 1997). Indeed, its revival has captured a strong hold on many people.[149]

Attempts at accounting for the phenomenon of the veiling that has emerged in the 1970s vary in approach and conclusions. MacLeod (1993) focused her study on eighty-five women from various neighborhoods of "lower-middle-class" women in Cairo, many of whom held clerical jobs. She formulates an argument about a double bind to describe the adoption of Islamic veiling among them. Her argument is that women from this sector need to work, for economic reasons, but that gender ideology (which she equates with an overarching gender construct) opposes work, thus posing a conflict for these women. Veiling reflects this dilemma, but is also the solution to it, as it allows them to work while they still claim traditional respect. Finally, a Western feminist argument is made that the veiling is not really going to liberate them, because it is "dangerous and double-edged," and hence the protest quality in veiling is lost, since by adopting traditional identities they are reproducing inequality.

There are problems with this argument and how it is made; that is, there are methodological flaws and there are doubts about the asserted content of the gender and work ideology. In general, conflict and stress deriving from the fact that women combine two jobs (the home and family and public work) is not unique to Cairo's lower middle class, and has been a focus of discussion in the United States, referred to these as "the latch-key problem." American working women did not resort to veiling to resolve the conflict. They began to "impose" equality in domestic work on men. No satisfactory solution has been found. It is temporarily solved by assistance from childcare facilities and from the cheap labor provided by other women (the legal and illegal workers from developing countries or needy immigrant women). Nor do we have to dig deep into gender constructs to identify the conflict.

Furthermore, while MacLeod narrowly focuses her pool of evidence down to a small representation of one sector of society any suggestions to account for so pervasive a phenomenon such as Islamic veiling derived from it cannot be adequate, since it cannot explain why women from other sectors also adopt Islamic veiling. Why have women from the higher strata, who are under no pressure to work, also adopted the *hijab*? This Islamic trend is a sweeping phenomenon entering its third decade, and has gradually and proportionally included middle- and upper-middle-class women, working and nonworking women.

There is a problem also when an Islamic movement is reduced to women's veiling. What about the men in the movement? They too adopted different dress. How will this double bind for women explain men's participation in the movement and adoption of its moral and dress code?

MacLeod dismisses the factor of Islamic revival in favor of the economic factor. The basis given for this dismissal is the fact that the women interviewed did not state revival as a factor behind their adoption of veiling. Here we have a methodological problem whereby "local knowledge" is confused with analysis, and conversational comments are taken for explanations.

Another problem with the notion of a "double bind" derives from its assumption of "distress" that is purported to be caused by a general cultural ethos that results in a new dress code. Numerically, the women who adopted the veil constitute a small number relative to the population at large. There is incongruity in explaining a "small," though significant, trend by a pervasive cultural ethos. The phenomenon is much more complex and is a consequence of local, regional and global factors, and the interplay of cultural, social and economic realities.

Let us situate gender ideology and work in social and cultural context. In Arab culture identification with the family and kin group is the bedrock of an individual's identity. And this is true for both sexes. This premise is reflected in the naming patterns for men and women, for example. The last names of families, whether commoner or ruling elite families, are often preceded by 'al-' (meaning "belonging to the family of"), as in the al-Khalifa ruling family in Bahrain, the al-Sabbah in Kuwait, or the al-Saud in Saudi Arabia. Another usage used for affiliation is *bin, bani,* or *awlad* (variants of words meaning "offspring of"). This naming practice both reflects and reinforces an individual's identity, not as an autonomous individual as in American culture, but as a member of a kin group. Furthermore, name patriliny applies equally to men and women – a woman, like her brother, keeps her maiden name irrespective of marital affiliation. Officially there is no name change for women after marriage. She is identified with her natal kin for life. In contrast, among Greeks "a woman's surname . . . is always given in the genitive (possessive) case: . . . 'Mr Black, Black's Mrs'. This applies equally to her maiden name, so that she is her father's; i.e. 'Smith's Miss' . . ." (Hirschon 1993: 71, n. 5).

Because this is a culture that recognizes the family as vital to society and of primary relevance to individual lives, it entrusts individuals with protecting their families. Relatives are collectively in charge of building and guarding its reputation. Family reputation is of primary concern to both sexes in Arab societies.[150] It is relational – the responsibility to build and guard it is interdependently held by kin and across gender. They carefully and complementarily cultivate it. It functions as the glue that keeps individual members connected and as a social barometer that measures a family's public behavior.

Its importance among traditional groups is demonstrated in ethnography.

For example, among the Rwala bedouins of the Syria–Jordan–Arabia region studied by William Lancaster (1981), reputation derives from daily and ritual demonstrations of honorability, mediation skills, courage, generosity and hospitality (1981: 43–5). Among the Rashayda bedouins of the Sudan studied by William Young (1996), a woman's reputation is woven skillfully into tents and veils. The highly skilled among them are publicly rewarded. A woman is the guardian (or shepherd) of the tent, or *ra'iyat al-bayt*. Her reputation is central to the group's public identity. The centrality of the women in Arab groups is further substantiated in the study on rural and urban Lebanon by Michael Gilsenan (1982). If women are central to a family's sacred identity it follows that they would be central to its reputation.

Whether in bedouin, rural or urban communities a narrow circle among the many relatives share more directly both benefits and risks from family reputation. To uphold this major cultural trust, relatives give support and hold controls over individual members. In terms of gender, male relatives are obligated by Arab tradition and Islamic law to provide a woman with tangible and intangible forms of support and security irrespective of her marital or financial status. It is in the context of the customary and legal obligations of men to women that the asymmetry in the Islamic law of inheritance must be understood. According to Islam, a man's share in inheritance is twice that of his sister. But he is also under a binding obligation to support financially her, his wife, his daughter, his mother, and any other dependent female relative, as well as the elderly males.[151] In Islam, the woman is a lifetime beneficiary, and she is under no similar obligation. In theory, and under the protection of the law, a woman is guaranteed the equivalent of a package of modern institutionalized plans: lifetime income, insurance, pension, retirement, unemployment, and disability.

The quality of support is also part of this obligation. The husband is required to maintain the standard of living his wife was accustomed to in her father's home, which may include an obligation to provide domestic help, child care, or even (as was more common in the past) a wet nurse, should the wife so desire. If it is not consistent with her premarital lifestyle and status, she may neither be required to perform domestic labor nor even to nurse her own babies. Rather, upon marriage she becomes *Sitt el-bait*, or the lady of the house – a term that corresponds more accurately to her role as head manager of the household, and represents a different notion from that of "housewife" in the West (see Rassam 1980).

Extending the premise further, this guarantee of male support and financial responsibility can, and often does, prevent a woman from *needing* to work for wages. A crucial economic stimulus is removed for those who can afford it, and employment becomes optional. Naturally, for the wealthy there is no need to work for wages. Poor women (and men) need to work for a livelihood, and are therefore not bound by the cultural constraints. However, the local population in the traditional urban sectors (the local neighborhoods made famous by Nobel Laureate Egyptian novelist Naguib Mahfuz and known for their folk men, and particularly women, known as *banat al-balad*) [152] still shares the same general cultural ideal.

In an ethnographic study of these women in Cairo, Sawsan el-Messiri describes the *bint al-balad* (sing. "folk woman"), her strong sense of self and the kind of work she engages in. In a case study described by el-Messiri there appears a typical *bint al-balad* who has been working as a butcher for the past twenty-five years, "independently of her husband. She supervises all activities in her own butcher shop five days a week, from early morning to late at night. She tends to her customers, directs her apprentices, and helps them to cut up meat when the shop is crowded" (1978: 527). Women like her tend to be wealthy, but are proud to live in these local alleys, disdaining both rural life and the urban aristocratic lifestyle. El-Messiri describes her as extremely coquettish in manner, typically strong, and reputed to have high status in the community. Not any job is accepted. Domestic service is looked down upon, and women working as domestic servants conceal the fact and try to work far away from their local neighborhoods. Local women also look down on the government and clerical jobs that younger women are increasingly taking for not being worth (in terms of their low pay and regular hours) the indignity of leaving one's home and family. Baladi women have similar concerns about reputation to those of middle- and upper-class women. Their behavior must accord with local expectations, and they view support of the family as the full responsibility of the husband and part of his identity as a man. "Husbands who insist that their wives work are looked down upon" (el-Messiri 1978: 536).

The stigma is not so much from work as from being unprotected by a family that can afford to support its members but doesn't. The stigma attaching to working for wages derives from the cultural interpretation that kinsmen are either unable or unwilling to support their women and fail to meet their obligations. There is a preference for avoiding culturally devalued work or employment held in low esteem. In ideal terms, the family prefers to protect a woman from employment in which she is subordinate, or in which a superior has power over her. In other words, there is no objection to employment in which the woman is in a superior position (see Forget 1962). Self-employment is desirable. Consistently with this, we find that Egyptian women of all classes have had a long history of owning and managing valued property (see Sayyid-Marsot 1995).

Traditionally, elite women all over the modern Arab East performed public social services on a volunteer basis. They worked indefatigably in charities and participated in feminist and nationalist struggles. In contrast to wage employment, voluntary work by women was not disapproved of. The early feminist movement of 1919 in Egypt was run by a group of such gentlewomen (Marsot 1978; Badran 1995a). It was not in the too distant past in the Arab East that the support jobs usually associated with females in industrial societies, such as secretary, typist, and nurse, were exclusively male or foreign women's jobs. Middle-class and wealthy families discouraged their women from having such jobs (Youssef 1974). Since the 1960s local women in the less wealthy Arab countries such as Egypt have filled these jobs. But in affluent Arab countries change is not yet significant. No observer traveling on a Gulf Arab airline will have failed to notice the absence of native women stewardesses. Either all-male stewards or foreign (mostly European) stewardesses occupy these positions on the airlines of wealthy Gulf countries.

A study using qualitative and quantitative data for patterns of women's employment and education that compares Egypt, a country in which women need to work, and Bahrain, a wealthy country in which this need is absent, shows that Arab culture does not oppose work for women *per se*, but rather indignity to women, as culturally and even subculturally defined. Work that does not subject women to indignity is not opposed – a factor that tends to push women to higher education and higher positions to escape subordination (El Guindi 1985b, 1986b). In Bahrain and other wealthy Arab countries domestic and unskilled jobs are generally filled by imported labor. The idea of stigma from paid employment and the goal of protecting women from subordinate positions and low-status jobs are key factors leading to low rates of employment for Arab women. These factors were evident for decades in the oil-rich Arab countries, where kinsmen can afford to pay the price of protectiveness, and do.

Contemporary Egyptian feminists recognize that, despite achievements "the idea of women working remained linked with poverty and necessity, or at least with a lack of means of financial security" (Sa'id 1977: 388). The major shift in attitude toward employment in Egypt occurred after the 1952 revolution, when work for women of all strata gradually lost its stigma and was seen more as a national duty. Current economic and population pressures in Egypt make it difficult to sustain older patterns. With its population size expanding exponentially Egypt cannot afford the luxury of protecting women.

MacLeod's argument that working-class women adopted veiling because they are in a double bind from a gender ideology that opposes work does not hold. Poor women have always worked, and society accepts that. But until the end of the 1970s they had not adopted the *hijab* in order to work. Why would the double bind begin to apply only after the 1970s?

The common reaction to this Islamic revival, whether by men of religion (the learned men of al-Azhar, or the *'Ulama),* university professors, the rest of the population, the press, or social scientists, was to look at the trend as a "problem." Other observers denied its significance altogether, or provided simplistic reasons and proposed facile solutions. Al-Azhar[153] is the millennium-old Islamic mosque-university built in 970 in the heart of premodern Cairo as a center for Islamic learning and authority. Although the guardian of Islam, it initially faced the new trend with silence, presumably because it was put in a bind by the populist movement. Islamic reform is enjoined by the authorities of al-Azhar down to the people, not, as in this case, the other way around. Moreover, al-Azhar was in no position to object to a dress and a code rooted in Islamic notions of modesty.

Especially confused, ambivalent and disturbed were the parents of this new woman. They wondered: where did we go wrong? Our daughter is not married yet; who will marry her now that she is hidden under a "tent"? After the long struggle by the founding feminists of Egypt (Q. Amin 1976 (1900); Badran 1995a; Nasif 1909, 1962; Nelson 1996; Sha'rawi 1981), and the successful lifting of the traditional face veil at the turn of the century, it simply did not make sense for young educated college women half a century later to *voluntarily* return to the *veil.*

But of course they did not (Williams 1979). This is neither a return to an early veil nor a return to an early Islamic community. It was not the same veil or the same woman or the same community. The "New Woman" of Qasim Amin's Egypt in 1900 (Amin 1976 [1900]) was not the new woman of contemporary Egypt in 1975 (El Guindi 1981a).[154] The contemporary college woman adopting a conservative appearance and demeanor continued to be active and visible in mainstream society, competitively enrolled in higher education, majoring in "nonsoft" professional fields, asserting her Muslim identity, career-oriented, modern and veiled.

Veiling by college women, which many had dismissed as a temporary fad, turned out to be a strong, resilient social and political movement. Though perhaps begun by women, the trend developed and grew among women and men who had a strong message to communicate. Dress embodied a sociomoral code and served as a central vehicle for this message. To understand this message contexts in which veiling developed are discussed. In these contexts local, regional, and global factors interplay as men and women (of Algeria, Egypt, Palestine, and Iran) struggle for independence from colonial control or the colonial legacy and women strive for emancipation.

11

Contexts of Resistance

Algeria's Struggle for Independence

A "historic dynamism of the veil" (Fanon's phrase) was dramatically played out in Algeria's struggle for independence. Fanon wrote: "The veil helped the Algerian woman to meet the new problems created by the struggle" (1967: 63). The role of the veil in liberating Algeria from French colonial occupation is popularly known, idealized, romanticized, ideologized, and fictionalized, but nonetheless real. When the French landed in Algeria in 1830 most inhabitants were Arabic-speaking Sunni Muslims (following the Malikite school of law). Inhabitants included the large Berber population (indigenous to Africa) and later descendants of the first wave of Arabs entering Algeria in the eighth century and then again of another wave in the eleventh century.

The gallicization of Algeria began on several fronts. French law was imposed on Islamic law, and from the beginning penal matters came under French law (Gordon 1968: 37). A French social plan was imposed on local custom (Gordon 1968). "Denied identity and representation, the approximately 10,000,000 Algerians – who were called the 'Muslims' – found themselves forbidden by law to study their language, Arabic, in the public schools" (Minces 1978: 160). Most teaching was about the history and geography of France. Algerian children in the countryside did not attend school at all (Minces 1978: 160). As Harlow puts it, the French conquest of Algeria that began in 1830 "was less a conquest than a deformation of the social order" (1986: xiii).

In the economic sphere there was a similar dispossession. The Europeans colonialists (known as the *colons*) had monopolized the best land and, exploiting Algerian labor, cultivated crops Algerians do not consume – for example, vineyards for making wine. French settlers dominated Algeria and kept Muslim Algerians at a distance, excluded from education and desirable employment (Gordon 1968: 36–58). They held positions as public functionaries, all the higher administrative posts, all positions in the tertiary sector and the overwhelming majority of subordinate posts (Minces 1978: 161).

"Administratively, Algeria was France, but it was a France populated by a majority of second-class citizens" (Minces 1978: 160), while all the political weight was held by the 10 per cent who were European colonizers (Minces 1978: 160). This occupation was not a simple picture of an imposed apartheid, but rather one of a total appropriation of Algerian resources and an absolute denial of a people and their culture.

To make this take-over complete another front was activated. In the late 1800s the Church and the White Fathers engaged in aggressive missionary proselytizing. However, this failed completely (Gordon 1968: 38–9). In Algeria, as in the rest of the Arab world, missionary Christianity could not replace Islam. And during the years 1930–1935 Algerian nationalist movements were beginning to take shape. The French administration began to strike at any anti-French impulse, largely by taking measures to undermine Algerian culture.

Another strategy was to assimilate upper-class Algerians by gallicizing the Algerian woman. The underlying premise is that were the woman to become uprooted from her culture the rest would follow. The veil became the target of the colonial strategy to control and uproot – to persuade the Muslim woman to unveil. The occupier was bent on unveiling Algeria. Fanon described the unveiling ceremony in May 1958, which was accompanied by cries of "Vive l'Algérie Française" (long live French Algeria), "as a theatrical performance involving only some intimidated prostitutes and maids" (1967: 59). Women's organizations were encouraged and supported. "Algerian men were made to feel guilty about having veiled wives . . . scorn was shown to French-educated Muslim professionals who kept their wives in seclusion, and teachers in class encouraged their students to unveil" (1967: 58). It can be argued that those measures were intended to modernize Algeria to match the colonists' taste; but Algerians, as do all nationalist Arabs, considered them tactics to undermine cultural roots. Algerians saw among settler Europeans a hidden desire to rape, literally and figuratively. The European woman who first encouraged Algerian women to unveil now looked down on the *evoluée* (the modernized evolved Algerian woman of her making) now as a loose woman.

Such tactics led Arabs to link the deveiling of Muslim women with a colonial strategy to undermine and destroy the culture (see Fanon 1967). The effect was the opposite of that intended by the French – it strengthened the attachment to the veil as a national and cultural symbol on the part of patriotic Algerian women, giving the veil a new vitality.

According to reports by the Algerian journalist Mouloud Feraoun posthumously published in his *Journal* after his assassination by the French Secret Army Organization (OAS), and summarized in Gordon (1968), the French assault on Algeria's women was devastating: "a contingent of French soldiers . . . [arrived at] a village one night . . . [and] the following day twelve women admitted they had been raped. At another village French soldiers behaved for three nights as if they were in a bordello. . . . attractive women were forced to sleep with French soldiers. One woman was forced to see her daughter and her daughter-in-law raped before her eyes" (1968: 52). According to the testimony of women in one village attacked by hundreds of French soldiers: "the men and women were grouped separately, but in one place an old man of seventy five was forced to dance naked in front of them. They were ordered to beat time, applaud, and cry out 'Vive la France'. Women who tried to hide their faces out of shame had their shawls ripped from their faces" (Gordon 1968: 53).

Rape is an ultimate violation designed to break Muslims by dishonoring their families and humiliating Muslim men. This was demonstrated in recent conflicts when Serbs attacked Muslim Bosnians. In traditional Arab culture, the family is the center around which the sociomoral universe exists. Women are the center of the family's sacred identity and the guardians of the Arab family's honor and reputation. Motherhood is considered sacred. Nationhood is expressed in "motherland" terms. The Arabic words for women, household and sacred sanctity are close derivatives of the same root. To undermine or attack the Muslim woman destabilizes the core of the sociomoral system. The Arab-Islamic judicial system long recognized rape as a serious crime that received capital punishment – at a time when rape in America was considered sex, not crime. That is precisely why those at war with Muslims and trying to break them choose the path of raping and killing Muslim women. A cultural strength, Islam's placing women at the heart of sacredness, is turned into a grave human rights violation in times of conflict and crisis. These are not random acts. They are systematic, racist and sexist and they violate international human rights (El Guindi 1998b).

When the OAS decided to abandon their policy of shooting only men, Henry Tanner of the *New York Times* wrote in his dispatch: "European terrorist gunmen opened fire on Muslim women in the streets of Algiers. . . . A veiled woman was shot dead this morning on her way to work . . . In all five attacks on women the gunmen deliberately chose their victims" (*New York Times*, 7 May 1962, as quoted in Gordon 1968: 53).

On 1 November 1954 a handful of little-known men solidly but clandestinely based in their home regions launched the insurrection. The peasant population supported the movement and the National Liberation Front (FLN) was born (Minces 1978: 161). By 1956 "a revolt by a relatively small number had turned into a national revolution" (Gordon 1968: 51) in which women, instead of dwelling on being victims, played a significant role that captured the imagination of the world. They were nurses, food providers, weapon concealers, and heroines in combat action, and suffered persecution and torture. Gordon describes the Algerian woman of the resistance this way: "scenes . . . of black-robed women fleeing razed villages; serving as nurses and even combatants with the FLN (National Liberation Front) . . . hiding [Algerian fighters] in cellars of the Casbah; . . . sitting in European dress at fashionable cafés with bombs in their handbags; suffering torture at the hands of French soldiers; marching in demonstrations, [ululating] and crying 'Algérie musulmane' [Muslim Algeria] during de Gaulle's tour of Algeria in 1958; . . . brutally shot down in the streets of Algiers in the last desperate days of the OAS (the secret army organization that sought through terror to delay Algerian independence); and, of course, just waiting in detention camps . . . and in refugee camps" (1968: 51; for more on the history see Abu-Nasr 1975; Berque 1967; Gordon 1962; Laroui 1977; Lucas and Vatin 1975).

Hal Lehrman of the *New York Times Magazine* described how the veil played a central role, calling it the "Battle of the Veil" (13 July 1958: 14–18). The veil again was at the center of the struggle against occupation and the center of traditional culture, a symbol of both resistance and tradition. The French occupation attacked it. The Algerian woman clung to it – a symbol of indigenous tradition and culture in the face of the colonial encounter. The veil won and Algeria was liberated. The French sociologist Pierre Bourdieu was partly right when he stated that "traditional traditionalism" was destroyed for many women by the revolution. So was Fanon, when he wrote that the veil lost its "purely traditional dimension."

This is so because the veil is a complex symbol of many meanings. Emancipation can be expressed by wearing the veil or by removing it. It can be secular or religious. It can represent tradition or resistance. Today Algeria is still liberating itself from the legacy of a long and brutal French dominance and occupation.[155] Alloula examines the French imagery of Algeria not only as a subject, but to use Barthes's phrase, "as a wound" (1982: 74). In interpreting the colonial postcards on Algeria, Alloula exposes thirty years of French colonial presence and its distorting effects on Algerian society (Harlow 1986: xiii) through the photographer's studio and the native models who re-enact exotic rituals in costumes, hence representing the French fantasy of the Oriental female and her inaccessibility. The postcards of exotic Arab women sent to the "mother countries ever hungry for raw materials" become a correlate of colonialism and domination. "Possession of Arab women came to serve as a surrogate for and means to the political and military conquest of the Arab world" (Harlow 1986: xv). And, as Alloula puts it, "I attempt . . . to return this immense postcard to its sender" (1986: 5).

By 1993, the Islamic Salvation Front had galvanized a wide and popular Algerian base of support and was expected to win elections. The Arab street, a popular and growing force of public opinion and nonmilitant resistance, had expressed desire for political change. Had the will of the people been allowed to take its course democratically, the world would have seen a different political landscape in Algeria. Instead, more than 60,000 people have reportedly died in the civil war between the government and the Islamic opposition since the voided 1993 election. In more recent developments, many innocent Algerian civilians in villages – mostly women and children – have been killed in brutal attacks blamed on Islamic groups.

The veil is now a symbol of resistance against the legacy of foreign occupation, against the contemporary occupation of Palestinian land, and against local unelected regimes, while still reaffirming Algerian tradition and identity. The struggle is ongoing. In 1998 Algeria is still liberating itself from the legacy of French colonialism, despite formal independence in 1956. In July 1998 (thirty-four years after gaining independence from France) Algeria has just established (perhaps re-established) Arabic as the official language of the land. The history of Algeria is still being written, and the veil is at the center of it.

Palestine: From *Intifada* to Islamic Resistance

The Palestinian context is another struggle, and again women's veiling is integral to it (Hammami 1990). "[B]efore the Intifada in Gaza there was wide variation in the forms and uses of the hijab worn by women of different social classes and groups . . . varying by class, regional background, religion or age" (1990: 24). According to Hammami, "since 1948 there has been a reinvention of various traditions of clothing and headcoverings" (1990: 24). She observes that older camp women in Gaza wore dress and headcovering that communicated both "their peasant origins" and "their contemporary status as camp women." The identity expressed through dress is that of class/group rather than gender. "In everyday life, camp women from both north and south wear a black cotton skirt (*da'ir*) and a white or black shawl (*shasha*). They adopted these after 1967, when materials for the traditional southern Palestinian dress were no longer available. These women . . . do not view their own dress as oppressive. Their point of reference is the older camp women" (Hammami 1990: 25, italics added).

In the late 1970s, "new Islamic movements, most notably . . . an Islamic group [that] later became Islamic Resistance Movement, or Hamas sought to . . . 'restore' the *hijab*" (1990: 25, italics added). This primarily concerned urban educated women in Gaza who were petit bourgeois and were not wearing any form of headcovering. "Women affiliated with the movement started to wear long, plain, tailored overcoats, known as *shari'a* [Islamic] dress . . . In the 1980s *Shari'a* dress proliferated in Gaza – at the workplace, within religious families or on the Islamic University campus. . . . Only during the Intifada was this social pressure transformed into an active campaign to impose the *hijab* on all women" (1990: 25).

The Islamic dress had no precedents in indigenous Palestinian dress (Seng and Wass 1995) and was introduced as a return to a more authentic Islamic tradition. Hammami describes it as "an invented tradition in both form and meaning" (1995: 25). It is a movement developing in the context of occupation and resistance, subjugation and struggle in which the *hijab* is ideologized and transformed into a symbol of resistance.

Iran's Islamic Revolution

The issue of the *hijab* in Iran must be placed in the context of the pre-Islamic regime's policies (Mir-Hosseini 1996a: 153). In his Westernizing crusade, Reza Shah banned the veil in 1936, and the police were arresting women who wore the veil and forcibly removing it. Clerics were outraged. To ordinary women "appearing in public without their cover was tantamount to nakedness" (1996a: 153). This move was welcomed by Westernized and upperclass men and women, who saw it in liberal terms as a first step in granting women their rights. "Since then, the *hejab* [*hijab*] issue has become a deep wound in Iranian politics, arousing strong emotions on all sides. It also became a major arena of conflict between the forces of modernity and Islamic authenticity, where each side has projected its own vision of morality" (Mir-Hosseini 1996a: 153).

Iran, like other areas in the Middle East, is known for sartorial variety. Differences are seen in dress from different regions, tribes, religious groups, and social classes. Chehabi (1993) observes that for men, hats were often the markers of group identity, while for women the "veil" varied according to province and social stratum. Europeanized upper-class Iranian men gradually adopted European clothing. With the Pahlavi rule, dress reform began to be imposed.

In the 1920s it was suggested that Iranian women should imitate Turkish women and replace the veil with a kerchief. There was uproar in Tehran. In 1927 dress reform for men was issued – the "Pahlavi hat," adopted from a French form, was to be the official hat for Iranian men. This was accomplished by ceremony. Then the government took on the veil issue (Chehabi 1993: 209–10). To use Mir-Hosseini's phrase, dress code in Iran is a "field of operation" (Mir-Hosseini 1996a: 143) for the State.

Eventually rules of dress code were relaxed, and after Reza Shah's abdication in 1941 the compulsory element in the policy of unveiling was abandoned, though the policy remained intact throughout the Pahlavi era. According to Mir-Hosseini "[b]etween 1941 and 1979 wearing *hejab* [*hijab*] was no longer an offence, but it was a real hindrance to climbing the social ladder, a badge of backwardness and a marker of class. A headscarf, let alone the *chador*, prejudiced the chances of advancement in work and society not only of working women but also of men, who were increasingly expected to appear with their wives at social functions. Fashionable hotels and restaurants refused to admit women with *chador*, schools and universities actively discouraged the *chador*, although the headscarf was tolerated. It was common to see girls from traditional families, who had to leave home with the *chador*, arriving at school without it and then putting it on again on the way home" (Mir-Hosseini 1996a: 153). One of the enduring legacies of Reza Shah is the problematization of dress as integral to Iranian politics (Chehabi 1993). Women's dress was placed center stage.

In the 1970s *hijab*, a symbol of virtue (see Higgins 1985), represented to the Pahlavis rejection of their rule and resistance to their forced Westernizing. Many middle-class urban working women voluntarily took up the scarf (see Betteridge 1983). In March 1979, when the intentions of the new regime became clear, these women once again took to the streets, this time to protest against the veil. It was too late. Gradually, *hijab* became compulsory. "In 1983, appearing in public unveiled became an offence, punishable by . . . up to seventy-four lashes. In 1994, there was not a single bareheaded woman to be seen in public anywhere in Iran. No woman could imagine venturing out without a head cover" (Mir-Hosseini 1996b: 153–4). Just as Reza Shah "unveiled" women before the Islamic Revolution, the Islamic Republic "veiled" women after the Revolution.

According to Chehabi, changing the dress code and Europeanizing women and men was not all there is to it: the idea was to desegregate society, to de-Islamize the system. This resulted in a catastrophic dislocation of people's lives that was not commensurate with socioeconomic progress. There was no fit between the cultural transformations and the socioeconomic reality of Iran (Chehabi 1993). In Iran, as in Ottoman Turkey (Quataert 1997; Norton 1997) and then Afghanistan, state reform seems always to focus primarily on dress reform (Baker 1997). The woman's veil is centered in the process. I agree with Mir-Hosseini that *hijab* is a powerful metaphor, capable of taking many shades of meaning and performing many functions. The enforcement of *hijab* can be as empowering as its ban. While it undoubtedly restricts some women, it emancipates others by legitimizing their presence in public life.

As elsewhere in the Islamic East, the current form of *hijab* is largely an urban phenomenon – for educated and working women, a populist anti-Western symbol. "Many women today owe their jobs, their economic autonomy, and their public persona, to compulsory *hejab* [*hijab*]. There are women who have found in [it] a sense of worth and a moral high ground, especially ... [in a social climate that] was self-consciously obsessed with the display of wealth" (Mir-hosseini 1996b: 156). "In a bizarre way *hejab* has even empowered those whom it was meant to restrain: Westernized middle-class women" (1996b: 157).

The battle began when Islamic groups politicized their agenda after gaining a large popular base of support. They demanded a change to Islamic values and a rejection of Western dominance. Battles were bloody in Egypt, and continue to be in Algeria. The veil pales in this climate. But it is there to communicate its message of silent resistance to forces governments have become passive about.

Veiling and Feminism

12

The Egyptian feminist movement at the turn of the century was described as a secular movement that "brought together Muslim and Christian women of the upper and middle classes[156] who identified [themselves] as Egyptians" (Badran 1995b: 45). Leila Ahmed does not see it in such monolithic terms. In a discussion linking Western colonialism and feminism, Ahmed distinguishes two strands of feminism represented by Egypt's "First Feminists" (1992: 169–88). There is the Westward-looking feminism espoused by Huda Sha'rawi (1879–1947)[157] and another, advocated by Malak Hifni Nasif (1886–1918),[158] that did not affiliate itself with Westernization.

Groundedness of feminists in their own culture has been largely overlooked in the discourse on feminism.[159] Fundamental to a genuine Arabo-Islamic society are mastery of the Arabic language (formal not colloquial) and access to Islamic knowledge. Huda Sha'rawi[160] admitted: "I memorized (*khatamt*) the Qur'an and everyone around me thought I mastered the Arabic language and Islam, whereas in fact I could not read Arabic, other than the Qur'an, and did not know any Islamic knowledge other than how to cleanse, pray and fast" (1981: 44; see also Fernea and Bezirgan 1977).

This had not always been the case in Egypt. Sayyid-Marsot mentions that in the eighteenth century the larger mass of both sexes were illiterate, but "[a]mong the elites both men and women were literate in religion and in language . . . [and] the *ulama* [male religious scholars] and *alimat* [female religious scholars] were more educated than any other sector of society" (1995: 14–15, italics added). Colonial and missionary pressures at the turn of the century as well as consumerist and secularizing trends in the twentieth century led women away from rights they already had in Islam – most importantly the right (with precedents in Islam) to full participation in the Islamic process, teaching, and worship. By submitting to these distancing trends, women excluded themselves from the two most relevant spheres (the Arabic language and Islamic studies) that most crucially regulate and sanction their lives, engender dignity and respect, and legitimize their rights and privileges. These became dominated by men.

As early as the 1870s and 1880s, before Egyptian organized feminism developed, Egyptian women were publishing their writings and were engaged

177

in public speaking. Women had already begun to debate their position on these issues when men, in search of factors behind the demise of their country, began questioning existing social practices with regard to gender and formulated what many considered to be feminist positions in the process. These men were highly educated, had legal training, and had been exposed to European thought. Consequently, a men's discourse on women's issues (questionably characterized as feminist) emerged in the Arab world (Badran 1995a: 13–16). Unlike its position in women's organized feminism, the veil was central to men's "feminist" discourse. Women were drawn into the debate, and popular periodicals became partisan publications. Three periodicals[161] were "staunch defenders of the veil . . . [and two][162] condemned the veil . . . Muslims, Jews, and Christians . . . all wrestled with the question of veiling" (Baron 1989: 372, 379).

A prominent Egyptian man who provoked heated controversy and debate was Qasim Amin, who came to be regarded by many as the founder of feminism in Arab culture. The response to his book *Tahrir Al-Mar'a (The Liberation of Woman)*, published in 1899, was intense, and opposition to its message was vociferous. A closer look reveals that Amin called not for feminist reforms but rather for a fundamental social and cultural change for Egypt and other Muslim countries, a Europeanization of Arab culture as it were, in which women's issues were embedded. Central to this reform, proposed as key to change and progress in society, was the call for abolishing the veil.

Tal'at Harb, a wealthy Egyptian industrialist entrepreneur who pioneered modern banking in Egypt, responded strongly to Amin (see Harb 1899 [1905], 1901). As Ahmed (L. Ahmed 1992) puts it: "In the course of making his argument, Amin managed to express . . . a generalized contempt for Muslims . . . often in lavishly abusive detail" (1992: 156).

Veiling was not a practice confined to Muslims; it was an urban phenomenon associated mostly with the upper classes. The Coptic intellectual Salama Musa noted in his memoirs that his mother and two married sisters wore the long veil until about 1907 or 1908, and that it was from missionary influence that Christian women began to drop the practice. Also Qasim Amin's wife continued to wear the veil. He tried to enforce unveiling on his daughters against efforts to the contrary from his own uncle.[163]

Both Amin and Harb claimed to be concerned with women's liberation. They differed in their frameworks, but reached similar conclusions. One exception is the veil. Harb's women must veil, and Amin's must unveil. The argument between Harb and Amin was not, as it is commonly characterized, feminist versus antifeminist,[164] but rather between two muddled versions of domesticity, a Western female domesticity versus an indigenous man's vision of female domesticity. Islam was not in any serious way the ideological basis for either position.[165] Contradictions abound in both. In appropriating a women's issue, men polarized discourse surrounding the veil.

By 1910 sensitivity toward the nuances of veiling and unveiling was established. The newspaper *al-'Afaf* began publication in Cairo in 1910 "proclaiming itself the mouthpiece of women" (Baron 1989: 370). In the twenty-sixth issue of its first volume it uses as a frontispiece a drawing of a woman standing in front of the pyramids and the sphinx, holding her arm aloft with a banner "modesty is my motto." Across her face she wore a light, translucent veil. The mouth and nose were revealed through the transparent fabric and the eyes were not covered. Baron (1989: 28) notes that the paper was criticized (see *al-'Afaf* 1911: 1)[166] and that three issues later the image was revised. The redrawn veil was thick and nontransparent, and the nose, face and chin were not revealed through it. Revealed, however, are the complex subtleties entailed in the reaction to this visual imagery of the veil and womanhood.

Interestingly, removing the veil was not part of the official feminist agenda at the time. According to Badran, unveiling, which had been of concern only to urban women, "had never been part of the EFU's (Egyptian Feminist Union's) formal agenda" (1995a: 94–6). The phrase used in the discourse surrounding the context of lifting the "veil" was *raf' al-higab* (the lifting of the *hijab*). Ironically, what secular feminists lifted was the traditional face veil (*burqu'*), which is rooted in cultural tradition and history rather than in Islamic sources, not the *hijab*. In her speech at the Feminist conference in Rome, Sha'rawi specified the face-veil (*burqu'* or *yashmik*), not the *hijab*, as a barrier to women's advancement (253, 254; see Kahf 1998). When Huda Sha'rawi dramatically cast off the veil in 1923, it was the face-veil she removed, not the *hijab*. Further, the act mirrored a change already taking place, as the debate over the issue of veiling and unveiling shows.

It is not trivial that Huda Sha'rawi only removed the face-cover (*burqu'* or *yashmik*), but kept the head-cover. Technically, therefore, Sha'rawi never "lifted the *hijab*." Some attribute her success in feminist nationalist leadership, compared to Doria Shafiq (1914–1976)[167] for example, to the fact that she respected tradition and remained *muhajjaba*. In her *Memoirs* there is a section in which she mentions being congratulated for "my success in arriving at lifting the *hijab* . . . but wearing the *hijab shar'i* (the lawful *hijab* – used specifically to mean the Islamic *hijab*) (Sha'rawi 1981: 291). The distinction made is important, and becomes central to the debate on contemporary veiling.

Sha'rawi lifted the traditional customary veil, and wore the *hijab* in a manner that finds support in Islamic sources.[168] Significantly, she was decorated with the state's highest honor, *Nishan al-Kamal* (the Medal of Perfection).

Badran (1995a) describes how in the first two decades of the twentieth century feminist women like Huda Sha'rawi and Malak Hifni Nasif (Bahithat al-Badiya) retained the veil because "uncovering the face was premature [and] society was not ready for it" (Badran 1995a: 22, 23).

Of the early feminists, Nabawiyya Musa, the first college graduate and the one who was not from the aristocracy, removed her face-cover unceremonially around 1909. "Bahithat al-Badiya died in 1918 without having unveiled" (Badran 1995a: 23). The comment by Nasif that after social change "I would approve of unveiling *for those who want it*" (Nasif 1962: 275–9, emphasis added) confirms, contrary to falsely publicized claims, the tolerant stance of early twentieth-century Egyptian feminism with regard to veiling. It also brings out an element in Nasif's feminism absent in other programs – choice by women.

Huda Sha'rawi unveiled ceremonially in a public political feminist act in 1923 upon returning from a feminist meeting in Rome – an act of far-reaching symbolic significance.[169] Its impact and ripple effect was felt beyond her narrow circle of the elite.[170] The gesture has entered the lore on women's liberation and, as lore, is alive and is continually embellished. Evidence in photographs and reports reveals how girls had begun to appear unveiled in schools,[171] in the streets,[172] and in protests[173] between 1910 and 1919 (Baron 1989: 379). It has been observed that in Cairo before the First World War Egyptian women were far more advanced than their Lebanese counterparts. Egyptian women, it was observed by a Lebanese writer, are "more emancipated than us . . . they saw the world with unveiled eyes [unlike our women] who did not see the world except from behind black veils" (al-Khalidi 1978: 64). So unveiling was already publicly visible before 1914. While Sha'rawi's dramatic gesture did not mark the beginning of unveiling, her social and political position in society gave the process celebrity and legitimacy.

The *hijab* worn by Muslim and Christian women at the turn of the century is different in meaning from the *hijab* worn by college women in the 1970s. The first was characterized as "a national Egyptian dress for upper-class women, then called *al-habara*" (al-Nabarawi 1979).[174] It consisted of a full-length skirt, a head cover, and *al-burqu'* (face-cover from below the eyes down to the chest), and was worn by Muslim and Christian women. In her memoirs, Huda Sha'rawi used the term *izari* ("my cloak") in referring to what she commonly wore as a wrap when she went out. She did not seem to use the term *hijab* except in the context of the political act of lifting the veil (Sha'rawi 1981: 89). *Izar* is a piece of white calico that covers the whole body, like the *habarah,* which for a married woman is made of glossy black silk. According to *A Dictionary of Islam*, the *izar* is worn by "females of the middle classes, who cannot afford to purchase a *habara*" (*A Dictionary of*

Islam 1885: 95). This latter comment indeed cannot be applicable in this case, since Huda Sha'rawi was a wealthy woman from a family belonging to the gentry of Egypt. More probably, *izar* was used to refer to the more casual attire worn in nonceremonial outings.

Reacting to the writings of European-influenced Egyptian men who advocated the lifting of the veil for women, Malak Hifni Nasif saw a nuanced "male domination being enacted in and through the [then] contemporary discourse of the veil" (L. Ahmed 1992: 179). She opposed mandatory unveiling. The two leading women (Sha'rawi and Nasif) espoused two feminist views: one more authentically Egyptian, the other Western-influenced. This differentiation is important, because research increasingly shows that feminism is rooted in culture.

Nasif's agenda stressed two significant elements absent in Sha'rawi's feminist agenda. First, she demanded that all fields of higher education be opened to women. Information on the specific fields that were closed to men is significant here. In the West the fields that were "open" for women were mostly the "soft" fields of art and home economics. American women until recently did not tend to go into the professional schools of medicine and engineering or majors such as mathematics or economics. In the Arab world, studies of patterns in higher education (El Guindi 1985b, 1986b) show that when higher education became widely accessible in the 1950s, enrollments were balanced between the sexes. The distribution in "soft" fields and professional majors was similar for both sexes. While women were significantly present in medicine and engineering (valued for modern society), they were absent in two particular majors: Arabic Studies and Islamic Studies. This is where cultural context is important in determining which obstacles facing women are relevant for their liberation. When Nasif demanded that *all* fields be made open to women, was she concerned about Arabic and Islamic Studies? This very issue would become relevant several decades later in the 1970s.

Secondly, she demanded that space be made in mosques for women to participate in public prayer. By demanding that mosques be made accessible to women, Nasif had established an agenda that recognizes what is core in the culture. Her agenda was Islamic, her goals feminist. These premises presupposed a strong populist movement that is Islamic feminist.

The discourse of colonialism incorporated a language of feminism and used the issue of women's position in Islamic societies as the focus of attack on those societies. Men serving the colonial administration, such as Cromer in Egypt,[175] who ironically opposed feminism in his own country, England, espoused in the colonial context a rhetoric of feminism that attacked Egyptian men for upholding practices that degraded their women. This posture of subversion and appropriation of the colonized culture can be interpreted as the colonizer's attempt to legitimize its own domination and justify its occupation policies. The kind of feminism emerging out of this colonial context becomes an alternative form of dominance that gives its men and women a sense of superiority. By adopting it, Egyptian men accepted and Egyptian women reproduced their own subordination within their culture as well as their country's subordination to European dominance.

It is within an Arabo-Islamic cultural model that we locate the conception of gender relevant to an objective understanding of Muslim women's activism. Approaching Muslim women's rights through liberal feminist agendas cannot be effective because these agendas are based on the Western experience and derive from Western values; hence they are irrelevant to most issues of concern to Muslim women. Matters pertaining to women and the family are based on scripturalist-derived decrees and laws. To be effective, these issues must be dealt with within the same framework that created them. Feminism within the context of Islam can provide the only path to empowerment and liberation available without challenging the culture as a whole.

But there is another point. Reaffirmation of traditional values and identities also feeds from the same Arabo-Islamic source. One can choose either the liberal feminist or the Islamic feminist path, but in neither can reform be effected, or goals be achieved, without direct access to the primary Islamic knowledge in Arabic. This point had not escaped Doria Shafiq, who struggled to find legitimacy for her feminism even among feminists. She recognized the need to master Islamic knowledge and to communicate in the Arabic language. Any Europeanized activities were considered marginal (see the ethno-biography of Doria Shafik by Nelson 1996; also Nelson 1986).

The Egyptian college women who pioneered the Islamic movement in the 1970s penetrated precisely these culturally relevant realms. They were reading primary sources, although much of their energy was spent in justifying their newly constructed dress and defending their posture *vis-à-vis* society. Their dress gradually became a uniform and a model for public demeanor and cross-sex relations. Mainstream society and Islam began to accommodate them. Increasingly, Egyptians dressed more conservatively. Islamic dress was mass-produced and made available at a low cost. Commercial stores specialized in its sale, thereby making it chic and appealing, and hairdressers opened special sections for the *muhaggabat* (see Figure 25).

Islamic feminism set itself unambiguously apart when the prominent pioneer, Zaynab al-Ghazali, carved an alternative path. Hoffman-Ladd (1995: 64–6) gives a summary of her life. Al-Ghazali was born in 1917, the daughter of an al-Azhar-educated independent religious teacher and cotton merchant. She was privately tutored in Islamic studies in the home, and afterwards

Figure 25 Hairdresser in Cairo, with a sign: "For Women, For *Muhajjabat*. A special section – Manicure, Pedicure." Ethnographic photo by F. El Guindi, 1995. Courtesy El Nil Research.

attended a public secondary school. Her father encouraged her to become an Islamic leader. She obtained certificates in *Hadith* and *Tafsir* (see also Ghazali 1977).

She founded, at the age of eighteen, *Jama'at al-Sayyidat al-Muslimat* (the Muslim Women's Association), which was active from 1936 to 1964[176] and published and "gave weekly lectures to thousands of women at the Ibn Tolon Mosque . . . The Association published a magazine, maintained an orphanage, offered assistance to poor families, and mediated family disputes" (1995: 64). Clearly, therefore her public activism and mastery and leadership in Islamic issues set her apart – she qualified, as it were, to lead women within the Islamic fold.

The movement that emerged in the 1970s is different. Above all, it is populist. It is also grounded in culture and in Islam, and had no formal organization or membership. It erupted everywhere in the main urban centers of Egypt, particularly in the universities, ultimately spreading outward. It was a grass-roots, voluntary youth movement, possibly begun by women, that mixed backgrounds, lifestyles and social boundaries. Its impact was powerful. Out of it emerged a grass-roots Islamic Feminism (El Guindi 1982a, b, 1983, 1992a, 1996a, 1997).

This thread of Islamic Feminism is left out of chronicles of Egyptian feminism. Secularist-bound scholars either deny its existence or ideologically dismiss any scholarly discussion of such formulations (even empirical studies) as apology.[177] Nevertheless, it is feminist because it seeks to liberate womanhood; it is Islamic because its premises are embedded in Islamic principles and values. Yet in some senses, the liberal Western-influenced feminism of the aristocracy and the Islamic one are not far apart. Both are about the emancipation of women. The early feminist lifting of the face-veil was about emancipation from exclusion; the voluntary wearing of the *hijab* since the mid-seventies is about liberation from imposed, imported identities, consumerist behaviors, and an increasingly materialist culture. Further, a principal aim has been to allow women greater access to Islamic literacy.

In the 1980s the movement shifted from establishing an Islamic identity and morality to asserting Islamic nationalism, engaging in participatory politics, and resisting local authoritarian regimes, colonial occupation and Western dominance. Embedded in today's *hijab* is imagery that combines notions of respectability, morality, identity, and resistance. Women (and men) who oppose the *hijab* are opposing the absence of choice, as in Iran, Turkey, Algeria, and Palestine. Resistance through *the hijab* or against it, in tangible form as attire or in intangible form as a code of behavior, has generated a dynamic discourse around gender, Islamic ideals, Arab society, and women's status and liberation.

The Current Climate

Three major events occurring in succession demonstrate this shift[178] in the regional political landscape: (1) Arab States boycotting the Doha (MENA) Conference held in Qatar against pressure from the United States to participate; (2) Arab States attending The Islamic Summit Dec. 9–11 1997 held in Tehran and chaired by Iran against pressure from the United States not to participate; (3) the refusal by Arab States to support President Clinton's campaign for a strike against Iraq during conflict over the inspection of Iraqi sites.

The agenda for the region was reset by these events. Foremost in it are: (1) a Palestinian State with Jerusalem as its capital, and (2) a coordinated front against cultural and economic domination of the region. Two unities, forming apart, converged – an Arab unity within an Islamic unity. This is a shift at the State level that would please both the Arab Street and Islamic activists (El Guindi 1998a: 9). Recent, apparently baseless, heavy-handed provocations (in Sudan and Afghanistan) are not helpful. A reaffirmation of tradition and culture might again be played out in the near future through the idiom and politics of the veil. It is of course being played out now in Afghanistan, as the Taliban are consolidating their power. The hysterics in the Western media about women in Afghanistan feeds from ethnocentrism and arrogance, and feeds into a reaction of extremism. The emergent regional political landscape that merges nationalism, cultural pride, and Islam is perhaps what the veil has come to represent in the 1990s.

Notes

1. Fieldwork for data on which this book is partially based was conducted in Egypt on many research trips (1976, 1979, 1980, 1981–2), and annual research trips from 1984 until 1997). Support was provided by a faculty grant from UCLA African Studies Center (1976), a Ford Foundation grant No. 770-0651 (1979, 1980) as part of the UCLA Interdisciplinary Ford Foundation project, *Rich and Poor States in the Middle East*, (directed by the late Malcolm Kerr under the auspices of the Center for Near Eastern Studies), and a Fulbright Fellowship (Islamic Civilization Senior Research Scholarship) grant No. 80-006-IC (1981–2). Subsequent trips are funded by El Nil Research, Los Angeles, a nonprofit center for ethnographic study and visualization of Arab culture. I acknowledge with gratitude the permission to use the ethnographic photos from its archives.

2. A good example of this point can be viewed in my film, *Ghurbal*, in which an Egyptian peasant and master craftsman spontaneously discusses the religious (Islamic) dimensions, citing Hadith sources, of the traditional sieve as he is crafting it in the courtyard of his own home. The same film is also a good example for demonstrating the interweaving of sacred and ordinary space and time in daily life.

3. The ruling dynasty of Persia from about 550 BC to 330 BC. It was named for Achaemenes (Hakhamanish, a minor ruler of Anshan in southwestern Iran), but the real founder of the dynasty was his great great grandson, Cyrus the Great, creator of the Persian Empire. The dynasty ended with the death of Darius III (*Microsoft Encarta Encyclopedia* 1993–7).

4. Parthia is the ancient empire of Asia, "in what are now Iran and Afghanistan. The Parthians were of Scythian descent . . . Parthia was subject successively to the Assyrians, Medes, Persians, and Macedonians under Alexander the Great, and Seleucids. About 250 BC the Parthians succeeded in founding an independent kingdom that, during the 1st century BC, grew into an empire extending from the Euphrates River to the Indus River and from the Oxus River . . . to the Indian Ocean. . . .

After the middle of the 1ˢᵗ century BC Parthia was a rival of Rome" and several wars weakened it (*Microsoft Encarta Encyclopedia* 1993–7).

5. In 224 AD a Persian vassal-king rebelled and conquered Parthia and founded a new Persian dynasty of the Sassanids. Khosrau II, who reigned from 590 to 628, began a long war against the Byzantine Empire and by 619 had conquered almost all southwestern Asia and Egypt. The last of the Sassanid kings reigned until 651, when the Arabs invaded Persia, replaced Zoroastrianism with Islam and incorporated Persia into the caliphate (*Microsoft Encarta Encyclopedia* 1993–7).

6. As an example of the inappropriateness of generalization and lumping of phenomena Ahmed (1992) writes: "In an urban Middle East with already well articulated misogynist attitudes and practices [various prejudices against women and the mores degrading women that were part of one or other tradition indigenous to the area before Islam] Islam lent itself to being interpreted as endorsing and giving religious sanction to a deeply negative and debased conception of women. As a result, a number of abusive uses of women became legally and religiously sanctioned Muslim practices in a way that they were not in Christianity" (L. Ahmed 1992: 87). These are grossly reductionist comments, in which Islam is presented as responsible for how it is interpreted. Who is doing the interpretation in this case?

7. Again Ahmed (L. Ahmed: 1992: 12–13) repeats wholesale simplified versions of complex historical and archeological developments. She connects the growth of complex societies (Mesopotamia, as an example) to the patriarchal family, male control of women and property, the emergence of prostitution, increased specialization, and a decline in women's economic contributions, leading to the decline of goddesses and the rise of the supremacy of gods. Aside from the tautology of such an argument, which assumes a pre-existing male dominance and ends with it, one might ask why has not the growth of complex urban society in Egypt led to the same path?

8. See for example Ahmed when she states that " Veiling and the confinement of women spread throughout the region and became the ordinary social practices, as did the attitudes to women and to the human body (shamefulness of body and sexuality) that accompanied such practices" (L. Ahmed: 18).

9. Some interesting facts brought up by Ahmed are good examples of how subtle and nuanced influences can be between traditions. She mentions "the fact that Hasan al-Basri (d.728), the eminent early Muslim mystic, was the son of Persian Christian parents ... and the fact that Harun ibn Musa, a convert from Judaism, was the first to write

down the variations in oral renderings of the Quran" (L. Ahmed 1992:
87). Ahmed recognizes these as suggestive of discrete contributions
from converts from outside Islam to the ideas that became part of
Islam.

10. This work challenges the non-differentiating approach taken by Leila
Ahmed, in which she asserts that veiling *"in those areas [in Syria and
Palestine], as in Arabia, . . . was connected with social status, as was
its use among Greeks, Romans, Jews, and Assyrians, all of whom
practiced veiling to some degree"* (1992: 55, emphasis mine). I argue
that it is neither the same veil nor does it have the same meaning,
although good analysis can discern some patterns among them.

11. In her account of Lady Mary Montagu's letters describing Turkish
society, Fernea (1981: 330–8) characterizes Montagu's Letters (see
Montagu 1893; Halsband 1965a) as ethnography. Ethnography, however, does not refer to a literary exercise of writing about culture, no
matter how sensitive or nonethnocentric. Ethnography is a study based
on systematic research that utilizes premises and principles from within
the discipline of anthropology. Nevertheless, the *Letters* contain valuable information about both Turkish and British society. Regarding
the fact that Muslim women of the upper classes owned property in
their own right she wrote that they are therefore less at the mercy of
men than their Christian sisters (Halsband 1965a: 1: 328; see also
Halsband 1956).

12. Rugh 1986 is on rural dress; and MacLeod 1993 is primarily on working women's economic status.

13. Some of these are Makhlouf (1979); Abu-Lughod (1986); MacLeod
(1993) in ethnography and Fernea (1965); L. Ahmed (1982); Hammami
(1990); Zuhur (1992) in Women's and Middle East Studies. The ethnography on Oman by Unni Wikan (1982) is among the more detailed
on the subject – a chapter (pp. 88–108) of 20 pages out of a book of
318 pages. Abu-Lughod (1986) subsumes veiling to discussions on
modesty in 33 pages (134–67) out of a 317-page book.

14. These are Antoun (1972), Lancaster (1981), Gilsenan (1982) and most
recently Young (1996).

15. As a visual anthropologist I distinguish between documentary and
ethnographic film. The difference lies in the field within which it is
embedded, the methodology that the discipline brings into the work
and the different production contexts. My three visual works: "El
Sebou': Egyptian Birth Ritual," "El Moulid: Egyptian Religious Festival,"
and "Ghurbal" are visual ethnographies embedded in the discipline of
anthropology. Documentary comes out of either broadcast journalism

or cinema (see the films by El Guindi 1986, 1990, 1995; El Guindi 1993a; 1998c).

16. The Rashayda Arabs are a "tribe" (*gabila*) of about forty thousand people who live near Sudan's eastern border with Ethiopia. Prior to 1965, most Rashayda were nomadic pastoralists, moving with their herds to desert pastures during the rainy seasons and forming large camps near wells during the dry seasons. Since then perhaps a quarter of the Rashayda have abandoned pastoralism: there is no longer enough pastureland to support the entire nomadic population of eastern Sudan (Young 1996: 61).

17. Purdah is not the same as veiling, but is as frequently used, often interchangeably in publications on South Asian society and culture; see Papanek (1973) on purdah, Sharma (1978) on veil.

18. *The Original Roget's Thesaurus of English Words and Phrases* (Americanized Version) is licensed from Longman Group UK Limited. Copyright © 1994 by Longman Group UK Limited. All rights reserved.

19. For perspective, note that during Wikan's fieldwork 60 men were considered *khanith* out of a population of approximately 11,000 men in Sohar, Oman.

20. His full name is Abu 'Abdullah Muhammad ibn Muhammad al-'Abdari ibn al-Hajj. He is a fourteenth-century conservative Islamic jurist and scholar.

21. Two documentaries, more than a decade apart, were made on the subject of women's *hijab* in Cairo, Egypt – Fernea's *The Veiled Revolution* (Fernea 1982) and a video by Kamal-Eldin *Covered* (Kamal-Eldin 1995). The former is sympathetic and the latter is feminist, orientalist.

22. Examples of titles with veil (or references to hiding or the hidden) in them are: *Veiled Sentiments* (Abu-Lughod 1986), *At the Drop of a Veil* (Alireza 1971), "Veiling Infitah with Muslim Ethic" (El Guindi 1981a), "Veiled Activism" (El Guindi 1983), *The Hidden Face of Eve* (El Saadawi 1980), "A Look Behind the Veil" (Fernea and Fernea 1979), *Accommodating Protest: Working Women, the New Veiling and Change in Cairo* (MacLeod 1993), *Changing Veils* (Makhlouf 1979), *Beyond the Veil* (Mernissi 1975),*The Veil and the Male Elite* (Mernissi 1987), "Social Distance and the Veil" (Murphy 1964), "Veil of Illusion" (Nelson and Olesen 1977b), *Reveal and Conceal* (Rugh 1986), "The Veil as a Symbol of Separation" (Sharma 1978), *Behind the Veil in Arabia* (Wikan 1982), "A Return to the Veil in Egypt" (Williams 1979, 1980), "Return to the Veil" (Hoodfar 1991); *Veiled Half-Truths* (Mabro 1991; *Revealing Reveiling* (Zuhur 1992), "Veiled Discourse – Unveiled

Bodies" (Najmabadi 1993), *Veils and Words* (Milani 1992) and perhaps a few more, most published in the 1970s and 1980s.

23. The source of this comment is Yvonne Haddad, personal communication.

24. Indeed some were motivated by timely career considerations, as "women in the Middle East" was a marketable topic, and careers were forged out of such a focus.

25. Good ethnography includes El-Messiri 1978; Antoun 1972; Lancaster 1981, and more recently Young 1996. Nelson's conceptual critique and analysis is exceptional (Nelson 1991, Nelson and Olesen 1977a, b).

26. T. Lichtenstadter, *Aiyam al-'Arab*, 1935, pp. 81 ff. (Stern 1939a: 108).

27. Information is sparse, and interpretations given in the early literature (such as veiling as a protection from envy) must be re-examined against more current ethnography.

28. Warmest thanks to my colleague and friend from Barcelona, Spain, Elisenda Ardévol, who, upon learning of my book on veiling, gave me this book as a gift.

29. In a future analysis I plan to include the use of wigs in ancient Egypt as a form of headcover.

30. According to Hansen 1967: "from about 1880 the theory was advanced that the Bahrain Islands could be identical with the land of Dilmun, mentioned in the Sumerian epics of Gilgamesh as the Land of the Living or the Island of the Living, well known from Assyrian and Babylonian cuneiform texts, in which visitors from Dilmun are mentioned coming from a land situated some days' journey south of the mouth of the twin rivers Euphrates and Tigris" (see Hansen 1961, 1967). The identification of Bahrain with the land of Dilmun has been supported by the Danish archeological excavations, begun in 1954. For more detail on the excavations see Glob (1954: 92-105; Glob 1959: 133-239).

31. Pearling in the Gulf has been known to exist from thousands of years ago. In Sumerian inscriptions references are made to "fish eyes," interpreted to mean pearls (see Wilson 1928: 5; Hansen 1967: 16; El Guindi 1985b: 76). Pre-Islamic poetry referred to them as "the tears of the beloved," and many Arab poets, historians and geographers wrote detailed accounts of pearls and of the boats, divers, merchants and entrepreneurs (see Khuri 1980: 56). Pearling has evidently not only existed as an economic activity from ancient times, (approximately 2000 BC), but been the center of a major complex of interdependent activities – pearling, trading, shipbuilding – until its decline during the colonial era of Bahrain.

32. In their commentary, the editors state: "The date of these Laws cannot be precisely determined, although it can be fixed within certain fairly wide limits . . . somewhere between 1450 and 1250 BC" (Driver and Miles 1935: 4).

33. Apparently the original tablets from which Law 40 came were in bad condition, and the missing words and question marks are inserted by the editors to indicate uncertainties in the translation of some parts of the text.

34. For perspective Ahmed gives the following timeline: "Between [539 BCE and] . . . 640 CE . . . the region was conquered by Alexander, then by the Parthians, and finally . . . [by] the Sassanians, who reigned from 224 CE until the Muslim conquest" (1992: 17). After defeating King Darius of Persia in 333 BCE Alexander vastly increased the size of his harem. "The harem he captured from Darius consisted of the king's mother and wife, each traveling in her own car and attended by her own troop of women on horseback . . . The size of royal harems grew very large and by Sassanian times . . . numbered in the thousands" (1992: 17).

35. The Hellenistic period begins with the death of Alexander the Great, King of Macedon, and ends with the death of Cleopatra VII, Queen of Egypt.

36. Some feminist Christians consider celibacy liberating for women. "Celibacy, or *renouncing the world,* offered women immediate rewards on earth, not just rewards in heaven," wrote Elaine Pagels, to retain "control of their own wealth, travel freely as *holy pilgrims,* devote themselves to intellectual pursuits" (Pagels 1988). Noteworthy in this regard is that the liberating elements of the "renounced world" for women as indicated are: freedom to travel and control of one's wealth. The latter is interesting as the implication is that had these women not renounced worldly life in favor of celibacy and instead chosen marriage, they would not have control over their own wealth. This is, of course, a culturally grounded expectation, since in Islam, for example, a woman can both be active heterosexually in marriage and legally retain credit and unshared control over her wealth, independently of her husband.

37. See Ahmed's citation from Michael Psellos about the negative reception at the birth of girls (1992: Chapter 2). She describes women "cloistered as prisoners" and always supposed to be veiled in order to be distinguished from prostitutes.

38. For further discussion from these sources see L. Ahmed 1992: 24, 25, 27.

39. Tertullian was born about 155 AD and died about 222 AD (Tertullian 1869: xviii, 179).

40. Note the book and motion picture *The Last Temptation of Christ* and the controversy surrounding them in the United States.

41. Relevant to this point is the English public response to Princess Diana's life and death and the popular participation in her funeral after her tragic accident. Also interesting in the US is the obsessive congressional and media response to President Clinton's admitted sexual encounter in the White House Oval Office in 1995. Both are related to sexuality. In Princess Diana's case the British population embraced her rejection of the royal stiff upper lip, aloofness and distance from the public as well as the characteristic repressed emotion. She represented a new openness. In the case of President Clinton, the Republicans in the Congress are the ones who rejected the American sexual revolution of the 1960s and hence were not transformed by it. Their obsessive preoccupation with the sex detail and its exposure, believing it would produce a negative public response, is more about conservative attitudes of repressed emotion and sexuality. The November elections and the polls confirmed the voters' different attitude. The Republicans could not comprehend how the public, which has been transformed, was so nonchalant about it.

42. Note that the Abbasid dynasty ruled in Baghdad from 750–1258 C.E. and Byzantine rule lasted from 330–1453 C.E.

43. Mernissi's first book (Mernissi 1975) was the most sociological of her books. Later ones tend to be more polemical. The value in her recent works lies largely in her extensive use of original Arabic sources (unfortunately rarely used in Western-language sources, which is a great loss).

44. Doumato does recognize the presence of seclusion for commoners in Arabia, but does not account for it. It is presented as an anomaly. No explanation is advanced for what seems to contradict the conclusions she herself arrived at.

45. In her *Memoirs* Huda Sha'rawi describes the role of Sa'id Agha – her perception of his sternness combined with his warmth and care for her and her brother.

46. For information on the role of Jews in supplying and trading European boys as eunuchs and Christians in castrating them for use in Muslim (and other) homes, courts, and sacred places see Mez 1937 (English translation), 1947 (Arabic translation), although I cannot assess the reliability of documentation in this Orientalist source. Note that according to the *Qur'an* it is forbidden in Islam to castrate animals, let alone humans.

47. Goodwin writes that in Cyprus in the seventeenth century a record shows that "two-thirds of the white slaves sold were male whereas only half the black slaves were male. Slaves came from Russia, Caucasia, Hungary [and were] Greek, Georgian and Croatian " (Goodwin 1997: 106; also see Garnett 1896; 1909)).

48. While the Turkish language is not gendered, Arabic is. The term in Arabic for a woman sultan is *sultana*. *Valide* is a Turkish adaptation of the Arabic term for a *jarya* (slave) who begets a son in the imperial household. In Arabic, as in Turkish, a distinction is made between *umm walad*, mother of boy, used for a *jarya*, versus *umm banin* (mother of sons) for a free woman (Mernissi 1993: 57).

49. *Qat* is a small shrub widely grown in Yemen and wild elsewhere in the Arab world, the leaves of which are chewed by men and women to produce a pleasant stimulation.

50. For an anthropological analysis of contemporary Arab women's world and the role of family and privacy for women see El Guindi 1986b (225–42).

51. Homosexuality is not the focus of the present analysis and does not negate the dominant public dual-gendered cultural model of sexuality.

52. Robert Withers "The Grand Signior's Serraglio" in *Purchas His Pilgrim*, 9: 51, cited in Ahmed 1982. Goodwin (1996) goes to great length to determine the authenticity of Withers as a source. According to Goodwin, "there was an original version of the manuscript published in 1625 and a new version with additions in 1650." Withers, according to Goodwin, took liberty in translating Bon's documents, adding and omitting information, and is suspected to have never himself gained entry into the private quarters of the Saray, a fact claimed in the 1625 version and omitted in the 1650 version (see Goodwin 1996: 18). He also seemed to mysteriously disappear. Goodwin acknowledges that even Bon, who came from a distinguished Venetian family and who was educated at the university of Padua, "did not visit the harem – nor did any male other than the eunuchs – but he did visit private areas of the Saray where no foreigner and only the highest-ranking officers at the sultan's court had ever penetrated" (1996: 13). Goodwin considers "Bon's account [to be] based on as accurate information as he could obtain" (1996: 11). "Of all the accounts by western diplomats and travellers between 1453 ... and the end of the seventeenth century, Bon's is the most reliable in every respect" (1996: 13; see Bon 1996).

53. A. B. Clot Bey, *Aperçu général sur L'Egypte (1840)*, vol. 2, p. 395. He is Antoine-Barthélemy Clot, originally from Marseille, who went to

Egypt in 1824 and was appointed the physician of Muhammad Ali Pasha. He remained in Egypt for thirty years after he was appointed Inspector General of Health Services of Egypt.

54. In Fernea's article (1981) on Lady Mary Montagu and her writing in the 1700s on Turkish life, Montagu comes across as at ease with the subject. She is non-judgmental and comfortable when she describes how women are "objects of obsession" in Western attitudes and writing.

55. In a contemporary adaptation in theater, *Arabian Nights* (Zimmerman 1997).

56. The notion in Catholic ideology that celibacy does not deny marriage, since women are believed to marry Christ, does not contradict the notion of impurity discussed here.

57. The view of the Orient in terms of "despotism," "splendor," "cruelty," "sensuality," to use Edward Said's (1978) terms, was to be "domesticated for local European use" by France and Britain from the beginning of the nineteenth century until the end of the Second World War, and since the Second World War has been taken over by the United States (1978: 3). This complex of attitudes (and consequent policy) characterizes the United States' approach to the Arab East, most dramatically reflected in every aspect of the Gulf War (see El Guindi 1991a, b, 1992c).

58. See S. Amin (1989) on this subject. Further, in an interesting and provocative book by James Cowan (1996) called *A Mapmaker's Dream: The Meditations of Fra Mauro, Cartographer to the Court of Venice* [brought to my attention by colleague Elisenda Ardévol] there is this quote and comment on it: "The Saracens, it appears, have other ways of defining such things. Probably one has to accept their idea of the veil if one is to understand their antipathy toward us. Calling us infidel is also an old Saracen trick. True meaning lies as if hidden behind a series of waxed seals on an edict, each bearing the stamp of authority. Breaking one open only inspires the need to break open another. As each meaning crumbles under the pressure of knowing, so too does the essential meaning still await revelation. This is the principle of the veil well known to the Saracens" (1996: 110). To clarify, Cowan adds this note: "Probably Mauro is alluding to a Koranic exposition of the Seventy Thousand Veils, where it says, *Allah has Seventy Thousand Veils of Light and Darkness: where He to withdraw their curtain, then would the splendors of His aspect surely consume everyone who apprehended Him with their sight*" (1996: 10). Leaving aside racist remarks, upon consulting the *Qur'an* no such text could be found. The *Qur'anic* reference on this subject can be found in *Sura al-Shura*, which states in

translation: "God addresses humans only as apparition, from behind the *hijab*, or via a messenger" (42: 51).

59. Laws of the two countries of Morocco and Algeria are presented interchangeably as examples of the influence of Islam; and Central Africa as an example of idol worship and fetishism.

60. It has been custodian of over 250,000 photographs since the formation of its Education and Cultivation Division in the early 1970s. The collection contains material created and collected from 1860 through to 1925 by a United Methodist predecessor denomination (Kaplan 1984: 61).

61. A note written below the photo states: The penciled notations and/or revisions in the text accompanying art were made for an audio-visual presentation in 1981 (Kaplan 1984: 65). So these slide shows continued into the 1980s and may still be operating.

62. Liberal versus Marxist and socialist, etc.

63. The author remarked that this fact – that they are unveiled – should cause any viewer to sigh in appreciation. This reflects the author's own perception about veiling.

64. The photo with its caption was printed in Kaplan 1984: 66. It is reprinted here by permission from the *Journal*.

65. It ought to be noted that "Christian" refers to Western Christianity. Eastern Christians were not in the picture one way or the other.

66. The ethnographic data on the Rashayda are from William Young's published works. He uses the term "costume" to refer to traditional dress. We differ in the analysis of the data.

67. It is significant to mention that William Young has mastered the Rashidi dialect of Arabic as well as standard spoken and written Arabic – skills that are absolutely critical for a systematic study of any group in the Arabic-speaking cultural region.

68. According to Young (1994, 1996) there are three forms or shapes of brands used to mark camels and livestock, each pertaining to a tribal branch of the Rashidi tribe. Each branch has a named ancestor and a distinctive brand used by all members of a branch.

69. The common translation of Ibn Khaldun's contrast (*'umran badawi/ 'umran hadari*) is "primitive culture/civilized culture." But as we consider carefully the notion *badawi*, I lean more towards a translation that is closer to the Arabic meaning. *Badawi* derives from the root that means "beginning" or "elementary" and is related to another derivative, *badiya*, which means "desert." In his cyclical theory of change he does not use lineal progress, a notion embedded in nineteenth-century evolutionary thought. Culture develops from a *badawi* phase

to a *hadari* phase. I find it closer to the original intent to translate these two phases as "elemental" and "civilizational" rather than the more commonly use translations "primitive" versus "civilized."

70. Within the paradigm of social evolution nineteenth-century evolutionists considered the civilized state to have reached its peak in the industrialized Western European nations and Victorian Christianity. The notion of progress was embedded in the paradigm of evolution.

71. Goffman acknowledged this debt in an article "Symbols of Class Status" (1951) and in his book *Relations in Public* (Goffman 1971).

72. Zuhur's 1995 entry for dress in *The Oxford Encyclopedia of the Modern Islamic World* (383–8) is too general, and by anthropological standards, too simple.

73. In some contexts in US society it might be appropriate to include the car in the complex of emblems.

74. See the section on the "Anthropology of Dress" for a survey of early anthropological works.

75. "Seven" recurs as a theme throughout the ceremony – seven grains are sprinkled around the house to spread prosperity, and the mother crosses seven times over the newborn in a bonding rite, among other instances.

76. A big candle is placed in the neck of the pot and is lit after sunset, to be put out by midnight. Some believe that the angels register the newborn's life-span, and this is reflected in the duration of the flame.

77. I made a visual ethnography (ethnographic film) on the *El-Sebou'*, called *El-Sebou': Egyptian Birth Ritual* (El Guindi 1986) in which the newborns were a pair of twins, one boy and one girl; both pots are shown in the sequence just described.

78. The familiar pink for girls, blue for boys are Western colors, which are now imported and are being absorbed along with other local colors in Egypt. Pink and blue were the colors of the two big candles purchased in the bazaar for the two pots of the twins that were the subject of the visual ethnography *El-Sebou': Egyptian Birth Ritual*.

79. This is an at least 150-year old pottery village in the heart of Old Cairo, known as Fustat. The potter in the film is Hag Saleh. Only recently has the government removed the village, because of the Islamic monuments that it was obscuring. So this particular pottery village, which was in the heart of Cairo, is no more.

80. The baby's cloth diaper is rolled and put aside for use later, in a ceremony to ensure the baby's protection from harm. As shown in the film *El-Sebou': Egyptian Birth Ritual* , in a rite of bonding the ritual leader holds the baby's diapers along with some sharp metal tool (a knife or scissors) as she counts loudly while the baby's mother steps

over the baby seven times. The baby lies in the *ghurbal,* or ceremonial sieve. This is a ceremony that bonds mother and child.

81. *Fustan* is a foreign word (Italian) that became incorporated in spoken Arabic and is commonly used only to refer to modern-style everyday dress for women. It is not ordinarily used for men's clothing. The present usage is in the ceremonial context of a gender-neutral baby.

82. For further analysis of this ceremony see El Guindi 1986 (film), 1996b; for analysis of the film as representing the ceremony see El Guindi 1998c.

83. The *Sunna,* which means "the path," with reference to the path of the Prophet, consists of actions, sayings, and deeds by Prophet Muhammad as transmitted by reliable sources close to him. The compilation of the *Sunna,* which occurred long after the death of the Prophet, is a scholarly process of verifying narratives transmitted by eyewitnesses conducted by Imams, and is published in written form. Women were among the major transmitters of *hadiths*; the *hadith* compilers and interpreters are all men. The written books containing the *Sunna* are called *Hadith,* a word translating as Prophetic Narratives. There are nine recognized Hadith Volumes. Each is divided into books by subject and chapters by constituent topics. Certain *hadith* compendia have been established as more reliable than others. The two reputed to be the most reliable are *Sahih Muslim* and *Sahih al-Bukhari.*

84. See El Guindi 1980, 1981a, b c, 1982a, b, c, d, 1983, 1984, 1985a, 1986a, 1987, 1992a, b, 1993b, 1996a.

85. It is interesting that according to Brenner (1996) the word *jilbab* is preferred in Indonesia to *hijab.* Brenner stresses, however, that *hijab* is an Arabic word. Of course both *jilbab* and *hijab* are Arabic words.

86. The word *Qur'an* derives from words that mean both "recite" and "read." It is based on the oral revelations transmitted to God's messenger, Muhammad, which were recorded upon his request on any available material: cloth, leather, bone, stone, etc. These were meticulously compiled and written down. The *Qur'an* is divided into *Suras* and the *Suras* into *Ayahs.*

87. For a glossary of Arabic words denoting forms of clothing for both sexes see *The Encyclopedia of Islam* (*Encyclopedia of Islam* 1986: 745–6).

88. Arabic is a major Semitic language spoken by approximately 260 million people, and is the religious language of over a billion people in the world today. Hebrew, which is a member of the same language group, resembles Arabic. The words for the Western rendition "Eve" are *hawwa'* in Arabic and *havva* in Hebrew.

89. The Qur'anic *Sura* 49: 13 appears to be similar to Genesis 1: 27, which states: *So God created man in his own image, in the image of God he*

created him; male and female he created them. The stress in Genesis is on two aspects: man in God's image and God as creator of male and female. The phrase "male and female he created them" represents a separate thought about God being creator, not about gender simultaneity of primordial creation. (David Phelps alerted me to a possible parallel in Genesis.)

90. I am grateful for Lila's gracious and immediate response to my telephone call when I requested the original bedouin-dialect tapes of women's poetry. She generously and immediately sent them to me. I was experimenting with community ethno-theater, and the first play selected was a performance of *ghinnawas* collected by Lila during her fieldwork. The tapes indeed helped the community women actors capture the bedouin style, although the performance was in the English language. I must note how the play provoked some Arab men in the audience, who saw the poetry as being radical feminist. That resulted in some lively debate in the Arab-American papers in Los Angeles. Otherwise the *Al-Funun al-Arabiya* theater ensemble (*Masrah*) and the audience enjoyed both performance and subsequent discussion with the actors.

   Lila Abu-Lughod's study of Awlad 'Ali women's performed poetry (1986: 28) begins with a discussion of gender. She uses the premise of sexual modesty to interpret patterns of women's veiling (1986: 34). In doing so, Abu-Lughod draws upon Mediterraneanist ideas of "modesty," "shame," "honor," and "impurity." Stripped of their cultural uniqueness, the Awlad' Ali read very much like a Greek village or a Balkan community – culture is a major dimension of people's lives.

   Masking passions (a bedouin quality of reserve characterizing their public persona and described in systematic detail by Lancaster (1981) and Young (1996) among others) is different from the claim of denial of sexuality (which is not Arabo-Islamic).

91. Gilsenan, in his observations on rural Lebanon, stresses the opposite point that "the organization of space insists on discontinuities, separations, opposed categorizations " (Gilsenan 1982: 166).

92. Among the Zuni of America north is thought of as blue, south as red, and east as white (Durkheim and Mauss 1903: 44; Needham 1973: 33).

93. In his early, pioneering article on modesty, Antoun acknowledged that he coined the phrase "modesty code" as a "short hand term" (1968: 672) to refer to this complex pattern.

94. Perhaps it might be more applicable to Christian Arab communities, although differences between them and Muslim Arabs tend to be minor, except for the areas of worship and theology. I contend that these

ethnocentricities do not properly capture Christian Arab cultural ideas either.

95. However, I do disagree with Antoun when he characterizes women in Islam as having limited capacity for right conduct, ritually impure (1968: 674), incapable of reflection and management (1968: 678), legally inferior (1968: 674), irrational (1968: 678), and of doubtful ethical capability (1968: 678). Nor do I concur with the assertion that there is in Islam an ideology of women's inferiority (1968: 675). One must consider the mix of sources that produced these interpretations and translations, and I fault him for the procedure he used to elicit rather haphazardly the Islamic vision of womanhood. The value of Antoun's analysis lies in identifying a pervasive code and trying to bring the textual into the village study.

96. According to Mernissi 1993 *mahram* refers to the person with whom the law of incest forbids marriage, "the person with whom there is a uterine (*rahm*) relationship, which makes that person forbidden. Territory, a man's haram, is that which belongs to him, that which he defends against the covetousness of others. The haram of a well is the space that surrounds it and to which access is forbidden: a well which a man has taken the pains to dig is forbidden to others, and one may not challenge his monopoly of it, and it is called *muharram* because its use is forbidden to all except the one who dug it. We see that the word harim in fact expresses an idea of threshold, of boundary, of separation between two territories. It is rooted in the idea of space as a field linked to life (sexuality) and to death (war) the ability to defend oneself and to protect. It is a threshold which organizes the universe and distributes beings in space, according to the relationships of power, their power to kill and defend threshold" (Mernissi 1993: 66). I find this entire section questionable in fact and in analysis. For example, if we take the phrase about those in relationship of incest taboo to a woman, Mernissi writes: "the person with whom there is a uterine (rahm) relationship, which makes that person forbidden." In fact, the relatives specified in Islam are both consanguineal and affinal (see Figure 8). And her analysis of "a field linked to life (sexuality) and death (war)" is a conceptualization that cannot stand up to ethnographic evidence.

97. Young traces the use of this term and finds that it is uncommon among Arabic-speaking groups except among West Arabians, where it is still in use, suggesting Arabian roots to the Rashayda of the Sudan (Young 1996).

98. It is interesting that Abu-Lughod (1986) makes such sweeping generalizations about bedouins and Muslims, whereas when she "writes women's worlds" (1992), she uses a "personalist narrative approach"

that Soheir Morsy, in her review of it, describes as "personalist hermeneutics . . . a postmodernist anthropology [which distances] anthropologists from responsibility for specific conclusions [and] shield anthropologists from critical commentary [from those] in a position to contest authoritative expertise" (1995: 424). Schweizer (1998) also criticizes Abu-Lughod's orientation. In the *Handbook of Methods in Cultural Anthropology*, he states that Abu-Lughod (1991: 149–57; 1992: Introduction) has "argued against generalizations in anthropology and has launched a project of writing 'ethnographies of the particular' . . . It is hard to believe how she can depict the individuality of particular Others without rendering information on the general ethnographic and historical context that gives each selected persona her or his particularity. Some sort of generalization is unavoidable; otherwise, the difference between the particular and the general does not become revealing" (1998: 60).

99. Another value related to *sharaf* and often misinterpreted is *'ard*. The same analysis can include it as part of the sanctity–reserve–respect complex and in relation to reputation. I do not include it in this treatment.

100. Among other groups, as those embracing the Judaic faith, the relation between dress and identity is exclusionary (tribal). According to Maimonides, in a translation of *The Book of Adoration*, there is a precept in the Torah "to attach fringes to the corners of the garment [but that] *cannot be made by or exchanged with persons outside the Israelite tribe*" (Maimonides 1965: 14a, emphasis added).

101. Young (1993) cites the detailed description in the works of Ibrahim Rif'at Basha, who was the *Amir al-hajj* (chief of pilgrimage rites in Cairo) in 1903, 1904, and 1908. The use of original sources in Arabic makes Young's presentation especially valuable. For details of the rites of transport of the *kiswa* and the "dressing" of the *ka'ba* in Makka see Young (1993).

102. Mamluks are an "Egyptian warrior caste dominant for over 700 years. They were originally slaves brought to Egypt by Fatimid caliphs in the 10th cent. Many were freed and rose to high rank. Aybak was the first Mamluk to actually become ruler (1250). For 250 years after that, Egypt was ruled by Mamluk sultans chosen from the caste of warriors. In 1517 the Ottoman Turks captured Cairo and put an end to the Mamluk sultanate. The Mamluks maintained their vast landholdings and their private armies, however, and remained provincial governors. As Turkish rule weakened, they reasserted their power, and by the 18th century they were virtual rulers again. Napoleon

I defeated them in 1798, but their final defeat came in 1811 when they were massacred by Muhammad Ali." (Microsoft Bookshelf '95 1983–5).

103. *Khawnad* is a Mamluk title for women of rank, but particularly the wives of Sultans.

104. It is not clear in the sources when this incident occurred. Omar Ibn Al-Khattab is one of the *sahaba,* the original followers of Prophet Muhammad, who became second Caliph after Muhammad's death. The association of face-veiling with high rank and free-born women has roots in earlier history in the region, particularly in Mesopotamia.

105. The reference here is probably to Makkan Arabians prior to their Islamization.

106. *Gina'* is Rashidi dialect for *qina'*. Note the cultural nuancing that differentiates dress articles on the basis of degrees of maturation. Among the Ghunyari, at least on the basis of the existing ethnography, the differentiation in women's clothing follows broad strokes. In general, mature women "wear a loose shirt (*kamiz*), over baggy trousers (*salwar*) with a wide scarf or shawl (*dupatta*) drawn about the head and shoulders" (Sharma 1972: 218).

107. This is not unique to the Rashayda among Arab groups. It is characteristic of traditional Arab groups. However, most ethnographies do not contain sufficient systematic and rigorous data on the subject of clothing and the life cycle. Scattered information on other groups exists as evidence of Young's point about maturity. Most ethnography that has some description of clothing and particularly of women's veiling shows evidence of differentiation of clothing in connection with the life cycle transitions.

108. The Rashidi dialect equivalent of *niqab*.

109. Sharma gives an extreme feminist analogy when she sees similarity between *ghungat* "footbinding in China, sexual teasing in Herefordshire (Whitehead 1976: 193), seclusion among Muslims and the myth of the perfect housewife in western capitalist societies" (Sharma 1978: 229).

110. Sharma explains *ghungat* as reflecting a contradiction in the social position of women in north Indian villages, which is a result of men's being in control of property (land) and women's consuming the product. In the north Indian village continuity in control of land depends on clear definition of relationships. Those between men are of subordination and superordination of two kinds: senior–junior (intracaste) and ritually pure/impure (intercaste), both expressed in terms of agnatic kinship. Women who use the idiom of affinity are

kept from threatening the male bond that glues the society together (Sharma 1978: 223).

111. There are secondary sources, however, that tend to repeat Western notions of womanhood and impose them on Muslim women. Original sources are clear on this issue.

112. "In ancient times, the Tuareg controlled the trans-Sahara caravan routes, taking the goods they helped to convey and raiding neighboring tribes. In modern times, their raiding was subdued by the French who ruled Algeria. The political division of Saharan Africa since the 1960s has made it increasingly difficult for the Tuareg to maintain their pastoral traditions. . . . Many Tuareg starved in droughts in the 1970s, and others have migrated to cities. Today more than 300,000 Tuareg live in Algeria, Tunisia, Mali, Libya, Burkina Faso, and Niger" (*Microsoft Encarta Encyclopedia* 1993–7).

113. Murphy argues that veiling is about shame, withdrawal and social distance. This sociopsychological position is not the one adopted in my analysis.

114. Sharma explains veiling in India from a feminist perspective. Others explained it in terms of structural ambiguity and ambivalence. This is not the position adopted in this work.

115. The informant was a male student, 21 years old, in his third year in veterinarian medicine at the University of Cairo, Coptic, from an upper-middle-class urban family. The interview was conducted on campus in January 1979.

116. A miraculous apparition, particularly of the Virgin Mary, is not uncommon cross-culturally. The Virgin Mary appeared on Mexico's Hill of Tepeyac in 1531 after the Spanish Conquest of Tenochtitlan. The shrine of the Virgin of Guadalupe, Mexico's patron saint, on Tepeyac remains to this day. Interestingly, in pre-Hispanic times Tepeyac had another shrine – a temple of the native American earth and fertility goddess Tonantzin. In the Mexican case, the appearance of the image of the Virgin Mary represented a synthesis in symbol and ritual between elements from pre-Hispanic beliefs (Tonantzin) and elements in the conqueror's religion (Catholicism), reflecting the nature of this newly meshed relationship between the two.

117. Umm Kulthum is the most beloved and famous Egyptian female singer, whose symbolism goes beyond her voice and artistic performance (see Danielson 1997), much like the symbolism associated with Nasser.

118. This theme was overplayed by the late President Sadat, using Islamic ideology to counter the predominant Nasserist ideology on university campuses. Mohammad Heikal wrote in his memoirs of the 1973 war

and with regard to the *'UBUR* (the Crossing): "A day or two after the crossing of the canal, the army information services had a leaflet printed which was distributed to all serving soldiers. This was couched in the most flowery language of piety: 'in the name of God, the merciful, the compassionate: the Prophet is with us in the battle. O Soldiers of God . . . one of the good men had had a dream in which he saw the Prophet Muhammad dressed in white, taking with him the Shaykh of Al-Azhar, pointing his hand and saying "come with me to Sinai." Some of the 'good men' were reported to have seen the Prophet walking among the soldiers with a benign smile on his face and a light all around him. So it went on, ending up: 'O soldiers of God, it is clear that God is with you'" (Heikal 1975: 236, 237). Heikal, a secularist Nasserist who was advisor to Nasser and Sadat, found this incident inappropriate. "By implying that the success of the crossing was due to a miracle, it diminished the part played by the troops who had been engaged in the battle and who had behaved with such conspicuous bravery and enterprise." There were signs of growing religious fanaticism as war fever mounted, so that eventually the President felt obliged to announce publicly that the commander of the first infantry brigade to cross the canal was a Copt, Major-General Fuad Ghali – who then became commander of the Second Army.

119. See Hamza 1981 for a personal account by a television personality who herself made the journey from *sufur* (uncovered head/face) to wearing the *hijab* (See note 141). She continued as host of the television program in both phases.

120. For interpretation many activists read primarily the works of Sayyid Qutb (1906–1966) and Abu al-'Ala al-Mawdudi (1903–1979), Islamic ideologues. See Qutb's *Fi Thilal al-Qur'an* ("In the Shade of the Qur'an"), 1974 and *Ma'lim fil Tariq* ("Milestones"), 1982. On Qutb see Haddad 1983. See al-Mawdudi 1972, 1985; and on Mawdudi see Adams 1983.

121. The Islamic vision was woven gradually out of fragments of occurrences, stories, wise sayings and exemplary acts during the days when the Islamic community itself (the *Umma*) was emerging and gradually forming its rules and traditions. Oral tradition was the divine medium of transmission. But it was also the community's traditional medium. The tradition of Arabic oral literacy is strongly associated with early Arabia. Other than the oral transmission of divinely revealed messages, it includes story telling and the high art form of poetry, which ranges from spontaneously improvised to highly formal. Sacred text is recited

or chanted, ritually and publicly, by both men and women. Some forms of poetry, called *ghinnawas*, are composed and performed by Bedouin women to send messages that qualify to be considered "feminist." Just as the highest form of formal Arabic is embedded in the sacred scriptural text, the highest art form of recitation is embodied in the *Qira'ah* (rhythmic oral recitation of Qur'anic text). The *Krayas* (a local dialect variant of same word) described for groups in Iraqi villages and elsewhere in the Arab world are group *Qira'ah(s)* held and attended by women. This kind of activity appeared during the past decade in Los Angeles among immigrant Muslim women, wives of wealthy Arabs who regularly met during *subhiyat* ("little mornings"). These all-women social gatherings gradually shifted from being purely social to combined social/religious events in which religious readings and performances were led by one woman (referred to as *Shaykha*) accompanied by female percussionists, and then followed by individual and collective prayers and lavish catered meals. The *Shaykha* leads in religious chanting and gives a moral sermon guiding women's lives in their new immigrant setting. Oral performances continue to be important for both sexes.

122.   The *Sunna,* which means "the path" with reference to the path of the Prophet, consists of actions, sayings, and deeds by Prophet Muhammad as transmitted by reliable sources close to him.

123.   Bürgel, a Christian (?) moralist by self-description: "a moralist [who treats] the topic with the view of a moralist" (1979: 86), describes erotic relations as reflected in literary sources. His selection of sources and generalizations from writings strongly reflect his ethnocentrism. He concludes from the incident reported in the *Hadith* (about a woman complaining to the Prophet about the poor quality of sex life with her current husband in comparison with that with her previous husband) that "voices were raised against this kind of candor" (1979: 82). I contend that, contrary to what Bürgel says, the important point is Islam's natural acceptance of sex as an important part of normal life. Another important point is the woman's right in Islam to sexual pleasure in matrimony.

124.   It is most certainly not suggestive of the eroticism of women's breasts (as in American culture) as there is no ethnographic evidence to that effect. While they are considered part of the beauty of a woman's body, in Arab culture (as is the case in many cultures outside the Euro-American culture) breasts are traditionally more associated with maternity and femininity than with sex. The monothematic sexualization of breasts is a Western influence.

125. Objection to exhibitionism in dress and behavior has a parallel in the Bible (*The Holy Bible: Revised Standard Version*, 1952) in Isaiah 3: 16-26. However, note the striking difference in content and meaning between these passages and the Qur'anic passages mentioned earlier about public demeanor, particularly 7: 27. First, the biblical rendition confines its reference to women only, whereas the Qur'an explicitly addresses men and women. Secondly, the Judaic Lord vengefully punishes women for their exhibitionist behavior and dress: "Because the daughters of Zion are haughty . . . glancing wantonly with their eyes . . . tinkling with their feet" (Isaiah 3: 16), "the Lord will smite with a scab the heads of the daughters of Zion, and the Lord will lay bare their secret parts" (Isaiah 3: 17). Vengeful punishment by the Lord against the women continues in Isaiah 3: 18 until Isaiah 3: 26. The women's men are referenced in 3: 23 as part of the women's punishment. Third, terms such as shame and secret body parts are used in the English rendition in the same context of punishment with reference to women only

126. This is the signification proposed by *Tafsir* (Islamic Exegesis). There is a gradation in Islamic moral evaluation between *haram* (taboo, unlawful) and *halal* (permissible). *Tafsir* has nuanced and subtle differentiations in determining the "intent" of behavior. *Tafsir* on the Qur'anic segment regarding anklets explicates the reference about "striking their feet while walking." If the intent of the woman is to "show off" her jewelry or *tabarruj* (exhibitionist dress or display of the body, and behavior such as to draw attention to one's body) then the act is considered *makrouh* or *mathmum* (reprehensible). Equivalently for men, if they flap their slip-ons for the purpose of flirting with women, then it is *haram* (taboo), and if they do so out of *tabarruj* it is *la yajouz* (not permissible). Again, this restriction applies to both sexes, and the notion of *tabarruj* applies to men as well as women.

127. Another part of a Middle Eastern woman's body culturally considered erotic is her eyes. Popular culture in song and poetry is full of references to the infatuating effect of women's eyes.

128. For a holistic discussion of *hijab* see El Guindi 1995b. For the first analysis of hijab as a concept that extends beyond women's clothing see El Guindi 1981a, in conclusions based on a field-based ethnography.

129. Sahih al-Bukhari 10: 710.

130. Sahih Muslim 38: 3857,3866,3867, 3878, 3879, 3886, 3887, 3888, 3890, 3892, 3895, 3910, 3972, 3973.

131.   Sahih Muslim 38: 3847,4874, 3876, 3896, 3897, 3898, 3899.
132.   Sahih Muslim 38: 3848, 3849, 3851, 3852, 3857, 3858, 3859, 3860, 3861,3862, 3864, 3868.
133.   Sahih Muslim 38: 3876.
134.   Sahih Muslim 38: 3880, 3879, 3870.
135.   Sahih Muslim 38: 3857, 3872, 3874, 3875, 3876, 3926, 3921, 3922, 3969; Sahih al-Bukhari 11: 837; 11: 926.
136.   Other commonly misunderstood notions include *qawwam*, as in the phrase "*al-rijal* qawwamun" and *hijab, tabarruj,* and *sufur,* among others.
137.   Prayer is the second of the five essential duties enjoined upon observing Muslims. A Muslim prays five times daily, facing Makka from anywhere. The five times are: at dawn, at noon, in midafternoon, at dusk, and in the evening. The human call for prayer from the minarets announces the moment at which the new prayer period begins, but it is also a way to mark the end of the period of the previous prayer. While it is preferred, when possible, to perform prayer upon the end of the call, it is permissible to pray at any time between two calls. In other words, the calls for prayer are structuring devices representing fixed points in the day, which mark the end of one prayer period and the beginning of another, at the same time giving a distinctive rhythm to the day as the sacred and the ordinary moments and spaces interweave. Other than prayer, there are the duties of declaration of faith, fasting, almsgiving and pilgrimage. In Arabic, the five duties required of Muslims are: *shahada, salat, sawm, zakat,* and *hajj.*
138.   Sahih al-Bukhari 8: 339, 352,354, 423; 9: 549; 10: 772; Sahih Muslim 38: 3877, 3878, 3879, 3880, 3916, 3917, 3918, 3919.
139.   Sahih al-Bukhari 10: 772.
140.   *Sura*s 4: 36; 17: 37; 28: 83; 31: 18; 40: 75; 57: 23.
141.   The dress in both phases is referred to in general as *tahaggub* (spoken Egyptian Arabic for *tahajjub*) and the woman in either phase is considered *mithaggiba* (spoken Egyptian Arabic for *muhajjaba).* Both *tahajjub* and *muhajjaba* derive from the root *h-j-b,* which is the root that *hijab* is derived from. *Tahajjub,* which was used to mean dress and general demeanor, was contrasted with both *tabarruj* (excess and immodesty) and *sufur* (uncovered head/face). The vocabulary is rooted in early Islamic language about dress and was used during the first decade of the movement for reference and as a control mechanism within the group.
142.   This is notwithstanding Fra Mauro's describing Islam as "the infidel religion of Mohammed" (Cowan 1996: 38). I hesitated long before

using quotations from him.

143. Goitein mentions Moses Maimonides, the Jewish Arab physician in the Ayyubid court who wrote many treatises in Arabic, such as the *Code of Law* and the *Guide for the Perplexed*. Goitein does not see past the superficial similarity of head covers when he writes that "a similar attitude [to that of the Jews] toward head cover was alive in Islam" (Goitein 1967: 159). Meaning can only derive from close ethnographic exploration, not by conjecture from textual evidence alone, nor should assumptions be extended on the basis of a mere similarity in form.

144. This is a change from his previous argument that the reference to separate women's quarters, called *haramiyya (h-r-m)*, in some of the Geniza documents was not evidence for a Jewish practice. In the earlier volume he conjectured that Jews probably bought homes already designed and built by Muslims (1967: 71).

145. al-Tabari died in 310 AH, al-Zamakshari in 538 AH, al-Baidawi in 685 AH, and as-Suyuti in 911 AH. AH means after the *Hejira*. The word *Hegira* or *Hejira* (from "abandon" or "migrate") marks when Prophet Muhammad left his native Makka, where he and his followers were persecuted, and headed for Yathrib, later named Madina. This was in September 622 AD. The Islamic calendar dates from the first day of the lunar year in which the *hejira* took place.

146. This arrogance is interesting, in the light of the fact emerging out of the records (see Sha'rawi 1981) that many European women who went to Egypt during that era were of "low class" origins and had gone there to seek wealthy husbands or household employment (particularly as nannies) in upper-class Egyptian homes, or for health reasons, or to "have fun" in the sun and subsequently write Memoirs and Letters about it. Melman (1992, 1995) who continues the Orientalist colonial European tradition, only gendering encounter by "writing" in "women travelers'" gaze and experience of the East, states that colonial "women had engaged in the colonial project" (1992: xxv) in ways different from men, even though they "adhered to imperialist and racist ideas" (1992: xxiv).

147. It was conducted by the National Center for Sociological and Criminological Research in Cairo, Egypt.

148. Zuhur's limited survey (1992) was also framed in the same terms of class, rural/urban origin, etc.

149. In a review of two books, Wikan (1996) and an edited collection that includes a 1993 article by MacLeod, Myntti (1997) criticizes Wikan for dismissing the Islamic trend by stating that "fundament-

alism" has no attraction for the poor people in Cairo. She praises MacLeod's notion of the double bind facing rising middle-class women as a good explanation for these women's veiling. The review points to contradictions in Wikan's view, since one of her chapters show that her informants were quite religious.

150. Wikan (1984) rightly challenges the oppositional quality of honor/ shame and its applicability to the Gulf Arab community of her study. I might add that the Arabic term *'ayb*, which is commonly used in social interactions, cannot be reduced, as it always is, to the simple translation of "shame." When used in contexts of socializing children a better English translation would be "behave," not shame. In adult situations the word *'ayb* is almost always accompanied by the phrase *ma yisahhish*, meaning inappropriate or improper. Together the reference is more to improper conduct or inappropriate behavior rather than shameful behavior, which has Euro-Christian moral connotations.

151. Nowadays structures of male support are dismantled and men are not meeting their legal financial obligation toward the women in the family, which was the premise underlying the justification for the asymmetry in Islamic inheritance laws, which grant a woman half the share of her brother. It is common for fathers to get around the law and find alternative ways to protect the rights of their daughters. Increasingly in Egypt, for example, fathers are distributing their wealth in their lifetime in the form of *hiba* (gifts) rather than *mirath* (inheritance), which becomes effective only after their deaths. There is no "will" in Islam.

152. *Bint al-Balad* (folk woman) and *ibn al-Balad* (folk man) represent a lifestyle independent of the level of wealth. They live in the old traditional urban quarters of Cairo. Their appearance is marked by a distinct dress and style of public behavior.

153. See Reid (1995: 168–71a) for more detail on al-Azhar's shifting role in Islamic society and its relation to power and the state.

154. Using the word "reveiling" (see Zuhur 1992) in reference to this contemporary phenomenon is misleading and inaccurate.

155. It is rather ironic that in this year's World Cup (July 1998) held in France the final victory of the French team was due to a masterful Muslim Algerian soccer star who is a citizen of France. In a sense France continues to benefit from Algerian resources.

156. The classist characterization of Egypt using the tripartite classification of lower, middle, and upper that is used in most writings on Egypt is too simple and too ethnocentric to be of value in understanding groupings in modern urban and traditional urban quarters and rural

Egypt. Wealth, education, religion, etc. do not lend themselves to neat (US-like) "class" membership. There are very wealthy butchers proud of their "Baladi" identity and living in traditional urban quarters, for example. There are educated, Westernized, urbanized individuals with strong rural backgrounds who visit their relatives in the villages. For the purposes of discussion of urban movements and class organization prior to the Revolution of the 1950s, which is the point where one can (though still simplistically) talk about an emergent middle class, it is best to use the dichotomy that has gone out of use: ascribed-status class and achieved-status class. This would be particularly useful in discussions on the Western-influenced feminist movement.

157.   Huda Sha'rawi was born Nur al-Huda Sultan in 1897 in Minya in southern Egypt, the daughter of Sultan Pasha, a wealthy landowner, and Iqbal Hanim, a woman of Circassian origin. She was tutored at home and was proficient in French, but learned enough Arabic to memorize the *Qur'an* (Badran 1995b: 44–6).

158.   Malak Hifni Nasif, born 1886 and died 1918, is a feminist activist and writer, known by her pen name Bahithat al-Badiya ("Researcher of the Desert"). The daughter of a scholar, she entered primary school when the state opened a section for girls in 1895 and received a diploma in 1901. She also enrolled in the Teachers' Training Program at Saniyah School and received a certificate in 1905. After marriage she published and lectured. She sent a list of feminist demands to the Egyptian Congress in 1911 (Badran 1995c: 229–30).

159.   Through African-American, Asian-American, Arab-American, and Native-American women's voices and voices from the non-Western world, discussion of different feminisms is gaining momentum in scholarly debates and activist forums. The dominance of the Western model of feminism is being challenged. See Warhol and Herndl 1997 and Mohanty *et al.* 1991.

160.   It is mentioned in Sha'rawi's *Memoirs* (see Sha'rawi 1981: 45) that she secretly bought popular novels from women peddlers. She writes (1981: 43) that she yearned to learn Arabic and that she completed memorizing (*khatma*) the *Qur'an* as she turned nine years old (1981: 44). Her mother gave a *khatma* celebration to mark the event. According to her *Memoirs*, private lessons were given in the Arabic, Turkish and French languages. When she asked the teacher to teach her Arabic grammar, Sa'id Agha, the chaperon-eunuch who attended all lessons and chaperoned Sha'rawi everywhere, shrugged it off, telling the teacher (sarcastically) not to do so, as "she will not become a lawyer one day" (Sha'rawi 1981: 43). She describes her resentment both of

Sa'id Agha and of all the controls on her. The eunuch chaperon played a role close to that of a governess and different from that of a nanny, though one of those also formed part of the domestic staff in Sha'rawi's home. For a perspective on the *Memoirs* as literature see Kahf (1998). Kahf notes how the first eleven chapters of the *Memoirs* "tell the story of the journey to acquisition of voice by the girl who had been left outside the door of Arabic self-articulation" (1998: 65). The question is: what was the role of Huda's secretary, Abd al-Hamid Fahmi Mursi? Was he a passive ghostwriter or a subordinate "editor" of her orally transmitted chronicle? The latter is the most likely.

161. These were: *Tarqiyat al-Mar'a* (1908), *al-'Afaf* (1892), and *Fatat al-Nil* (1913).

162. They were: *al-Jins al-Latif* (1908) and *al-Sufur* (1915). The writer and editor Abd al-Hamid Hamdi founded the last, which endorsed complete unveiling and progress and reform in all domains (1915: 1(1), 1, 2).

163. This observation is made in the article by Beth Baron (1989: 379; see also Baron 1994).

164. Ahmed 1992 observes that analysts (such as Cole 1981: 394–407) routinely treat the debate as one between "feminists," that is, Amin and his allies, and "antifeminists," that is, Amin's critics: those who called for the veil's abandonment were feminist, and those opposing its abandonment were antifeminists (1992: 162).

165. Ahmed (1992) describes the dominant political groups in Egypt at the time Amin's work was published. One group strongly supported the British occupation and Europeanization; dominant in it were Syrian Christians, who founded the pro-British newspaper *al-Muqattam*. At the other end of the spectrum, a group strongly opposed Westernization, supporting instead an Islamic tradition. Their views were published in the newspaper *Al-Mu'ayyad* of Sheikh 'Ali Yusuf. Led by Mustapha Kamil, the National Party (al-Hizb al-Watani) also opposed the British and Westernization, but took a secularist position. To them, expelling the British was the priority. Then there was the People's Party (al-Umma), influenced by the thought of Muhammad 'Abdu, which espoused combining Western technology and knowledge, including the European notion of the nation-state, with the Islamic heritage and Islamic reform. The goal was ultimately Egypt's independence from the British. Ahmed describes their approach as that of "measured collaboration." Ahmad Lutfi al-Sayyid and Za'd Zaghloul were prominent leaders in this last party (1992: 144–68).

To sum up the various ideological political threads: there was (1) one that supported Europeanization and British colonialism, (2) one that opposed Westernization and reaffirmed tradition and Islam, (3) one that opposed colonialism and Westernization, choosing a secular path, and (4) one that called for adopting Western technology and knowledge, but chose to revitalize the Islamic heritage, and to reform women's position within it.

166. Sulayman al-Salimi, *Didd al 'Afaf* ("Against *Virtue*"), Vol. 1, No. 28 (29 May 1911), p. 14. This is cited in Baron 1989: 383.

167. A contemporary yet opposite of Zaynab al-Ghazali, in that the former had internalized the superiority of Europe and European ways.

168. Kahf's notion of *hijab*'s two layers of meaning: concealment versus covering, is polemical and analytically unproductive (1998: 79).

169. Baron, like many writers, makes a link between women's veiling, seclusion, and the "harem system." This linkage hinders analysis. She mistakenly interprets Huda Sha'rawi's dramatic unveiling as "the signal for the end of the harem system" (1989: 371).

170. Here I disagree with Baron, who suggested that the dramatic unveiling act may have been "a significant gesture only to those of the elite" (1989: 371).

171. A 1910 photograph in the collection of *al-Mathaf al-Markazi al-Qawmi li-Buhuth al-Tarbiya* (the Central National Museum for Educational Research), of Wizarat al-Tarbiya (the Ministry of Education) in Cairo shows students from Abbas girls' school with their faces uncovered. This was noted in Baron (1989).

172. "A Student in the House," Aflaha Tullab al-Sufur, al-'Afaf, 1 (20), 24 March 1911. This is noted in Baron (1989).

173. A photograph taken during the 1919 Revolution shows an unveiled schoolgirl addressing the crowd (Shaarawi 1987: 115).

174. This was in a taped interview I carried out with the feminist Ceza al-Nabarawi, a contemporary of Huda Sha'rawi, in February 1979 during our participation in the Symposium, "The Changing Role of Sudanese Women," held in Khartoum, Sudan (22–28 February 1979), in celebration of the 75th anniversary of the founding of the Al-Ahfad Schools and Girls' Education.

175. Earl Cromer, *Modern Egypt*, 2 vols. (New York: Macmillan, 1908) 2: 146, cited in Ahmed 1992.

176. This is separate and different from the Society of Muslim Sisters (*al-Akhawat al-Muslimat*), a branch organization of the Muslim Brothers. According to Ahmed "women who joined the . . . Muslim Sisters . . . wore a head covering," (1992: 194) but the position of

the organization differed little from the general modernist position (1992: 194).

177. The bias built into secularist scholarship is not addressed. It raised the question for my theoretical formulation of feminism of whether an individual Muslim woman's personal experiences (childhood abuse or rape) or ideological positions (such as atheism) qualify her formulations to enter a culture-free spectrum of feminisms? To what extent is one individual's account of abuse only that? To what extent does an atheist position prejudice discussion on religion? The case of the Bangladeshi physician/writer Taslima Nasrin comes to mind.

178. The jubilation among Arab populations, including those in the Gulf countries, over Iran's recent (June 1998) victory over the United States in the recent World Cup held in France is another manifestation of the shift. Further, the decision by the United Nations General Assembly on 7 July 1998 that granted Special Status to Palestine (alongside the Vatican and Switzerland) is a crucial development.

Bibliography

Books and Articles

Abbott, Nabia (1941) 'Women and the State on the Eve of Islam,' *American Journal of Semitic Languages* 58.

Abbott, Nabia (1942) *Aishah, the Beloved of Muhammad*. Chicago: University of Chicago Press.

Abbott, Nabia (1946) *Two Queens of Baghdad: Mother and Wife of Harun al-Rashid*. Chicago: University of Chicago Press.

Abou-Zeid, Ahmed M. (1959) 'The Sedentarization of Nomads in the Western Desert of Egypt,' *UNESCO International Social Science Journal* 11: 550–8.

Abou-Zeid, Ahmed M. (1966) 'Honour and Shame Among the Bedouins of Egypt,' in J. G. Peristiany (ed.), *Honour and Shame*, pp. 243–59. Chicago: University of Chicago Press.

Abou-Zeid, Ahmed M. (1979) 'New Towns and Rural Development in Egypt,' *Africa* 49: 283–90.

Abu-Lughod, Lila (1986) *Veiled Sentiments: Honor and Poetry in a Bedouin Society*. Berkeley, CA: University of California Press.

Abu-Lughod, Lila (1991) 'Writing Against Culture,' in Richard G. Fox (ed.), *Recapturing Anthropology*, pp. 137–62. Santa Fe, NM: Santa Fe School of American Research Press.

Abu-Lughod, Lila (1992) *Writing Women's Worlds: Bedouin Stories*. Berkeley, CA: University of California Press.

Abu-Nasr, Jamil M. (1975) *A History of the Maghrib*. Cambridge: Cambridge University Press.

Abu-Zahra, Nadia (1970) 'On the Modesty of Women in Arab Muslim Villages: A Reply,' *American Anthropologist* 72(5), October: 1079–88.

Adams, Charles J. (1983) 'Mawdudi and the Islamic State,' in John L. Esposito (ed.), *Voices of Resurgent Islam*, pp. 99–133. New York and Oxford: Oxford University Press.

Ahmed, Akbar S. (1988) *Discovering Islam*. London and New York: Routledge and Kegan Paul.

Ahmed, Akbar S. (1993) *Living Islam: From Samarkand to Stornoway*. London: BBC Books Ltd.

Ahmed, Leila (1982) 'Western Ethnocentrism and Perceptions of the Harem,' *Feminist Studies* 8(3), Fall: 521–34.

Ahmed, Leila (1992) *Women and Gender in Islam: Historical Roots of A Modern Debate*. New Haven, CT: Yale University Press.

Alireza, Marianne (1971) *At the Drop of a Veil*. Boston: Houghton Mifflin.

Alloula, Malek (1986) *The Colonial Harem* (trans. of *Le Harem Colonial: Images d'un Sous-Erotisme* by Myrna Godzich and Wlad Godzich). Theory and History of Literature, Vol. 21, Minneapolis, MN: University of Minnesota Press.

Amin, Qasim (1976 [1899]) *Al-a'mal al-Kamilah li-Qasim Amin (Complete Works of Qasim Amin)*, Vol. 1, *Tahrir al-Mar'a (The Liberation of Woman)*, Reprinted and compiled in 'Amarah's work, ed. Muhammad 'Amarah, pp. 7–114. Beirut: al-Mu'assasa al-'Arabiyya lil-Dirasat wal-Nashr.

Amin, Qasim (1976 [1900]) *Al-A'mal al-Kamilah li-Qasim Amin (Complete Works of Qasim Amin)*, Vol. 2, *al-Mar'a al-Gadida (The New Woman)*, Reprinted and compiled in 'Amarah's work, ed. Muhammad 'Amarah, pp. 115–230. Beirut: al-Mu'assasa al-'Arabiyya lil-Dirasat wal-Nashr.

Amin, Samir (1989) *L'eurocentrisme*, trans. Russell Moore. New York: Monthly Review Press.

Anderson, Jon W. (1982) 'Social Structure and the Veil: Comportment and the Composition of Interaction in Afghanistan,' *Anthropos* 77: 397–420.

Antoun, Richard T. (1968) 'On the Modesty of Women in Arab Muslim Villages: A Study in the Accommodation of Traditions,' *American Anthropologist* 70(4), August: 671–97.

Antoun, Richard T. (1970) 'Antoun's Reply to Abu-Zahra,' *American Anthropologist* 72(5): 1088–92.

Antoun, Richard T. (1972) *Arab Village: A Social Structural Study of Transjordanian Village*. Bloomington, IN: Indiana University Press.

Apostolos-Cappaduna, Piane (1996) *Encyclopedia of Religious Art*. Oxford: Oxford University Press.

Ardener, Edwin (1975a) 'Belief and the problem of women,' in Shirley Ardener (ed.), *Perceiving Women*, pp. 1–17. London: Dent.

Ardener, Edwin (1975b) 'The voice of prophecy,' The Munro Lecture, delivered in Edinburgh.

Ardener, Shirley (1993) 'Ground rules and social maps for women: An introduction,' in Shirley Ardener (ed.), *Women and Space: Ground Rules and Social Maps*, pp. 1–30. Oxford: Berg.

Aristotle (1921) *The Works of Aristotle (12 volumes)*, ed. W. D. Ross, trans. Benjamin Jowett. Oxford: Clarendon Press.

Armstrong, Karen (1995) *Through the Narrow Gate*. New York: St. Martin's Press.

Asbahani, Abu al-Faraj al- (1927 [1868,1905]) *Kitab al-Aghani* (20 vols), 3rd edn. Cairo: reprint of Dar al-Kutub version.

Aswad, Barbara C. (1967) 'Key and Peripheral Roles of Noble Women in a Middle Eastern Plains Village,' *Anthropological Quarterly* 40: 139–52.

Aswad, Barbara C. (1974) 'Visiting Patterns Among Women of the Elite in a Small Turkish City,' *Anthropological Quarterly* 47: 9–27.

Aswad, Barbara C. (1978) 'Women, Class, and Power: Examples from the Hatay,

Turkey,' in L. Beck and N. Keddie (eds), *Women in the Muslim World*, pp. 473–81. Cambridge, MA: Harvard University Press.

Badran, Margot (1995a) *Feminists, Islam, and Nation: Gender and the Making of Modern Egypt*. Princeton, NJ: Princeton University Press.

Badran, Margot (1995b) 'Huda Sha'rawi,' in John L. Esposito (ed.), *The Oxford Encyclopedia of the Modern Islamic World*, Vol. 4. New York and Oxford: Oxford University Press.

Badran, Margot (1995c) 'Malak Hifni Nasif (1886–1918),' in John L. Esposito (ed.), *The Oxford Encyclopedia of the Modern Islamic World*, Vol. 3. New York and Oxford: Oxford University Press.

Baizerman, S., Joanne B. Eicher and C. Cerny (1993) 'Eurocentrism in the Study of Ethnic Dress,' *Dress* 20: 19–32.

Baker, Patricia L. (1997) 'Politics of Dress: The Dress Reform Laws of 1920–1930s Iran,' in N. Lindisfarne-Tapper and Bruce Ingham (eds), *Languages of Dress in the Middle East*, pp. 178–92. London: Curzon with The Centre of Near and Middle Eastern Studies, SOAS.

Barnes, Ruth and Joanne B. Eicher (1992a) 'Introduction,' in Ruth Barnes and Joanne B. Eicher (eds), *Dress and Gender: Making and Meaning in Cultural Contexts*, pp. 1–7. Providence, RI and Oxford: Berg.

Barnes, Ruth and Joanne B. Eicher, Editors (1992b) *Dress and Gender: Making and Meaning*. Providence, RI and Oxford: Berg.

Baron, Beth (1989) 'Unveiling in Early Twentieth-Century Egypt: Practical and Symbolic Considerations,' *Middle Eastern Studies* 25(3), July: 370–86.

Baron, Beth (1994) *The Women's Awakening in Egypt: Culture, Society, and the Press*. New Haven, CT and London: Yale University Press.

Barraclough, Steven (1998) 'Al-Azhar: Between The Government And The Islamists,' *The Middle East Journal* 52(2), Spring: 236–50.

Barthes, Roland (1957) 'Histoire et sociologies du vêtement,' *Annales*: ESC.

Barthes, Roland (1982) *Camera Lucida* (trans. by Richard Howard from the Fr. original *La Chambre Claire: Note Sur la Photographie*, Paris: Editions du Seuil, 1980). New York: Hill and Wang.

Basha, Ibrahim Rif'at (1925) *Mir'at al-Haramayn*. Cairo: Dar al-Kutub al-Masriyya.

Bateson, Gregory (1958 [1936]) *Naven*. Stanford, CA: Stanford University Press.

Berque, Jacques (1967) *French North Africa: The Maghrib Between Two World Wars* (trans. Jean Stewart). London: Faber and Faber.

Betteridge, Ann (1983) 'To Veil or Not to Veil: A Matter of Protection or Policy,' in Guity Nashat (ed.), *Women and Revolution in Iran*. Boulder, CO: Westview Press.

Bohannon, P. (1956) 'Beauty and Scarification Amongst the Tiv,' *Man* 56: 117–121.

Bon, Ottaviano (1996) *The Sultan's Seraglio: An Intimate Portrait of Life at the Ottoman Court* (From the Seventeenth-Century Edition of John Withers). London: Saqi Books.

Boucher, F. (1966) *20,000 Years of Fashion: The History of Costume and Personal Adornment*. New York: Harry N. Abrams.

Bourdieu, Pierre (1966) 'The Sentiment of Honour in Kabyle Society,' in J. G.

Peristiany (ed.), *Honour and Shame*, pp. 191–241. Chicago: University of Chicago Press.

Boxer, Marilyn (1982) 'For and About Women: The Theory and Practice of Women's Studies in the United States,' in N. Keohane, M. Rosaldo and B. Gelpi (eds), *Feminist Theory: A Critique of Ideology*, pp. 237–71. Brighton: Harvester Press.

Brenner, Suzanne (1996) 'Reconstructing Self and Society: Javanese Muslim Women and "the veil",' *American Ethnologist* 23(4): 673–97.

Brown, Peter (1988) *The Body and Society: Men, Women and Sexual Renunciation in Early Christianity*. New York: Columbia University Press.

Bukhari, Muhammad Ibn Ismail al- (1956) *Sahih al-Bukhari*, (eds), an-Nawawi, M. A. Ibrahim and M. Khafiji. Cairo.

Bukhari, Muhammad Ibn Ismail al- (1996) *Sahih al-Bukhari: English Translation with Arabic Text*. Alexandria: Al-Saasawi Publications.

Bürgel, J. C. (1979) 'Love, Lust, and Longing: Eroticism in Early Islam as Reflected in Literary Sources,' in Afaf Lutfi Al-Sayyid Marsot (ed.), *Society and the Sexes in Medieval Islam*, pp. 81–117. Malibu, CA: Undena Publications.

Burton, Richard F. (1964 [1855]) *A Personal Narrative of a Pilgrimage to al-Madinah and Meccah* (2 Vols). New York: Dover.

Campbell, J. K. (1964) *Honour, Family and Patronage: A Study of Institutions and Moral Values in a Greek Mountain Community*. Oxford: Oxford University Press.

Chatty, Dawn (1997) 'The Burqa Face Cover: An Aspect of Dress in Southeastern Arabia,' in N. Lindisfarne-Tapper and Bruce Ingham (eds), *Languages of Dress in the Middle East*, pp. 149–77. London: Curzon with The Centre of Near and Middle Eastern Studies, SOAS.

Chehabi, Houchang E. (1993) 'Staging the Emperor's New Clothes: Dress Codes and Nation-Building under Reza Shah,' *Iranian Studies* 26(3–4), Summer/Fall: 209–21.

Clot Bey, A. B. (1840) *Aperçu général sur L'Egypte* (2 vols), Vol. 2. Brussels: Meline.

Cole, Juan Ricardo (1981) 'Feminism, Class, and Islam in Turn-of-the-Century Egypt,' *International Journal of Middle East Studies* 13(4): 394–407.

Cowan, James (1996) *A Mapmaker's Dream: The Meditations of Fra Mauro, Cartographer to the Court of Venice*. Boston and London: Shambhala.

Crawley, E. (1912) 'Dress,' in *Encyclopedia of Religion*, Vol. 5, pp. 40–72. New York: Charles Scribner's sons.

Crawley, E.. (1931) *Dress, Drinks, and Drums: Further Studies of Savages and Sex*, ed. Theodore Besterman. London: Methuen.

Cromer, Earl (1908) *Modern Egypt*, 2 vols. New York: Macmillan.

Danielson, Virginia (1997) *The Voice of Egypt: Umm Kulthum, Arabic Song, and Egyptian Society in the Twentieth Century*. Chicago Studies in Ethnomusicology. Chicago: The University of Chicago Press.

Darwin, C. (1955 [1872]) *The Expression of the Emotions in Man and Animals*. New York: Greenwood Press.

Darwin, C. (n.d. (1859 and 1871, respectively)) *The Origin of Species* and *The Descent of Man, and Selection in Relation to Sex*. New York: The Modern Library.

Davenport, W. (1948) *The Book of Costume*. New York: Crown Publishers.

Davidoff, L. (1979) 'The Separation of Home and Work? Landladies and Lodgers in Nineteenth and Twentieth Century England,' in S. Burman (ed.), *Fit Work for Women*. London: Croom Helm.

Davis, Fanny (1986) *The Ottoman Lady: A Social History from 1718 to 1918*. Contributions in Women's Studies. New York: Greenwood Press.

Davis, Fred (1986) 'Clothing and Fashion as Communication,' in Michael R. Solomon (ed.), *The Psychology of Fashion*, pp. 15–27. Lexington, MA: Lexington Books, D. C. Heath.

Davis, Susan S. (1983) *Patience and Power: Women's Lives in a Moroccan Village*. Cambridge, MA: Schenkman.

de Matons, Jose Grosdidier (1967) 'La Femme dans l'Empire Byzantin,' in Pierre Grimal (ed.), *Histoire Mondiale de la Femme*, 4 vols. Paris: Novelle Librairie de France.

Dengler, Ian C. (1978) 'Turkish Women in the Ottoman Empire: The Classical Age,' in Lois Beck and Nikkik Keddire (eds), *Women in the Muslim World*, pp. 229–44, Cambridge, MA: Harvard University Press.

Dessouki, Ali E. Hillal, Editor (1982) *Islamic Resurgence in the Arab World*. New York: Praeger Publishers.

d'Huart, A. and N. Tazi (1980) *Harems*. Paris: Editions du Chêne.

Dorsky, Susan (1986) *Women of 'Amran: A Middle East Ethnographic Study*. Salt Lake City, UT: University of Utah Press.

Douglas, Mary (1970) 'Heathen Darkness, Modern Piety,' *New Society* 12 (March).

Douglas, Mary (1973a) 'Formal Correspondences,' in Mary Douglas (ed.), *Rules and Meaning: The Anthropology of Everyday Knowledge*, p. 249. New York: Penguin Books.

Douglas, Mary, Editor (1973b) *Rules and Meaning: The Anthropology of Everyday Knowledge*. New York: Penguin Books.

Doumato, Eleanor Abdella (1995) 'Seclusion,' in John L. Esposito (ed.), *The Oxford Encyclopedia of the Modern Islamic World* (4 Vols.), pp. 19–20. New York: Oxford University Press.

Dransart, Penny (1992) 'Pachamama: The Inka Earth Mother of the Long Sweeping Garment,' in R. Barnes and Joanne B. Eicher (eds), *Dress and Gender: Making and Meaning in Cultural Contexts*, pp. 145–63. Providence, RI and Oxford: Berg.

Driver, G. and John C. Miles, Editors (1935) *The Assyrian Laws*, trans. G. Driver and John C. Miles. Oxford: Clarendon Press.

Durkheim, E. and M. Mauss (1963 [1903, first published in France 1901–2]) *Primitive Classification*, trans. R. Needham. London: Cohen and West.

Early, Evelyn A. (1993) *Baladi Women of Cairo: Playing with an Egg and a Stone*. Boulder and London: Lynne Rienner Publisher.

Eicher, Joanne B. (1995a) 'Introduction: Dress as Expression of Ethnic Identity,' in Joanne B Eicher (ed.), *Dress and Ethnicity: Change Across Space and Time*, pp. 1–5. Oxford and Washington, DC: Berg.

Eicher, Joanne B., Editor (1995b) *Dress and Ethnicity: Change Across Space and*

Time. Ethnic Identities Series. Oxford and Washington, DC: Berg.

Eicher, Joanne, B. and M. E. Roach-Higgins (1992) 'Definition and Classification of Dress: Implications for Analysis of Gender Roles,' in Ruth Barnes and Joanne B. Eicher (eds), *Dress and Gender: Making and Meaning*, pp. 8–28. Providence, RI and Oxford: Berg.

Eicher, Joanne B. and Barbara Sumberg (1995) 'World Fashion, Ethnic, and National Dress,' in Joanne B. Eicher (ed.), *Dress and Ethnicity*, pp. 295–306. Oxford: Berg.

El Guindi, Fadwa (1980) 'Religious Revival and Islamic Survival in Egypt,' *International Insight* 1(2): 6–10.

El Guindi, Fadwa (1981a) 'Veiling Infitah with Muslim Ethic: Egypt's Contemporary Islamic Movement,' *Social Problems* 28(4): 465–85.

El Guindi, Fadwa (1981b) 'Is There An Islamic Alternative? The Case of Egypt's Contemporary Islamic Movement,' *Middle East Insight* 1(4): 19–24.

El Guindi, Fadwa (1981c) 'Religious Revival and Islamic Survival in Egypt (Reprinted),' *Middle East Insight* 2(1): 31–6.

El Guindi, Fadwa (1982a) 'From Consciousness to Activism: Dynamics of the Islamic Movement,' American Research Center Lecture Series. Cairo: ARCE Office.

El Guindi, Fadwa (1982b) 'The Killing of Sadat And After: A Current Assessment of Egypt's Islamic Movement,' *Middle East Insight* 2(5): 20–27.

El Guindi, Fadwa (1982c) 'Die Ruckkehr zum Schleier: Vom unaufhaltsamen Siegeszug eins konservativen Symbols. Nahost in Flammen,' *Der Monat* (285): 165–78.

El Guindi, Fadwa (1982d) 'Reveal and Conceal: Dynamics of Dress in Egypt,' *Fullbright (Cairo) Newsletter*.

El Guindi, Fadwa (1983) 'Veiled Activism: Egyptian Women in the Contemporary Islamic Movement,' *Peuples Méditerranéans (Femmes de la Méditerranée)* (22–3): 79–89.

El Guindi, Fadwa (1984) 'Veiled Activism: Egyptian Women in the Islamic Movement (Reprinted),' *Egypt Then and Now* II(1): 21–5.

El Guindi, Fadwa (1985a) 'The Sacred Divide,' paper presented at Middle East Studies Association Annual Meeting, New Orleans.

El Guindi, Fadwa (1985b) 'The Status of Women in Bahrain: Social and Cultural Considerations,' in J. Nugent and T. Thomas (eds), *Bahrain and the Gulf*, pp. 75–95. Sydney: Croom Helm.

El Guindi, Fadwa (1986a) 'The Mood in Egypt: Summer Heat or Revolution?' *Middle East Insight* 4(4 and 5): 30–9.

El Guindi, Fadwa (1986b) 'The Egyptian Woman: Trends Today, Alternatives Tomorrow,' in Lynne B. Iglitzin and Ruth Ross (eds), *Women in the World, 1975–1985: The Women's Decade*, pp. 225–42. Santa Barbara, CA: ABC-CLIO.

El Guindi, Fadwa (1986c) *The Myth of Ritual: Native Ethnography of Zapotec Life-Crisis Ritual*. Tucson, AZ: University of Arizona Press.

El Guindi, Fadwa (1987) 'Das islamische Kleid "al-hidschab,"' in G. Volger, K. V. Welck and K. Hackstein (eds), *Pracht und Geheimnis: Kleidung und Schmuck aus Palatina und Jordanie*, pp. 164–67. Köln: Rautenstrauch-Joest-Museum der Stadt Köln.

El Guindi, Fadwa (1991a) 'Images of Domination, Voices of Control,' *International Documentary: Journal of Nonfiction Film and Video*, Spring.

El Guindi, Fadwa (1991b) 'War "Game" Casts Iraqis as Losers,' *Media and Values*, Fall.

El Guindi, Fadwa (1992a) 'Feminism Comes of Age in Islam,' *Los Angeles Times (Op-Ed)*.

El Guindi, Fadwa (1992b) 'Distorted View Shrouds Image of Muslim Women (Op-Ed),' *The Atlanta Journal/The Atlanta Constitution (Sunday Edition)*.

El Guindi, Fadwa (1992c) 'Waging War On Civilization: Report on the Archeology of Mesopotamia,' in Ramsey Clark (ed.), *War Crimes: A Report on United States War Crimes Against Iraq*. Washington DC: Maisonneuve Press.

El Guindi, Fadwa (1993a) 'Charting Content, Freezing Structure: A Methodological Base for Visual Ethnography,' in Jack R. Rollwagen (ed.), *Anthropological Film and Video in the 1990s*, pp. 11–36. Brockport, NY: The Institute, Inc.

El Guindi, Fadwa (1993b) 'Mubarak Should Call an Election and Step Aside (Op-Ed),' *Los Angeles Times*.

El Guindi, Fadwa (1995a) 'Feminism Comes of Age in Islam,' in S. Sabbagh (ed.), *Arab Women: Between Defiance and Restraint*, pp. 159–61. New York: Olive Branch Press.

El Guindi, Fadwa (1995b) 'Hijab,' in John Esposito (ed.), *The Oxford Encyclopedia of the Modern Islamic World* (4 Vols.), pp. 108–11. Oxford: Oxford University Press.

El Guindi, Fadwa (1995c) 'Mawlid,' in John Esposito (ed.), *The Oxford Encyclopedia of the Modern Islamic World* (4 Vols.), pp. 78–82. Oxford: Oxford University Press.

El Guindi, Fadwa (1995d) 'Voice of Islam, Experience of Muslims: The Television Series, Review of Living,' *Anthropology Today* 11(1): 24–6.

El Guindi, Fadwa (1996a) 'Feminism Comes of Age in Islam,' in S. Sabbagh (ed.), *Arab Women: Between Defiance and Restraint*, pp. 159–61. New York: Olive Branch Press.

El Guindi, Fadwa (1996b) *Film Study Guide: Egyptian Celebration of Life Series – El Sebou'*. Los Angeles: El Nil Research.

El Guindi, Fadwa (1997) 'Islamic Identity and Resistance,' Middle East Institute Annual Conference. National Press Club, Washington DC, Friday, 3 October .

El Guindi, Fadwa (1998a) 'Gender in Islamic Activism: The Case of Egypt,' McLean, Virginia, 21 May.

El Guindi, Fadwa (1998b) 'UN Should Act to Protect Muslim Women,' *Newsday*, Monday, 13 April, A29.

El Guindi, Fadwa (1998c) 'From Pictorializing to Visual Anthropology,' in H. Bernard Russell (ed.), *Handbook of Methods in Cultural Anthropology*, pp. 459–512. Walnut Creek, CA: Altamira Press, Sage Publications.

Ellis, H. H. (1897) *Studies in the Psychology of Sex*. London: Society of Psychological Research.

El-Messiri, Sawsan (1978) 'Self Images of Traditional Urban Women in Cairo,' in

L. Beck and N. Keddie (eds), *Women in Muslim Society*, pp. 522–57. Cambridge, MA: Harvard University Press.

El Saadawi, Nawal (1980) *The Hidden Face of Eve*, trans. Sherif Hetata. London: Zed Press.

Ellis, H. H. (1897) *Studies in the Psychology of Sex*. London: Society of Psychological Research.

Fanon, Frantz (1967) *A Dying Colonialism*, trans. Haakon Chevalier. New York: Grove Press.

Faris, James C. (1972) *Nuba Personal Art*, Art and Society Series. London: Duckworth.

Fawwaz, Zainab (1896) *Kitab Al-Durr al-MantHur fi Tabaqat Rabbat al-Khudur*. Cairo.

Ferguson, Francis (1966) 'Myth and the Literary Scruple,' in John B. Vickery (ed.), *Myth and Literature*. Lincoln, NB: University of Nebraska Press.

Fernea, Elizabeth W. (1965) *Guests of the Sheik: An Ethnography of an Iraqi Village*. Garden City, NY: Doubleday, Anchor Books.

Fernea, Elizabeth W. (1981) 'An Early Ethnographer of Middle Eastern Women: Lady Mary Wortley Montagu (1689–1762),' *Journal of Near Eastern Studies* 40(4), October: 329–38.

Fernea, Elizabeth W. and Basima Q. Bezirgan (1977) 'Huda Sha'rawi: Founder of the Egyptian Women's Movement,' in Elizabeth W. Fernea and Basima Q. Bezirgan (eds), *Middle Eastern Muslim Women Speak*, pp. 193–200. Austin, TX and London: University of Texas Press.

Fernea, Elizabeth W. and Robert A. Fernea (1979) 'A Look Behind the Veil,' *Human Nature* 2: 68–77.

Forget, Nelly (1962) 'Attitudes towards Work by Women in Morocco,' *International Social Science Journal* 14(1): 92–124.

Foucault, Michel (1980) *The History of Sexuality*. New York: Vintage - Random House.

Fowler, Orson (1898) *Intemperance and Tight-Lacing*. Manchester: J. Heywood.

Garnett, Mrs M. J. (1896) *Turkish Life in Town and Country*. London: G. P. Putnam's Sons.

Garnett, Mrs. M. J. (1909) *The Turkish People*. London: Methuen and Co..

Gaudio, Attilio and Renée Pelletier (1980) *Femmes d'Islam Ou Le Sexe Interdit*. Paris: Denoil/Gonthier.

Geertz, Clifford (1968) *Islam Observed: Religious Development in Morocco and Indonesia*. Chicago and London: The University of Chicago Press.

Ghazali, Zaynab al- (1977) *Ayam min Hayati (Days from My Life) (Arabic)*. Cairo and Beirut: Dar al-Shuruq.

Gilsenan, Michael (1982) *Recognizing Islam: Religion and Society in the Modern Arab World*. New York: Pantheon Books.

Glob, P. V. (1954) 'Bahrain, oen med de hundrede tusinds gravhoje (Bahrain – Island of the Hundred Thousand Burial Mounds,' *KUML*.

Glob, P. V. (1959) 'Arkaeologiske undersagelser i fire arabiske stater (Archeological

Investigations in Four Arab States),' *KUML.*

Goffman, E. (1951) 'Symbols of Class Status,' *British Journal of Sociology* 2: 294–304.

Goffman, E. (1971) *Relations in Public, Microstudies of the Public Order.* New York: Harper and Row.

Goitein, S. D. (1967) *A Mediterranean Society: The Jewish Communities of the Arab World as Portrayed in the Documents of the Cairo Geniza* (5 vols.), Vol. I, *Economic Foundations.* Berkeley, CA: University of California Press.

Goitein, S. D. (1978) *A Mediterranean Society: The Jewish Communities of the Arab World as Portrayed in the Documents of the Cairo Geniza* (5 vols), Vol. III, *The Family.* Berkeley, CA: University of California Press.

Goitein, S. D. (1983) *A Mediterranean Society: The Jewish Communities of the Arab World as Portrayed in the Documents of the Cairo Geniza* (5 vols.), Vol. IV, *Daily Life.* Berkeley, CA: University of California Press.

Goldschmidt, A. Jr. (1983) A Concise History of the Middle East. Boulder, CO: Westview Press.

Goodwin, Godfrey (1996) 'Introduction', in Bon, Ottaviano, *The Sultan's Seraglio: An Intimate Portrait of Life at the Ottoman Court (From the Seventeenth-Century Edition of John Withers),* pp. 11–19. London: Saqi Books.

Goodwin, Godfrey (1997) *The Private World of Ottoman Women.* London: Saqi Books.

Gordon, David (1962) *North Africa's French Legacy, 1954–1962.* Harvard Middle East Monograph Series. Cambridge, MA: Harvard University Press.

Gordon, David C. (1968) *Women of Algeria: an Essay on Change.* Harvard Middle Eastern Monograph Series. Cambridge, MA: Harvard University Press.

Gordon, Lady Lucie Duff (1969) *Letters from Egypt (1862–1869).* London: Routledge and Kegan Paul.

Graham-Brown, Sarah (1988) *Images of Women: The Portrayal of Women in Photography of the Middle East, 1860–1950.* London: Quartet Books.

Haddad, Yvonne Y. (1983) 'Sayyid Qutb: Ideologue of Islamic Revival,' in John L. Esposito (ed.), *Voices of Resurgent Islam,* pp. 67–98. New York and Oxford: Oxford University Press.

Hajj, Abu 'Abdullah al-'Abdari Ibn al-', Author (1929) *Al-Madkhal* (4 vols.). Cairo: Al-Matba'a Al-Misriyya.

Hajj, Abu 'Abdullah al-'Abdari Ibn al- (1960) *Al-Madkhal,* Vol. 1. Cairo: Sharikat Maktabat wa-Matba'at Mustapha al-Babi al-Halabi wa-Awladih.

Hall, E. T. (1959) *The Silent Language.* New York: Doubleday.

Hall, G. Stanley (1898) 'Some Aspects of the Early Sense of Self,' *American Journal of Psychology.*

Halsband, Robert (1956) *The Life of Lady Mary Wortley Montagu.* Oxford.

Halsband, Robert, Editor (1965a) *The Complete Letters of Lady Mary Wortley Montagu* (2 Vols). Oxford: Clarendon Press.

Halsband, Robert (1965b) 'Preface,' in Robert Halsband (ed.), *The Complete Letters of Lady Mary Wortley Montagu,* (2 Vols), pp. i–vii. Oxford: Clarendon Press.

Hamdi, 'Abd al-Hamid (1915) 'al-Sufur (Unveiling),' *al-Sufur*, 21 May, 1–2.

Hamdy, Ahmad Mahmoud (1959) *Beautification Tools in Museum of Islamic Art*. Cairo: The Museum.

Hammami, Rema (1990) 'Women, the Hijab and the Intifada,' *Middle East Report (164/165)* 20(3 and 4), May–June/July–August: 24–28.

Hamza, Kariman (1981) *Rihlati min al-Sufur ilal-Hijab (My Journey from Exposure to Modesty)*. Cairo: Dar al-I'tisam.

Hanna, Nelly (1991) *Habiter au Caire*. Cairo: Institut Français d'Archéologie Orientale du Caire.

Hansen, Henry Harald (1961) 'The Pattern of Women's Seclusion and Veiling in a Shi'a Village,' *Folk* 3: 23–42.

Hansen, Henry Harald (1967) *Investigations in a Shi'a Village in Bahrain*. Copenhagen: The National Museum of Denmark.

Harb, Tal'at (1899 [1905]) *Tarbiyet al-Mar'a wa al-hijab (Socialization of Women and the Veil)*. Cairo: Matba'at al-Manar.

Harb, Tal'at (1901) *Fasl al-Khitab fi al-Mar'ah wa al-hijab (The Last Word on the Woman and the Veil)*. Cairo: Matba'at al-Manar.

Harlow, Barbara (1986) 'Introduction,' in *The Colonial Harem*, pp. ix–xxii. Minneapolis, MN: University of Minnesota Press.

Hasib, Laila (1996) ' Exotic western view of Muslim women,' http: //www.malaysia. net/muslimedia/, Multimedia International, 30 June.

Heikal, Mohamed (1975) *The Road to Ramadan*. New York: Quadrangle/The New York Times Book Co.

Hertz, R. (1973 [originally in French 1909]) *The Pre-eminence of the Right Hand* (originalay "Death and the Right Hand'), trans. And ed. R. Needham. London: Cohen and West.

Herzfeld, M. (1980) 'Honour and Shame: Problems in the Comparative Analysis of Moral Systems,' *Man*15: 339–51.

Herzfeld, M. (1987) *Anthropology Through the Looking Glass: Critical Ethnography in the Margins of Europe*. Cambridge, MA: Cambridge University Press.

Higgins, Patricia J. (1985) 'Women in the Islamic Republic of Iran: Legal, Social and Ideological Changes,' *Signs* 10(3): 477–94.

Hirschon, R. (1981) 'Essential Objects and the Sacred: Interior and Exterior Space in an Urban Greek Locality,' in Shirley Ardener (ed.), *Women and Space: Ground Rules and Social Maps*. London: Croom Helm.

Hirschon, R. (1993) 'Open Body/Closed Space: The Transformation of Female Sexuality,' in S. Ardener (ed.), *Defining Females: The Nature of Women in Society*, pp. 51–72. Oxford: Berg.

Hitchcock, J. and L. Minturn (1963) 'The Rajputs of Khalapur, India,' in B. Whiting (ed.), *Six Cultures*. New York: John Wiley.

Hoffman-Ladd, Valerie J. (1987) 'Polemics on the Modesty and Segregation of Women in Contemporary Egypt,' *International Journal of Middle East Studies* 19(1), February: 23–50.

Hoffman-Ladd, Valerie J. (1995) 'Zaynab Al-Ghazali,' in John L. Esposito (ed.),

The Oxford Encyclopedia of the Modern Islamic World, Vol. 2. New York and Oxford: Oxford University Press.

Hoodfar, Homa (1991) 'Return to the Veil: Personal Strategy and Public Participation in Egypt,' in Nanneke Edclift and M. Thea Sinclair (eds), *Working Women: International Perspectives on Laour and Gender Ideology*, pp. 104–24. London and New York: Routledge.

Ibn Khaldun, Abdul Rahman (1867–1868) *Kitab al-'Ibar*, ed. Shaikh Nasr af Hurini, 7 vols, Cairo: Bulaq.

Ibn Khaldun, Abdul Rahman (1958) *The Muqaddimah: An Introduction to History* (3 vols), Vol. 2, trans. Franz Rosenthal. Bollingen Series XLIII. Princeton, NJ: Princeton University Press.

Ibn Manzur (1883–1890) *Lisan al-Arab*. Cairo: Bulaq.

Ibn Sa'd (1905–1928) *Kitabu't-Tabaqat al-Kabir*. Leiden: Brill.

Ibrahim, Saad Eddin (1980) 'Anatomy of Egypt's Militant Islamic Groups: Methodological Notes and Preliminary Findings,' *International Journal of Middle East Studies* 12(4): 426–44.

Ibrahim, Saad Eddin (1982) 'The Islamic Alternative in Egypt: the Muslim Brotherhood and Sadat,' *Arab Studies Quarterly* 4(1 and 2).

Idlibi, Ulfat al- (1988) 'The Women's Baths,' trans. Michel G. Azrak, in Michel B. Azrak and M. J. L. Young (eds), *Modern Syrian Short Stories*, pp. 19–27. Washington DC: Three Continents Press.

Imarah, Muhammad, Editor (1976) *Al-a'mal al-Kamilah li-Qasim Amin (Complete Works of Qasim Amin)*, pp. 11–366. Beirut: al-Mu'assasa al-'Arabiyya lil-Dirasat wal-Nashr.

Jabarti, Abd al-Rahman al- (1882) *Ajaib al-Athar fi-l tarajim wa-l Akhbar*, 4 vols. Cairo: Lajnat al-Bayan al-'Arabi.

Jacobson, D. (1970) 'Hidden Faces: Hindu and Muslim Purdah in a Central Indian Village,' Dissertation, Columbia University, New York.

Jennings, Anne M. (1995) *The Nubians of West Aswan: Village Women in the Midst of Change*, Women & Change in The Developing World. Boulder, CO: Lynne Rienner Publishers.

Jubouri, Yahia (al-) (1989) *Arab Clothes in Pre-Islamic Poetry: A Descriptive Dictionary of Arab Garments*. Beirut: Dar al-Gharb al-Islami.

Jullian, Philippe (1977) *Les Orientalistes*. Paris: Office du Livre.

Kahf, Mohja (1998) 'Huda Sha'rawi's Mudhakkirati: The Memoirs of the First Lady of Arab Modernity,' *Arab Studies Quarterly* 20(1), Winter: 53–82.

Kanafani, Aida S. (1983) *Aesthetics and Ritual in the United Arab Emirates: The Anthropology of Food and Personal Adornment among Arabian Women*. Beirut, Lebanon and Syracuse, New York: American University of Beirut and Syracuse University Press.

Kaplan, Daile (1984) 'Enlightened Women in Darkened Lands – A Lantern Slide Lecture,' *Studies in Visual Communication* 10(1), Winter: 61–77.

Khalidi, 'Anbara Salam al- (1978) *Jawla fil-Thikrayat bayna Lubnan wa-Falastin (A Journey into Memories From Lebanon to Palestine)*. Beirut: Dar al-Nahar.

Khuri, Fuad I. (1980) *Tribe and State in Bahrain.* Chicago: University of Chicago Press.

Kimball, Michelle R. and Barbara R. von Schlegell, Editors (1997) *Muslim Women Throughout The World: A Bibliography.* Boulder, CO: Lynne Rienner Publishers.

Kramer, S. N. (1961) *Sumerian Mythology.* New York: Harper Torchbooks.

Kroeber, A. L. (1919) 'On the Principle of Order in Civilization as Exemplified by Changes in Fashion,' *American Anthropologist* 21, July: 235–63.

Kroeber, A. L. (1957) *Style and Civilization.* Ithaca, NY: Cornell University Press.

Kroeber, A. L. and J. Richardson (1940) 'Three Centuries of Women's Dress Fashions: A Quantitative Analysis,' *Anthropological Records* 5(2): 111–53.

Kunzle, David (1977) 'Dress Reform as Antifeminism: A Response to Helene E. Roberts's "The Exquisite Slave: The Role of Clothes in the Making of the Victorian Woman",' *Signs: Journal of Women in Culture and Society* 2(3): 570–9.

Lancaster, William (1981) *The Rwala Bedouin Today*, Changing Cultures. Cambridge, MA: Cambridge University Press.

Lane, Edward W. (1883) *Arabic–English Lexicon.* Cambridge, MA: The Islamic Texts Sociey.

Lane, Edward W. (1923) *Manners and Customs of the Modern Egyptians.* London: Dent.

Laroui, Abdallah (1977) *The History of the Maghrib: An Interpretive Essay* (trans. Ralph Mannheim). Princeton, NJ: Princeton University Press.

Lerner, Gerda (1986) *The Creation of Patriarchy.* New York: Oxford University Press.

Lewis, O. (1956) *Village Life in Northern India.* New York: Vintage Books.

Lhote, Henri (1955) *Les Touaregs du Hoggar.* Paris: Payot.

Lichtenstadter, Ilse (1935) *Women in the 'Aiyam al-'Arab: A Study of Female Life During Warfare in Preislamic Arabia.* London: Royal Asiatic Society.

Lindisfarne-Tapper, N. and Bruce Ingham, Editors (1997a) *Languages of Dress in the Middle East.* London: Curzon with The Centre of Near and Middle Eastern Studies, SOAS.

Lindisfarne-Tapper, N., and Bruce Ingham (1997b) 'Approaches to the Study of Dress in the Middle East,' in N. Lindisfarne-Tapper and Bruce Ingham (eds), *Languages of Dress in the Middle East*, pp. 1–39. London: Curzon with The Centre of Near and Middle Eastern Studies, SOAS.

Lucas, P. and Jean-Claude Vatin (1975) *L'Algerie des Anthropologues.* Paris: Maspero.

Mabro, Judy (1991) *Veiled Half-Truths: Western Travellers' Perceptions of Middle Eastern Women,* London: I. B. Tauris.

MacLeod, A. E. (1993) *Accommodating Protest: Working Women, the New Veiling and Change in Cairo.* New York: Columbia University Press.

Maimonides (1965) *Mishneh Torah: The Book of Adoration*, trans. Moses Hyamson. Jerusalem: Boys Town Jerusalem Publishers.

Makhlouf, Carla (1979) *Changing Veils: Women and Modernisation in North Yemen.* Austin, TX: University of Texas Press.

Maqrizi, Ahmad ibn 'Ali al- (1972 [1934[]) *As-Suluk fi Ma'rifat Duwal al-Muluk.* Bulaq: al-Mabu'at al-Mairiyah.

Marçais, W. (1928) 'L'islamisme et la vie urbain,' *Communication, Comptes Rendus, Académie des Inscriptions et Belles-Lettres.*

Marsot, Afaf L. al-Sayyid (1978) 'The Revolutionary Gentlewomen in Egypt,' in L. Beck and N. Keddie (eds), *Women in the Muslim World*, pp. 261–76. Cambridge, MA: Harvard University Press.

Marsot, Afaf L. al-Sayyid (1979) *Society and the Sexes in Medieval Islam*, ed. Afaf L. al-Sayyid Marsot. Malibu, CA: Undena Publications.

Maurel, Christian (1980) *L'Exotisme Colonial*. Paris: Laffont.

Mawdudi, Abu al-A'la al- (1972) *Purdah and the Status of Woman in Islam*. Lahore: Islamic Publications.

Mawdudi, Abu-al A'la al- (1985) *Al-Hijab*. Damascus: al-Dar al-Sa'udiyya.

Meek, Theophile J. (trans.) (1950) 'The Middle Assyrian Laws,' IN James B. Pritchard, (ed.), *Ancient Near Eastern Texts Relating to the Old Testament*, pp. 183–85. Princeton, NJ: Princeton University Press.

Melman, Billie (1992, 1995) *Women's Orients: English Women and the Middle East, 1718–1918, Sexuality, Religion and Work*. Ann Arbor, MI: University of Michigan Press.

Mernissi, Fatima (1975) *Beyond the Veil: Male–Female Dynamics in a Modern Muslim Society*. Cambridge, MA: Schenkman.

Mernissi, Fatima (1987) *The Veil and the Male Elite*. New York: Addison-Wesley.

Mernissi, Fatima (1993) *The Forgotten Queens of Islam*, English, trans. Mary Jo Lakeland (with the assistance of French Ministry of Culture). Cambridge, UK: Polity Press.

Mez, Adam (1937) *The Renaissance of Islam*, Trans. Salahuddin Khuda Bakhsh. Patna, India: The Jubilee Printing and Publishing House.

Mez, Adam (1947) *Al-Hadara Al-Islamiyya Fi'L-Qarn Al-Rabi' Al-Hijrı (Islamic Civilization in the Fourth Century of the Hijria)*, Trans. Muhammad Abdul Hadi Abu-Rida. Cairo.

Microsoft® '95 Bookshelf 1983–1995. Microsoft Corporation.

Microsoft® Encarta® 98 Encyclopedia 1993–1997. Microsoft Corporation.

Milani, Farzaneh (1992) *Veils and Words: The Emerging Voices of Iranian Women Writers*. Syracuse: NY: Syracuse University Press.

Miller, Arthur (1998) 'Opinioins'. *The Daily News*, 16 Oct. 1998.

Minces, Juliette (1978) 'Women in Algeria,' in L. Beck and N. Keddie (eds), *Women in the Muslim World*, pp. 159–71. Cambridge, MA: Harvard University Press.

Mir-Hosseini, Ziba (1996a) 'Women and Politics in Post-Khomeini Iran: Divorce, Veiling and Emergent Feminist Voices,' in Haleh Afshar (ed.), *Women and Politics in the Third World*, pp. 142–70. London and New York: Routledge.

Mir-Hosseini, Ziba (1996b) 'Stretching The Limits: A Feminist Reading of the Shari'a in Post-Khomeini Iran,' in Mai Yamani (ed.), *Feminism and Islam: Legal and Literary Perspectives*, pp. 285–319. New York: New York University Press.

Mohanty, Chandra, Ann Russo and Lourdes Torres (eds), (1991) *Third World Women and the Politics of Feminism*. Bloomington, IN: Indiana University Press.

Mohsen, Safia Kassem (1967) 'Legal Status of Women Among the Awlad 'Ali,'

Anthropological Quarterly 40: 153–66.

Mohsen, Safia Kassem (1975) *Conflict and Law among Awlad 'Ali of the Western Desert*. Cairo: National Center for Social and Criminological Research.

Montagu, Lady Mary Wortley (1893) *The Letters and Works of Lady Mary Wortley Montagu*, new edn revised by W. Moy Thomas, 2 vols, ed. Lord Wharncliffe. London: Swan Sonnenschein.

Moore, Alexander (1992) *Cultural Anthropology: The Field Study of Human Beings*. San Diego, CA: Collegiate Press.

Moore, Henrietta L. (1986) *Space, Text and Gender*. Cambridge, MA: Cambridge University Press.

Moore, Henrietta L. (1988) *Feminism and Anthropology*. Minneapolis, MN: University of Minnesota Press.

Morgan, Lewis Henry (1877) *Ancient Society*. New York: Holt.

Morsy, Soheir A. (1995) 'Review of "Writing Women's Worlds: Bedouin Stories" by Lila Abu-Lughod,' *American Ethnologist* 22(2): 424–5.

Murphy, Robert (1964) 'Social Distance and the Veil,' *American Anthropologist* 66(6, Part I), December: 1257–74.

Myers, James (1992) 'Nonmainstream Body Modification: Genital Piercing, Branding, Burning, and Cutting,' *Journal of Contemporary Ethnography: A Journal of Ethnographic Research* 21(3), October: 267–306.

Myntti, Cynthia (1997) 'Women in Cairo,' *American Anthropologist* 99(2), June: 394–5.

Nabarawi, Ceza al- (1979). Personal communication, Khartoum, Sudan, February.

Nader, Laura (1997) 'Controlling Processes: Tracing the Dynamic Components of Power,' *Current Anthropology* 38(5), December: 711–37.

Nagata, Judith (1984) *The Reflowering of Malaysian Islam: Modern Religious Radicals and Their Roots*. Vancouver: University of British Columbia Press.

Naggar, B. S. al- (1981) 'al-Mar'a wa-'Ilaqat al-Intaj fi Mujtama'at al-Khalij al-Taqlidiyya (The Woman and Production Relations in the Traditional Societies of the Gulf) (Arabic),' Second Regional Conference: Women in the Peninsula and the Gulf. Kuwait, March.

Najmabadi, Afsaneh (1993) 'Veiled Discourse – Unveiled Bodies,' *Feminist Studies* 19, Fall.

Nanda, Serena (1990) *Neither Man nor Woman: The Hijras of India*. Wadsworth Modern Anthropology Library. Belmont, California: Wadsworth Publishing Company.

Nasif, Majd al-Din Hifni (1962) *Athar Bahithat al-Badiyah Malak Hifni Nasif: 1886–1918*. Cairo: Wizarat al-Thaqafah wa-al-Irshad al-Qawmi.

Nasif, Malak Hifni (1909) *Nisa'iyyat (Feminist Texts)*. Cairo: Al-Jarida Press.

Needham, Rodney (1969) *Structure and Sentiment*. Chicago: University of Chicago Press.

Needham, Rodney, Editor (1973) *Introduction to Right and Left, Essays on Dual Symbolic Classification*. Chicago: University of Chicago Press.

Needham, Rodney (1979) *Symbolic Classification*. Santa Monica, CA: Goodyear

Publishing.

Nelson, Cynthia (1974) 'Public and Private Politics: Women in the Middle Eastern World,' *American Ethnologist* 1: 551–63.

Nelson, Cynthia (1986) 'The Voices of Doria Shafik: Feminist Consciousness in Egypt 1940–1960,' *Feminist Issues* 6(2).

Nelson, Cynthia (1991) 'Old Wine, New Bottles: Reflections and Projections Concerning Research on Women in Middle Eastern Studies,' in Earl L. Sullivan and Jacqueline S. Ismail (eds), *The Contemporary Study of the Arab World*. Alberta: Alberta University Press.

Nelson, Cynthia (1996) *Doria Shafiq the Feminist: A Woman Apart*. Cairo: American University in Cairo Press.

Nelson, Cynthia and Virginia Olesen (1977a) 'Introduction,' *Catalyst* (10–11), Summer: 1–7.

Nelson, Cynthia and Virginia Olesen (1977b) 'Veil of Illusion: A Critique of the Concept of Equality in Western Feminist Thought,' *Catalyst* (10–11), Summer: 8–36.

Nicolaisen, Johannes (1961) 'Essai sur la religion et la magie touaregues,' *Folk* 3: 113–62.

Norton, J. (1997) 'Faith and Fashion in Turkey,' in N. Lindisfarne-Tapper and Bruce Ingham (eds), *Languages of Dress in the Middle East*, pp. 149–77. London: Curzon with The Centre of Near and Middle Eastern Studies, SOAS.

Olson, E. A. (1985) 'Muslim Identity and Secularism in Contemporary Turkey: "The Headscarf Dispute",' *Anthropological Quarterly* 58(4): 161–71.

Ong, Aihwa (1990) 'State versus Islam: Malay Families, Women's Bodies, and the Body Politica in Malaysia,' *American Ethnologist* 17: 258–76.

Pagels, Elaine H. (1988) *Adam, Eve, and the Serpent*. New York: Random House.

Papanek, H. (1973) 'Purdah: Separate Worlds and Symbolic Shelter,' *Comparative Studies in Society and History* 15(3): 289–325.

Penzer, N. M. (1936) *The Harem*. London: G. Harrap.

Peristiany, J. G., Editor (1966) *Honour and Shame: The Values of Mediterranean Society*. Chicago: University of Chicago Press.

Pitt-Rivers, Julian A. (1954) *The People of the Sierra*. New York: Criterion Books.

Pitt-Rivers, Julian, Editor (1963) *Mediterranean Countrymen: Essays in Social Anthropology of the Mediterranean*. Paris: Mouton.

Pitt-Rivers, Julian A. (1965) 'Honour and Social Status,' in *Honour and Shame in the Mediterranean*. London: Weidenfeld & Nicolson.

Pitt-Rivers, Julian (1970) 'Women and Sanctuary in the Mediterranean,' in Jean Pouillon and Pierre Maranda (eds), *Echanges Et Communications: Mélanges Offerts à Claude Lévi-Strauss à L'Occasion de son 60ème Anniversaire* (2 vols), pp. 862–75. The Hague and Paris: Mouton.

Pomeroy, Sarah B. (1975) *Goddesses, Whores, Wives, and Slaves: Women in Classical Antiquity*. New York: Schocken.

Pomeroy, Sarah B. (1984) *Women in Hellenistic Egypt: From Alexander to Cleopatra*. New York: Schocken Books.

Quataert, Donald (1997) 'Clothing Laws, State, And Society in the Ottoman Empire, 1720–1829,' *International Journal of Middle East Studies* 29: 403–25.

Qutb, Sayyid (1974) *Fi Thilal al-Qur'an [In the Shadow of the Qur'an)* (6 vols). Cairo: Dar al-Shuruq.

Qutb, Sayyid (1982) *Ma'alim fil Tariq (Milestones)*. Cairo and Beirut: Dar al-Shuruq.

Radcliffe-Brown, A. R. (1952) 'A further note on joking relations,' in A. R. Radcliffe-Brown (ed.), *Structure and Function in Primitive Society*. London: Cohen and West.

Radwan, Zeinab 'Abdel Mejid (1982) *Thahirat al-hijab bayn al-jam'iyyat (The Phenomenon of the Hijab Among Islamic Groups) {Arabic}*. Cairo: Al-markaz al-qawmi lil-buhuth al-ijtima'iyya wal-jina'iyya (The National Center for Sociological and Criminological Research).

Rassam, Amal (1980) 'Women and Domestic Power,'*international Journal of Middle East Studies* 12(2).

Ratzel, F. (1896–1898) *History of Mankind*. London: Macmillan.

Raziq, Ahmad 'Abd ar- (1975) *al-Mar'a fi Misr al-Mamlukiyya (Women in Mamluk Egypt)*. al-Faggala: Dar al-Gil lil Tiba'a.

Reid, Donald Malcolm (1995) 'Al-Azhar,' in John L. Esposito (ed.), *The Oxford Encyclopedia of the Modern Islamic World*, Vol. 1, *ABBA–FAMI*. New York and Oxford: Oxford University Press, pp. 168–71.

Reinhart, A. Kevin (1995) 'Haram,' in John L. Esposito (ed.), *The Oxford Encyclopedia of the Modern Islamic World* (4 vols), p. 101. New York: Oxford University Press.

Reiter, R. R., Editor (1975) *Toward an Anthropology of Women*. New York and London: Monthly Review Press.

Roach, M.E. (1979) 'The Social Symbolism of Women's Dress,' in Justine M. Cordwell and Ronald A Schwarz (eds), *The Fabrics of Culture: The Anthropology of Clothing and Adornment*, pp. 415–22. The Hague: Mouton Publishers.

Roach, M. E. and Joanne. B. Eicher (1965) *Dress, Adornment, and the Social Order*. New York: John Wiley.

Roach, M. E. and Joanne B. Eicher (1973) *The Visible Self: Perspectives on Dress*. Englewood Cliffs, NJ: Prentice-Hall.

Roach, M. E. and Joanne B. Eicher (1979) 'The Language of Personal Adornment,' in Justine M. Cordwell and Ronald A. Schwar (eds), *The Fabric of Culture: The Anthropology of Clothing and Adornment*, pp. 7–22. The Hague: Mouton Publishers.

Roach-Higgins, M. E. and Joanne B. Eicher (1992) 'Dress and Identity,' *Clothing and Textile Research Journal* 10(4): 1–8.

Robinson, D. (1976) 'Fashions in Shaving and Trimming of the Beard: The Men of the Illustrated London News, 1842–1972,' *American Journal of Sociology* 8, March: 1133–9.

Roche, Daniel (1994) *The Culture of Clothing: Dress and Fashion in the 'ancien regime,'* English, trans. Jean Birrell. Cambridge, MA: Cambridge University Press.

Rosaldo, M. Z. (1974) 'Woman, Culture,and Society: A Theoretical Overview,' in

M. Z. Rosaldo and L. Lamphere (eds), *Woman, Culture, and Society*, pp. 17–42. Stanford, CA: Stanford University Press.

Rubinstein, Ruth P. (1986) 'Color, Circumcision, Tattoos, and Scars,' in Michael R. Solomon (ed.), *The Psychology of Fashion*, pp. 243–54. Lexington, MA: Lexington Books, D. C. Heath and Company.

Rugh, A. B. (1986) *Reveal and Conceal: Dress in Contemporary Egypt*. Syracuse, NY: Syracuse University Press.

Rumaihi, M. al- (1976) *Al-Bahrain: Mushkilat al-Taghayyur al-Siyasi wal-Ijtima'i (Bahrain: Problems of Political and Social Change)*. Beirut: Dar Ibn Khaldun.

Said, Edward W. (1978) *Orientalism*. New York: Vintage Books (Random House).

Sa'id, Aminah al- (1977) 'The Arab Woman and the Challenge of Society,' in Elizabeth W. Fernea and Basima Q. Bezirgan (eds), *Middle Eastern Muslim Women Speak*, pp. 373–90. Austin, TX and London: University of Texas Press.

Sandys, George (1905 [1619]) 'Relation of a Journey Begunne A.D. 1610,' in Samuel Purchas (ed.), *Purchas His Pilgrim: Microcosmus or, the Historie of Man*, p. 9: 347. London.

Sault, Nicole, Editor (1994) *Many Mirrors: Body Image and Social Relations*. New Brunswick, NJ: Rutgers University Press.

Sayyid-Marsot, Afaf Lutfi al- (1995) *Women and Men in Late Eighteenth-Century Egypt*, Modern Middle East Series. Austin, TX: University of Texas Press.

Schweizer, Thomas (1998) 'Epistemology: The Nature and Validation of Anthropological Knowledge,' in H. Russell Bernard (ed.), *Handbook of Methods in Cultural Anthropology*, pp. 39–88. Walnut Creek, CA: Altamira Press (Sage Publications).

Sciama, Lidia (1993) 'The Problem of Privacy in Mediterranean Anthropology,' in Shirley Ardener (ed.), *Women and Space: Ground Rules and Social Maps*, pp. 87–111. Oxford and Providence, RI: Berg.

Seng, Y. and B. Wass (1995) 'Traditional Palestinian Wedding Dress as a Symbol of Nationalism,' in Joanne B. Eicher (ed.), *Dress and Ethnicity*, pp. 227–54. Oxford: Berg.

Shaarawi, Huda (1987) *Harem Years: The Memoirs of an Egyptian Feminist (1879–1924)*, trans. Margot Badran. CUNY, New York: The Feminist Press.

Sha'rawi, Huda (1981) *Huda Sharawi: Muthakkirat Ra'idat al-Mar'a al-Arabiyya al-Hadith (Memoirs of Huda Sharawi, leader of modern Arab women) (Introduction by Amina al-Said) (Arabic)*, Kitab al-Hilal, Silsila Shahriyya. Cairo: Dar al-Hilal.

Sharma, U. (1978) 'Women and Their Affines: The Veil as a Symbol of Separation,' *Man* 13: 218–33.

Sidque, Ni'mat (1975) *Al-Tabbaruj (Exhibitionist Display of Dress and Body)*. Cairo.

Smith, Jane I. and Yvonne Y. Haddad (1975) 'Women in the Afterlife: Islamic View as Seen from the Qur'an and Traditions,' *Journal of the American Academy of Religion* 43(1): 39–50.

Smith, Jane I. and Yvonne Y. Haddad (1982) 'Eve: Islamic Image of Woman,' *Women's Studies International Forum* 5(2): 135–44.

Spellberg, D. A. (1996) 'Writing the Unwritten Life of the Islamic Eve: Menstruation and the Demonization of Motherhood,' *International Journal of Middle East Studies* 28: 305–24.

Spencer, H. (1879) *The Principles of Sociology, Vol. II-1*. New York: D. Appleton and Company.

Stern, Gertrude (1939a) *Marriage in Early Islam*. London: Royal Asiatic Society.

Stern, Gertrude (1939b) 'The First Women Converts in Early Islam,' *Islamic Culture* 13(3).

Stillman, K. (1986) *The Encyclopedia of Islam*, Vol. V, *Libas: The Muslim West*, New Edition, ed. C.E. Bosworth, E. van Donzel and B. Lewis Pellat. Leiden: E. J. Brill.

Stowasser, Barbara F. (1984) 'The Status of Women in Early Islam,' in Freda Hussain (ed.), *Muslim Women*, pp. 11–43. London and Sydney: Croom Helm.

Stowasser, Barbara F. (1994) *Women in the Qur'an, Traditions, and Interpretation*. New York: Oxford University Press.

Strathern A. and M. Strathern (1971) *Self-Decoration in Mount Hagen,* Art and Society Series. Toronto: University of Toronto Press.

Tertullian (1869) *The Writings of Q. S. F. Tertullianus*. Edinburgh: Ante-Nicene Christian Library.

Thevenot, Jacques (1980) *Voyage du Levant*. Paris: Maspero.

Tylor, E. B. (1871 [1958]) *Primitive Culture*. New York: Harper.

Vercoutter, Jean (1965–7) 'La Femme en Egypte ancienne,' in Pierre Grimal (ed.), *Histoire Mondiale de la Femme* (4 vols). Paris: Nouvelle Librairie de France.

Verier, Michelle (1979) *Les Peintres Orientalistes*. Paris: Flammarion.

Wallace, Anthony F. C. (1956) 'Revitalization Movements,' *American Anthropologist* 58: 264–81.

Warhol, Robyn R. and Diane P. Herndl (eds), (1997) *Feminisms: An Anthology of Literary Theory and Criticism*. New Brunswick, NJ: Rutgers University Press.

Wazir, Jahan Karim (1992) *Women and Culture: Between Malay Adat and Islam*. Boulder, CO: Westview Press.

Weir, Shelagh (1989) *Palestinian Costume*. London: British Museum Publications.

Wellhausen, J. (1897) *Reste arabischen Heidentums*, 2nd edn. Berlin: G. Reimer.

Westermarck, E. (1922 (1891)) *The History of Human Marriage*, Vol.1. New York: The Allerton Book Company.

Westermarck, E. (1926) *Ritual and Belief in Morocco* (2 vols). London: Macmillan.

Whitehead, A. (1976) 'Sexual antagonism in Herefordshire,' in Allen S. Barker (ed.), *Dependence and Exploitation in Work and Marriage*. London: Longman.

Wikan, Unni (1977) 'Man Becomes Woman – Transsexualism in Oman as a Key to Gender Roles,' *Man* 12(3).

Wikan, Unni (1978) 'The Omani Xanith – a Third Gender Role?' *Man* 13(3).

Wikan, Unni (1982) *Behind the Veil in Arabia: Women in Oman*. Baltimore, MD: Johns Hopkins University Press.

Wikan, Unni (1984) 'Shame and Honor: A Contestable Pair,' *Man* 19: 635–52.

Wikan, Unni (1996) *Tomorrow, God Willing: Self-Made Destinies in Cairo*. Chicago:

University of Chicago Press.

Williams, John Alden (1979) 'A Return to the Veil in Egypt,' *Middle East Review* XI (3): 49–54.

Williams, John Alden (1980) 'Veiling in Egypt as a Political and Social Phenomenon,' in John L. Esposito (ed.), *Islam and Development: Religion and Sociopolitical Change*, pp. 71–86. Syracuse, NY: Syracuse University Press.

Wilson, Arnold T. (1928) *The Persian Gulf.* London: Allen & Unwin.

Withers, Robert (1905 [1619]) 'The Grand Signior's Serraglio,' in Samuel Purchas (ed.), *Purchas His Pilgrim: Microcosmus or, the Historie of Man*, pp. 9–51. London.

Wolf, Eric R. (1951) 'The Social Organization of Mecca and the Origins of Islam,' *Southwestern Journal of Anthropology* 7(4): 329–56.

Yalman, Nur O. (1963) 'On the Purity of Women in the Castes of Ceylon and Malabar,' *Journal of the Royal Anthropological Institute* 93: 25–8.

Young, William C. (1993) 'The Ka'ba, Gender and the Rites of Pilgrimage,' *International Journal of Middle East Studies* 25: 285–300.

Young, William C. (1994) 'The Body Tamed: Tying and Tattooing among the Rashaayda Bedouin,' in Nicole Sault (ed.), *Many Mirrors: Body Image and Social Relations*, pp. 58–75. New Brunswick, NJ: Rutgers University Press.

Young, William C. (1996) *The Rashaayda Bedouin: Arab Pastoralists of Eastern Sudan.* Case Studies in Cultural Anthropology. Fort Worth, TX: Harcourt Brace College Publishers.

Youssef, Nadia Haggag (1974) *Women and Work in Developing Countries.* Berkeley, CA: Institute of International Studies.

Zainah, Anwar (1987) *Islamic Revivalism in Malaysia: Dakwah among the Students.* Pelaling Jaya, Malaysia: Pelanduk.

Zuhur, Sherifa (1992) *Revealing Reveiling: Islamist Gender Ideology in Contemporary Egypt*, SUNY Series in Middle Eastern Studies. Albany, NY: State University of New York Press.

Zuhur, Sherifa (1995) 'Dress,' in John Esposito (ed.), *The Oxford Encyclopedia of the Modern Islamic World*, pp. 383–8. Oxford: Oxford University Press.

Films (and Theater) Cited

El Guindi, Fadwa (1986) *El Sebou': Egyptian Birth Ritual.* El Nil Research, 27'; 16mm; color.

El Guindi, Fadwa (1990) *El Moulid: Egyptian Religious Festival.* El Nil Research, 38'; 16mm; color.

El Guindi, Fadwa (1995) *Ghurbal.* El Nil Research, 30'; 16mm; color.

Fernea, Elizabeth W. (1982) *A Veiled Revolution.*

Kamal-Eldin, Tania (1995) *Covered: The Hejab in Cairo, Egypt.* Herway Productions, 25' color; video.

Zimmerman, Mary (1997) *The Arabian Nights.* Looking Glass Theater Company.

Reference Works

A Dictionary of Islam (1885) 'Dress,' in T. Patrick Hughes (ed.), *A Dictionary of Islam*, pp. 92–9. Lahore: Premier Book House Publs. and Booksellers.

An Indonesian–English Dictionary, 3rd edn. (1989. ed. John M. Echols and Hassan Shadily, Ithaca, NY: Cornell University Press.

The American Heritage Dictionary (1994), ed. William Morris. Boston: Houghton Mifflin.

The Encyclopedia of Islam (1986) New Edition, Vol. 5, ed. C.E. Bosworth, E. van Donzel and B. Lewis, Pellat. Leiden: E. J. Brill.

The Holy Bible: Revised Standard Version (1952). New York: Thomas Nelson.

The New Columbia Encyclopedia (1975), ed. H. William and J. S. Levey Harris. New York: Columbia University Press.

Wehr, Hans (1994) *A Dictionary Of Modern Written Arabic: (Arabic–English)*, Milton Cowan. Ithaca, NY: Spoken Language Services.

Subject Index

'*awrah*, 140–3
  as blemish, 141, 142
Aghani (al-), 112, 120
Amin, Q., 178
Arab gender construct, 7–8, 64, 74

baladi, 5, 85, 137
Baron, B., 179
book methodology, xi, 66–67
Bukhari (al-), 112, 114, 135, 140
burqu', 7, 9, 88, 89, 95, 97, 98, 105, 114,
  126, 153, 179, 180

chador, 59, 129, 175
Chehabi, H., 174
Christian Missionary Project, 40–4
clothing laws, 9
  Turkey, 130
costume, clothing. see dress
creation
  Christian, 21, 71
  Islamic, 71–2, 74, 148
  Judaic, 70
  Sebou', 62, 63
  Sumerian, 14
critique
  of approach, xii, xiii, xv, xix, 26, 74, 79,
    83, 90, 109
  of study, xiv, 25, 75

dress. see also *libas*
  and birth, 64
  and costume, 55
  and sexuality, 31, 33, 36, 71, 74, 76
    Victorian, 45
  Andean origin, 52
  Arab gender construct, 8, 62, 64. see also
    El-Sebou'

as body art, modification, alteration, 56,
  57
as framework, 66, 69
body image, 56, 71
ceremonial
  krayas, 59
  Nubians, 60
  Palestine, 5
  Rashayda, 89
  religious festival (Egypt), 61
  Sebou', 62
  Yemen, 99
dual-gendered, 7, 61
for *hammam*, 39. see also *hammam*
Hebrew origins, 74
in anthropology, 49–57
  Crawley. see Crawley, E.
  Darwin. see Darwin, C.
  Eicher. see Eicher, J.
  Ibn Khaldun. see Ibn Khaldun, A.
  Kroeber. see Kroeber, A. L.
  Morgan. see Morgan, L. H.
  Spencer. see Spencer, H.
  Tylor. see Tylor, E. B.
  Westermarck. see Westermarck, E.
in missionary project, 43, 44. see also
  Christian Missionary Project
Islamic origins, 74, 75, 147
men's, 5, 52, 78, 105, 114, 119, 123, 129,
  130, 143, 175
Morocco, 61
neutral-gendered, 7, 9
Nubian, 60
Palestinian, 5, 58
Rashayda, 51, 109. see Rashayda
Sebou', 64
Shi'a Iraqi rural, 59
the *Ka'ba*, 95

Egyptian feminism, 26, 177, 180, 184
  Nasif, M., 177, 179, 181
  Sha'rawi, H., 161, 177, 179
El Moulid
  the visual ethnography, 61
El-Sebou'
  dress, 63
  etymology, 62
  folksong, 64
  gendered pots, 62
  life-cycle, 64
  the visual ethnography, 62
eunuch, 26, 27, 28, 29, 30, 96, 135, 141

face-veil, 111, 117, 118, 119, 120, 124,
  148, 152, 179, 184
fieldwork, xi, xv, xvii, xviii, 11, 51, 62, 67,
  79, 118, 199
  filming, n.15, 189
fieldwork n.19, 190

ghungat, 109, 111
Ghurbal
  interweaving between spaces, 68
  the visual ethnography, 67
Gordon, D., 171, 172

Hadith, 90, 106, 114, 140, 205, 231. see
    Bukhari (al-)
  Abu-Dawoud, 106
  as authority, 154
  as data source, ix, xi, 66
  as evidence, 120, 135, 152
  'awrah, 140, 142
  haya', 90
  hijab, 154, 155
  in ethnographic analysis, xiii
  in everyday life, 68
  Islamic dress code, 140
  libas, 70
  men's dress, 97, 114, 135
  veiling for power, 126
  womanhood, 137
  women as transmitters of, n.83, 198
  women's learning of, 183
hammam, 10, 34, 36
  as sexual, 10, 33, 37, 38
  Byzantine bath, 20

men's, 38
women's, 35, 103
  experience, 38–40, 38, 39, 40
haram
  and sanctity, 84
  etymology, 84
  meaning, 84
  versus halal, 84
haramlik. see harim
harem. see also harim
  Abbasid, 25, 29
  as aggregate, 3, 22
  as Byzantine institution, 28
    gynecea, 27
  as household, 25
    order and management, 29
  as sexual, 23, 25, 27, 36
  colonial gaze
    postcards, 45
    studio constructions, 37
  etymology, derivatives, 25
  eunuchs, 29
  Euro-Christian gaze, 10, 31, 34, 35, 37,
    38, 40, 45
  Fatimid, 30
  holistic approach, 22, 36
  in Western perception, 23, 30, 35
  Mamluk, 104
  of Alexander the Great, 192
  Ottoman, 27, 28, 29
    governance, 28
    pyramid structure, 29
    school of courtly arts, 28
    training school, 29
    woman's authority, 29
    women's ranking, 30
  seclusion fallacy, 25
  versus gate, 28
  women solidarity, 25, 26, 32
harim, 25. see also harem
  and gendered space, 151
  Arabo-Islamic construct, 85
  aristocracy, 96
  as sanctity-privacy, xvii
  etymology, derivatives, 25
  life in
    Sha'rawi memoirs, 26
    medieval Jews, 151. see also Goitein, S. D.

relational approach, 36
  men's quarters-*salamlik* (Turk.), 25
  women's quarters-*haramlik*(Turk.), 25
  seclusion fallacy, 12, 25
hasham, 92. see also hishma-tahashud
hijab, xi, xii, 46, 47, 69, 88, 155. see also
  dress, *libas*, *niqab*
  and feminism, 38, 179. see also Sha'rawi,
    Nasif
    versus *burqu'* or *yashmik*, 179. see also
      Egyptian Feminism
  and proposed explanations, 163–8
  as conversion, Indonesia, 69
  as dress, xii. see also *libas*
  as lifting veil, 153, 179
  as resistance
    Iran, 174, 175. see also *chador*
    Palestine, 173, 174
  as sacred, 147–48. see also *libas*
  as *satr*, 88. see also Mamluk Egypt. ,
    haram
  as separation, 148, 154, 157. see also
    khimar, jilbab
  Christian women, 180
  clothing laws
    Turkey and Iran, 130. see also turban
  compulsory, 175, 176. see also clothing
    laws
  etymology, 152, 157
  in films, n. 21, 190
  in *Hadith*, 155
  in Islamic movement, 143. see also
    tabarruj, sufur
    as women's dress, 143, 145. see also
      jilbab, khimar
    Mawdudi, A., 118
  in Islamic Movement, 69
    gendered space, 118
  in *Qur'an*, 139, 153, 155
    Sura al-Ahzab, 139
    Sura al-Nur, 119
  meaning, 152–57
  voluntary, 184. see also Islamic movement
hishma-tahashshud
  as restraint-respect-dignity, xvii, 90, 91
hurma. see *haram*, privacy

ihram. see haram

iltizam, 133
'*imamah*, 9, 105, 120, 121
Islamic activism. see Islamic Movement
Islamic architecture, 26, 82. see also
  mashrabiyya
Islamic dress, 69, 182
  as code, 134
  form, 143
  historical roots, 145
  in Egypt, 129
  in *Qur'an*, 135
  in Turkey, 130
  Palestine, 174
  uniformity in, 69
  voluntary, 145
Islamic feminism, 182
Islamic movement. see also *hijab, tahajjub*
  and veil, 46
  as revitalization, xvi, 5, 131–34
  as revival, xvi, xix, 131, 135, 143, 164,
    168
  Egypt in 1970s, 135
  El Guindi field study, xi, xv, xviii, 67, 68,
    118
  emergent contemporary, xvii
  Hamas, 173
  ideologue, 135
    Mawdudi, 135
    Qutb, 135
  in Indonesia, 139
  men, 163
  transitional phases, 129, 132
  versus fundamentalism, xix
  women, 182
Islamic Movement
  ideologue
    Mawdudi. n. 120, 204
    Qutb . n. 120, 204
Islamic text
  orientation, xiii
  superficial use of, xiii

jellaba. see jilbab
jilbab, 7, 61, 136, 139, 143, 152, 155
  meaning, 139

Ka'ba, 95, 126
  as sanctuary, 96

khanith. see Arab gender construct
khimar, 7, 85, 88, 97, 98, 120, 130, 135,
    136, 143, 155, 157
   Jewish, 150
   men's, 121
kiswa, 95, 96
   etymology, meaning, 95

Le Bain Turc, 35
libas, xii, 66, 69, 70, 117
   and *'imamah*, 105
   Arab dress, 66
   in *Qur'an*, 76, 142
   meaning, 69, 76
   of ashraf, 106
lithma, 97, 121
lived Islam, xiv, 67
   rural craftsman, 68

maharim. see mahram
mahram, 85, 98
   in *Qur'an*, 98. see also *haram*
Makka, xiv, 41, 78, 79, 84, 95, 112, 125,
    126, 201, 207, 208
   transliteration, ix
Mamluk Egypt, 4, 103, 151
mashrabiyya, 94, 95
men's veiling, 117, 119–24, 120, 125. see
   also turban, *'imamah, lithma, qina'*
mitdayyinin, 132, 133, 134
modesty, 50, 76, 83
   modesty-shame code, xiv, 71, 79, 83, 91,
    126, 157

Nelson, C., 190
niqab, 105, 114
Nuba, 56, 64

original analysis, xviii

primary data, xviii
privacy
   activated, 94
   and sexuality, 137
   and veil, 16
   Arab construct, 77, 81, 82, 94, 104, 136
   as experience, 94
   as right, 94

as sacred, 126
'awrah, 113
   dress, 60, 147
   etymology, 81
   in public, 81, 95
   in *Qur'an*, 113, 135, 141, 142, 154, 156
   in society and culture, 155
   individualism, 82
   Islamic construct, 113, 134, 140, 145,
    148
   Ka'ba, 126
   libas, 76
   of body in Islamic text, 112
   reserve-respect, 96
   sanctity-sanctuary, xvii, 74, 85, 143, 157
   seeing/not-seeing, 93, 94
   social and sacred, 46
   veil, 92, 96
   Western, 77, 81
   Western violation of, 37
   women solidarity, 32

qina', 97
Qur'an, 198, 206
   and creation, 71, 72, 74
   and Taliban, xvii
   as data source, xiii, 32
   as evidence, 98, 135, 157
   'awrah, 113, 140, 141
   both sexes, 114
   ceremonial reading, 59
   creation, 142, 147
   ethnographic analysis, xiii
   hijab, 139
   learning of, 177
   lived Islam, 78
   living document, xv, 67
   men and women interpreters, 136
   monogamy, 28
   revelation, 148
   sacred, 66, 135, 148
   sura 2, 187, 66
   transliteration, ix
   veil, 135, 152, 153

Rashayda, 93–94, 105, 108, 109, 110, 111,
   126
   life-cycle, 106–9

living Islam, xiv
reputation, 165
respect, 126
Rwala, 87, 91, 165
   reputation, 87, 165

salamlik. see harim
sanctuary. see *haram, harim*
satr. see veil as privacy
saw'ah, 73, 74, 113, 142, 147
Sayyid Badawi, 61
Sciama, L., 81
seclusion, 3
   Hellenic/Byzantine, xvi
   modesty-seclusion paradigm, xvii, 3, 90
spurious divides, xiv, 79
sufur, 143
Sultan's Serraglio (The), 33

tabarruj, 8, 156, 157
tahajjub, 207. See also *hijab*
the book
   methodology, xiii–xv
Tiv, 64
turban, 61, 98, 105, 106, 107, 108, 120,
   121, 123, 125, 130, 131

veil, 4, 10. see also *lithma, khimar*, turban,
   hijab, veiling
   "the verse of the veil", 153
   and *hammam*, 10
   and harem, 3
   and kinship relations, 98, 110
   and *mashrabiyya*, 102
   and respect, 109. see *ghungat*
   and sexuality
      Christian construct, 31
   and womanhood, 8
   anthropology of, xii, 5
   Arabic clothing terms, 7
   as book title, xi, xii
   as dress, xii, 6, 45
   as dress code, xvi. see also Islamic
      movement
   as identity, xii, 93. see also Rashayda
   as *lithma*, 61. see also turban
   as power, 14, 112
   as privacy, 86, 96. see also *satr, hurma*

as resistance, xii, xvii, xx, 46, 143, 172,
   173, 176, 184. see also *hijab*
as spatial divide, 6
Assyrian law, 11, 14–16
Assyrian nobility, 15
Christian analogy, 31
Christian construct, 6, 33–36
classification, 9
colonial violence, 23
critique of approaches to, 3–5, 10–12
embedded in
   complex of practices, 3
   culture and society, xvi, 82, 117, 119
   gender, 10, 11, 12
   women's studies, 3, 12, 117
ethnocentric perception, xi, xii, 3, 6, 10,
   23, 31
etymology, xi
   in Arabic, 6
   in English (Western), 6, 7
evangelist project
   lantern slides, 41. see also Christian
      Missionary Project
gap in study of, 10
   in communication paradigm, xvi
   in analysis, xiii
   in eating, 124
   in *Hadith*, 97, 152
   in Islamic worship, 114
   in Mamluk Egypt, 104
   in pre-Islamic Arabia, 111, 112
   in public space, 93
   in *Qur'an*, 85, 113
   in Yemen, 97, 99
invisible aspects, 70
Java, Indonesia, 69
life-cycle, 103, 108. see also Rashayda
   maturity, 124
   virgin's veil, 89
meaning, 88
men's, 11
   Tuareg, 121, 123
multiple contexts, 12
of commoners, 105. see Mamluk Egypt
of *Ka'ba*, 95, 126
origin, xvi
public-private dichotomy, 79
Rashayda *burqu'*, 89

relational
  not-veil, 148
  symbol of marriage, 110
  symbolism of, xvi
veil and gender ideology, xvi
  ancient Egypt, 13
  Aristotle, 16
  Byzantine, 11, 20
  Christian construct, 20–22
  complementarity, 13
  equality, 18
  exclusionary, 14
  Greek society, 17
veil and social space
  caste, 110, 111
  rank, 104
  status, 103, 124
veil as communication, 98, 103, 109
  flexible manipulation, 97, 98, 109, 125

veiling, 46, 126. see also veil
  Awlad 'Ali, 92
  by Prophet Muhammad, 119, 148, 152
  Christian, 178
  for femininity, 51, 52
  Judaic women, 13, 150
  Morocco, 61
  not-veiling, 110
  Nubians, 60
  proxemics, xvii
  Yemen, 93
visual analysis, 67, 88

yashmik, 179. see burqu'
Yemen, 4, 7, 10, 32, 51, 97, 102, 103, 109, 137

zawj. see also critique
  meaning, 72–73

Author Index

Abbott, N., 112

Abou-Zeid, A., 75, 91

Abu-Lughod, L., xii, 74, 92, 157

Abu-Zahra, N., 83, 84, 90, 92

Ahmed, A., 67

Ahmed, L., xvi, 7, 9, 10, 11, 13, 15, 16, 17, 18, 20, 25, 32, 33, 35, 150, 177, 178

Alireza, M., 32

Alloula, M., 23, 24, 25, 33, 35, 36, 37, 38, 45, 172

Amin, Q., 168

Anderson, J., 92

Antoun, R., xiv, 83, 84, 86, 126

Ardener, E., 11

Ardener, S., 77, 79, 81

Badran, M., xii, 26, 93, 178, 179

Baker, P., 175

Baron, B., 178, 179

Barraclough, S., 130

Barthes, R., 172

Bateson, G., xvii

Betteridge, A., 175

Bohannon, P., 64

Bon, O., 33

Bourdieu, P., 172

Brenner, S., 68

Brown, P., 19

Burton, R., 95

Campbell, J.,, 79

Chatty, D., 97

Crawley, E., 31, 49, 50, 51, 54, 58, 64, 85, 105, 120, 124, 125

Darwin, C., 52, 53

Davis, S., 61

Douglas, M., 75, 79

Doumato, E., 25

Durkheim, E. & Mauss, M., 77, 79

Early, E., 85, 86, 137

Eicher, J., xii, 40, 49, 52, 53, 54, 55, 56, 57, 58, 59, 61, 64, 105

El Guindi, F., xi, xviii, 7, 11, 14, 25, 61, 63, 64, 67, 68, 78, 82, 84, 98, 103, 126, 131, 132, 143, 153, 162, 163, 167, 168, 171, 181, 183, 184

El-Messiri, S., 137, 166

Fanon, F., 169, 170, 172

Faris, J., 56

Fernea, E., 7, 34, 35, 59, 93

Fernea, E. & Bezirgan, B., 177

Forget, N., 166

Foucault, M., 44

Geertz, C., xiii

Ghazali (al-), Z., 182

Gilsenan, M., 78, 88, 92, 93, 95, 165

Goitein, S. D., 13, 150, 151

Goodwin, G., 27, 28, 29, 30, 33

Gordon, D., 169, 170

Graham-Brown, S., 37, 85

Haddad, Y., 71, 72, 74

Hajj (al-), A., 9, 103, 104, 119, 120, 135

Hammami, R., 173, 174

Hamza, K., 143

Hansen, H., 11, 14

Harb, T., 178

Heikal, M., 204

Hertz, R., 79

Herzfeld, M., 80

Hirschon, R., 79

Hoffman-Ladd, V., 182

Ibn Khaldun, A., xiv, 53, 54, 103

Ibrahim, S., 162

Jabarti (al-), A., 104

Jennings, A., 60

Jubouri (al-), Y., 97

Kaplan, D., 40, 41, 43

Kroeber, A. L., 49

Lady Duff Gordon, 44
Lady Montagu, 33, 34, 35
Lancaster, W., 87, 165
Lichtenstadter, I., 12
Mabro, J., 23
MacLeod, A., 163, 164, 167
Makhlouf, C., 4, 10, 32, 51, 52, 93, 95, 97, 98, 99, 102, 103, 109
Maqrizi(al-), A., 103
Mawdudi (al-), A., 90, 118, 135
Melman, B., 27, 28, 38
Mernissi, F., xii, 25, 30
Minces, J., 169, 170, 171
Mir-Hosseini, Z., 174, 175
Mohsen, S., 75
Moore, A., 27, 28, 29, 30
Moore, H., 10, 11, 79
Morgan, L. H., 52
Murphy, R., 110, 121, 123, 124, 125, 126
Nagat, J., 69
Nasif, M., 168
Needham, R., 79
Nelson, C., 136, 168
Nicolaisen, J., 124
Olson, E., 130
Pagels, E., 20, 21
Papanek, H., 51, 98
Peristiany, J.,, 79
Pitt-Rivers, J., 75, 79, 91
Pomeroy, S., 17, 18

Qutb, S., 135
Radcliffe-Brown, A., 110
Radwan, Z., 162
Rassam, A., 165
Reinhart, A., 84
Sayyid-Marsot, A., xvi, 19, 29, 30, 31, 37, 40, 103, 136, 151, 177
Schweizer, T., xiii
Sciama, L., 79
Sha'rawi, H., 26, 38, 161, 168, 177, 179, 181
Sharma, U., 98, 102, 109, 110, 111, 112, 126
Sidque, N., 143
Smith, J. & Haddad, Y., 147
Spellberg, D., 70, 72, 74
Spencer, H., 53, 54
Stern, G., 11, 12, 111, 112, 120, 149, 150, 152, 153, 154, 155, 156
Strathern, A & M., 50
Tylor, E. B., 53
Wallace, A., 131, 144
Weir, S., 5, 58
Westermarck, E., 54, 120
Wikan, U., 4, 7, 8, 97
Williams, J., 161, 168
Yalman, N., 92
Young, W., xviii, 5, 51, 78, 79, 82, 86, 88, 89, 91, 92, 93, 95, 96, 105, 107, 108, 165
Youssef, N., 167